ALSO BY Edward M. Hallowell, M.D.

What Are You Worth?

*Finding the Heart of the Child: Essays
on Children, Families, and Schools*

...

DRIVEN
TO
DISTRACTION

...

Recognizing and Coping with
Attention Deficit Disorder from
Childhood through Adulthood

...

Edward M. Hallowell, M.D.

and

John J. Ratey, M.D.

A TOUCHSTONE BOOK
Published by Simon & Schuster
New York London Toronto Sydney

TOUCHSTONE
Rockefeller Center
1230 Avenue of the Americas
New York, NY 10020

First Touchstone Edition 1995
Published by arrangement with Pantheon Books,
a division of Random House, Inc.
Touchstone and colophon are registered trademarks
of Simon & Schuster Inc.

Manufactured in the United States of America

35 37 39 40 38 36

Library of Congress Cataloging-in-Publication Data
Hallowell, Edward M.
Driven to distraction :
recognizing and coping with attention deficit disorder
from childhood through adulthood /
Edward M. Hallowell & John J. Ratey.
p. cm.
"A Touchstone book."
Previously published: New York : Pantheon Books, 1994.
Includes bibliographical references and index.
1. Attention-deficit disorder in adults—Popular works.
2. Attention-deficit hyperactivity disorder—Popular works.
I. Ratey, John J., 1948– . II. Title.
RC394.A85H35 1995
616.85'89—dc20   94-40712
CIP
ISBN-13: 978-0-684-80128-5
ISBN-10:   0-684-80128-0

Grateful acknowledgment is made to Frank Wolkenberg and *The New York
Times* for permission to reprint excerpts from "Out of the Darkness," October
1987. Copyright © 1987 by Frank Wolkenberg. Reprinted by permission.

■ ■ ■

DEDICATION

We gratefully dedicate this book to seven teachers of ours, seven psychiatrists who shared with each other a liveliness of mind, an independence of thought, a love of the work, and an appreciation of play.

They taught us to listen and to see.

Doris Menzer Benaron, Jules Bemporad, William Beuscher, Thomas Gutheil, Leston Havens, Allan Hobson, and Irvin Taube all gave of themselves much more than this small dedication can acknowledge. During their years of teaching at the Massachusetts Mental Health Center in Boston, they taught us to be humble in our work. They taught us to go to where the patient is and to sit down and listen. They taught us to connect with the patient, person-to-person. They taught us to look for the heart of the patient, to look for the sorrow and for the joy. We thank them from our own hearts.

■ ■ ■

CONTENTS

■ ■ ■

A Personal Perspective

I have attention deficit disorder (ADD). I discovered I had ADD when I was thirty-one years old, near the end of my training in child psychiatry at the Massachusetts Mental Health Center in Boston. As my teacher in neuropsychiatry began to describe ADD in a series of morning lectures during a steamy Boston summer, I had one of the great "Aha!" experiences of my life.

"There are some children," she said, "who chronically daydream. They are often very bright, but they have trouble attending to any one topic for very long. They are full of energy and have trouble staying put. They can be quite impulsive in saying or doing whatever comes to mind, and they find distractions impossible to resist."

So there's a name for what I am! I thought to myself with relief and mounting excitement. There's a term for it, a diagnosis, an actual condition, when all along I'd thought I was just slightly daft.

As the lectures progressed, I devoured everything I could read on the topic. Not only did I realize that I had ADD, but I recognized the syndrome in the behavior of several members of my family as well, which made sense since it is genetically influenced. Then I heard Dr. Paul Wender, a pioneer in the field, give a talk, and soon after I read his book. I felt as if a boulder had been lifted from my back. I wasn't all the names I'd been called in grade school—"a daydreamer," "lazy," "an underachiever," "a spaceshot"—and I didn't have some repressed unconscious conflict that made me impatient and action-oriented.

What I had was an inherited neurological syndrome characterized by easy distractibility, low tolerance for frustration or boredom, a greater-than-average tendency to say or do whatever came to mind (called impulsivity in the diagnostic manual), and a predilection for situations of high intensity. Most of all, I had a name for the overflow of energy I so often felt—the highly charged, psyched-up feeling that infused many of my waking hours in both formative and frustrating ways.

At last there was a term to explain the conversations I tuned out of, involuntarily, for no apparent reason. For the rage I felt and the times I broke pencils and threw them around the room when I didn't immediately grasp a concept in grade school. For the seven attempts it can take me to read a page of a novel. For the nonsequiturs my wife says I've offered in the midst of intimate conversation. For forgetting the task at hand as I go off on the wings of a new thought or off in search of what I forgot. For the love of the chase, the new project, the hot idea, for the love of, the need for, something highly stimulating and riveting—whether it's doing psychotherapy with a paranoid, violent man or putting a high-stakes bet down at the racetrack. At last I had a name for these parts of me, parts I had chalked up to temperament or neurosis. Now with a name rooted in neurobiology I could begin to make sense of, in a forgiving way, parts of myself that had often frustrated or scared me.

I don't like the term "attention deficit disorder," although it sure beats its predecessor, minimal brain dysfunction. Technically, the correct current diagnostic label is attention-deficit hyperactivity disorder, which incorporates the symptom of hyperactivity into the diagnosis. It is an imperfect label for several reasons. The syndrome is not one of attention deficit but of attention inconsistency; most of us with ADD can in fact hyperfocus at times. Hyperactivity may or may not be present; in fact, some children and adults with ADD are quite dreamy and quiet. The very word "hyperactivity" is ambiguous; sedate evaluators label some simply active individuals "hyperactive," thus incorrectly diagnosing a normal state. Finally, the word "disorder" puts the syndrome entirely in the domain of pathology, where it should not entirely be. Although ADD can generate a host of problems, there are also advantages to having it, advantages that this book will stress, such as high energy, intuitiveness, creativity, and enthusiasm, and they are completely overlooked by the "disorder" model. The disorder didn't keep me from becoming a doctor, and it hasn't kept many others from far greater success in a wide variety of fields.

Although attention-deficit hyperactivity disorder is the official term used by the *Diagnostic and Statistical Manual of Mental Disorders* of the American Psychiatric Association, throughout this book we will use the term attention deficit disorder (ADD), which more clearly includes both the people who have the symptom of hyperactivity or excess energy and those who do not.

After that steamy summer ten years ago when I first learned about this intriguing syndrome, I began treating children and adults with ADD and studying the syndrome in its human details. I am still learning about ADD from my patients and from their families, teachers, and friends. Through extensive contact with people of all ages who have ADD, and with people who are close to them, like teachers, spouses, and friends, and through my own personal self-examination, I have developed a "feel" for ADD not just as a diagnostic entity but as a style of living.

It has become clear to me that while ADD is hard to define exactly, and while it almost never occurs in a pure form—that is, without some accompanying problem, such as a learning disability or low self-esteem— it is a distinct syndrome, greatly in need of detection and treatment. Un- treated, it leaves millions of children and adults misunderstood and unnec- essarily floundering, even incapacitated.

While subspecializing in the treatment of ADD, I have remained a general child and adult psychiatrist, seeing a wide range of human problems in my practice. Remaining a generalist has helped me preserve a balanced view, so that I do not see ADD behind every child's school problem or beneath every adult's work frustration. Although it is important to dissem- inate information about ADD, it is also important that ADD not become a diagnostic fad.

While *Driven to Distraction* is written entirely by me, some of the thought that went into it was the work of my collaborator, Dr. John Ratey. John was my chief resident when I started my training in adult psychiatry in 1979. He inspired me as a teacher then, and over the years we became close friends. His research led him into working with disorders of impulse control in adults and from there into working with adults with ADD. In addition to being an authority in the field, John also has ADD himself.

Our collaboration on this book grew out of conversations we had following our twice-a-week squash games, in which we noted how excited we both were in seeing our patients who had ADD get better. Many of these patients had been misdiagnosed as having other disorders. When the ADD was detected and appropriately treated, the results were often dramatic.

"More people should know about ADD," John said after a particularly strenuous game last winter.

"I've wanted to write about it for a long time," I responded. "Do you think we can pay attention long enough to get it done?"

"It's worth a try," John said. And so, helping each other plan our time, setting deadlines for each other, giving each other the external structure people with ADD so badly need, we shaped this book, a book about ADD by two psychiatrists who have ADD, written in the hope that the millions of other people out there with ADD can get the help they need to make the most of the lives they lead.

In explaining ADD, this book relies heavily upon examples drawn from life. Some of the accounts are composites, some are drawn directly from our patients' experience, and some are based upon interviews conducted for this book. In all cases the names are fictitious.

We would like to thank the many individuals who shared their experience so that this book could be possible.

—Edward M. Hallowell

Driven to Distraction

▪ 1 ▪

What Is
Attention Deficit Disorder?

Once you catch on to what this syndrome is all about, you'll see it everywhere. People you used to think of as disorganized or manic or hyper or creative but unpredictable, people who you know could do more if they could just "get it together," people who have bounced around in school or in their professional lives, people who have made it to the top but who still feel driven or disorganized, these may be people who in fact have attention deficit disorder. You may even recognize some of the symptoms in your own behavior. Many of the symptoms of ADD are so common to us all that for the term ADD to have specific meaning, rather than just be a scientific-sounding label for the complex lives we lead, we need to define the syndrome carefully. The best way to understand what ADD is—and what it is not—is to see how it affects the lives of people who have it.

In the cases that follow, and in the many case illustrations that appear in this book, one can witness the struggles individuals faced to break through inaccurate labels and unfair judgments. As their stories unfold, a definition of ADD emerges.

3

Case 1: Jim

It was eleven o'clock at night and Jim Finnegan was up pacing in his study. This was where he often found himself at night: alone, pacing, trying to get things together. Now approaching the halfway point of life, Jim was getting desperate. He looked around the room and took in the disorder. The room looked as if the contents of a bag lady's shopping cart had been dumped into it. Books, papers, odd socks, old letters, a few half-smoked packages of Marlboros, and other loose ends lay scattered about, much like the bits and pieces of cognition that were strewn about in his mind.

Jim looked up at the TO DO list that was tacked to the corkboard above his desk. There were seventeen items, the final one circled several times in black ink and marked with exclamation points: "Reorganization proposal due Tues., 3/19!!!" This was Mon., 3/18. Jim hadn't started on the proposal. He'd been thinking about it for weeks, ever since he told his boss that he had a plan that would increase productivity, as well as morale, in the office. His boss had said fine, come up with a written proposal and we'll see how it looks. His boss had also added a remark about how he hoped Jim would have enough "follow-through" to actually get something done this time.

Jim knew what he wanted to say. He'd known for months what he wanted to say. The office needed a new computer system, and the men and women out front needed more authority so they could make decisions on the spot so everybody's time wouldn't be wasted in unnecessary meetings. Efficiency would go up and morale would definitely improve. It was simple. Obvious. All the ideas were detailed on the various scraps of paper that dotted the floor of his room.

But all Jim could do was pace. Where do I start? he thought to himself. If it doesn't come out right, I'll look stupid, probably get fired. So what else is new? Why should this job be any different? Great ideas, no follow-through. That's me, good old Jim. He kicked the trash basket and added to the mess on the floor. OK, breathe in, breathe out, he told himself.

He sat down at his word processor and stared at the screen. Then he went over to his desk and began to straighten things up. The telephone rang and he barked at it, "Can't you see I'm busy?" When the answering machine came on, he heard Pauline's voice: "Jim, I'm going to sleep now.

I just wanted to see how your proposal is coming. Good luck with it tomorrow." He didn't have the heart to pick up the phone.

The night went on agonizingly. One minor distraction after another would knock Jim off-line as he tried to clutch onto the task at hand. A cat would meow outside. He'd think of something someone had said three days ago and wonder what they really meant by that. He'd want a new pencil because the one he had felt heavy in his hand. Finally, he got down the words "A Proposal for Office Reorganization at Unger Laboratories." Then nothing. "Just say what you want to say," a friend had told him. OK, say what you want to say. But nothing came. He thought of a new job he wanted to apply for. Maybe I should just bag this and go to bed. Can't do that. No matter how bad it is, I've got to finish this proposal.

By 4 A.M. he was beat. But not beaten. The words began to come. Somehow his extreme fatigue had lifted the censor in his mind and he found himself explaining his ideas simply and efficiently. By six he was in bed, hoping to get a little sleep before his meeting with his boss at nine.

The only trouble was that at nine he was still in bed, having forgotten to set the alarm before he went to sleep. When he arrived in a panic at the office at noon, he knew from the look on his boss's face that no matter how good the proposal was, his days at Unger were over. "Why don't you find a place with a little bit more flexibility?" his boss said, and thanked him for his proposal. "You're an idea man, Jim. Find a place that can accommodate to your style."

"I don't get it," he said to Pauline over drinks several weeks later. "I know I have more to offer than getting myself fired every six months. But it's always the same old story. Great ideas, but can't get it done. Even in high school, can you believe that? The guidance counselor, she was this really nice lady, she told me that I had the highest IQ in the class, and so she just couldn't figure out why I had such a hard time living up to my potential."

"You know what's not fair?" Pauline said, turning the stem of her Manhattan glass between her thumb and forefinger. "They took the ideas in your proposal and used them. Dramatic improvement. Everybody's happier and work is up. Those were your ideas, Jim, and you got fired. It's not fair."

"I don't know what's wrong with me," Jim said. "I don't know what to do."

Jim had attention deficit disorder. When he came to see me at the age of thirty-two, he had been living a life of chronic underachievement, falling short of his goals both at work and in relationships because of an underlying neurological problem that made it difficult for him to pay attention, sustain effort, and complete tasks.

ADD is a neurological syndrome whose classic defining triad of symptoms include impulsivity, distractibility, and hyperactivity or excess energy. About 15 million Americans have it today; most of them do not know that they have it. The condition occurs in children and adults, men and women, boys and girls, and it cuts across all ethnic groups, socioeconomic strata, levels of education, and degrees of intelligence. It used to be thought that this was a disorder of childhood alone, and that one outgrew it during adolescence. We now know that only about a third of the ADD population outgrows it; two-thirds have it throughout adulthood. ADD is not a learning disability or a language disability or dyslexia, and it is not associated with low intelligence. In fact, many people who have ADD are very smart. It's just that their smartness gets tangled up inside. Undoing the tangle to get a smooth run on the line can take more patience and perseverance than they can consistently bring to bear.

■ ■ ■

Where does the syndrome begin and normal behavior leave off? What is impulsivity? What is distractibility? How much energy is excess? These are the questions we will explore throughout this book, mainly in the context of individual cases, like Jim's. Considering the symptoms, can't we all recognize parts of ourselves? Yes. However, one bases the diagnosis of ADD not on the mere presence of these symptoms, but on their severity and duration, and the extent to which they interfere with everyday life.

When Jim came for consultation, he was at wit's end. He came into my office, sat down in one of the easy chairs, and began to run his fingers through his curly hair. He leaned forward, alternately looking at me or staring at the floor. "I don't know where to begin. I don't even know what I'm doing here," he said, shaking his head as if to say no, this won't help either.

"Did you have any trouble finding your way here?" I asked. He was twenty minutes late, so I figured he might have gotten lost.

"Yes, yes, I did," he said. "Your directions were fine, it wasn't your fault. I just turned left where I should have turned right and then I was gonzo, school was out. It's a miracle I got here at all. I ended up at some gas station in Somerville."

"Well, it can be pretty confusing," I said, hoping to let him relax a bit. Of the people who consult with me for problems related to ADD, probably about a half are either late for their first appointment or miss it altogether. I have come to expect it. It comes with the territory. My patients, however, usually feel very bad about it and so begin the session thinking that I am going to reprimand them in some way. "You certainly aren't the first person to get lost coming here," I said.

"Really?" he asked. "That's good to hear." He took a deep breath to say something, but paused, as if the words had crowded in his throat, then let his breath out in a long sigh, the words apparently dispersed. He went through the same cycle a second time before I asked him if maybe he could use a few moments just to collect his thoughts while I wrote down some bits of information about him like his name, address, and telephone number. That seemed to help. "OK," Jim said. "Let's start."

"OK," I responded, leaning back in my chair, folding my hands behind my head. There was another long pause, and another sigh from Jim. "I can see that it's hard for you to get started," I said. "Maybe we could focus on what the problem is that brought you here."

"Yes," he said, "OK." With that little bit of prodding from me, Jim began to fill in most of his history. A normal childhood, or so it seemed to him. But when I pressed for more detail, Jim acknowledged that he was quite rambunctious in grade school and enjoyed getting into mischief. He got good grades even though he never really studied. "I thought school was like playtime," he said. But with high school, things got tougher. His innate intelligence couldn't carry him so easily anymore, and he began to fall behind. He started to get lectures from his teachers and parents on his moral shortcomings, how he was letting himself and everyone else down, how in the long run he'd be the worse for it, and so forth. His self-esteem fell, although somehow his inborn temperament was buoyant enough to keep him fairly upbeat. After stumbling through college, he began a long series of jobs in various computer-related fields.

"You like computers?" I asked.

"I could have invented them," he said with great enthusiasm. "I love them. I just have this understanding of them, you know what I mean? I know what makes them tick, and I know how to get the most out of them. If only I could tell people what I know. If only I didn't screw up every time I get a chance—"

"How do you screw up?" I asked.

"How do I screw up?" he asked, then repeated the question again, turning it into a sorrowful statement by his tone of voice. "How do I screw up. I forget. I argue. I postpone. I procrastinate. I get lost. I get mad. I don't follow through. You name it, I do it. I'll get into these discussions with my boss, and I'll see my way is right, and the next thing you know, I'm calling him a stupid jerk for not seeing that I'm right. Tends to get you fired, calling your boss a stupid jerk. Or I'll have this idea, but I won't be able to find it, like it's a jumble lost in the closet or something. It's in there, I know it's in there, but I just can't get it out. I want to get it out, I try to get it out, but I can't. One of my old girlfriends told me before she left me that I should face it, I'm just a loser. Maybe she's right, I don't know."

"You cared about her?" I asked.

"For a while. But then she got fed up, like all the rest have. I mean, I'm pretty intense to be with."

"Where do you think that intensity comes from?" I asked.

"I don't know," he said. "It's always been there, though."

The longer we talked, the clearer it became how right Jim was, how the intensity had always been there, seldom harnessed, but always burning. That intensity may in part explain why ADD is common among people in high-energy fields, from sales to advertising to commodities to any high-pressure, high-stimulus kind of work. "Have you ever consulted a psychiatrist before?" I asked.

"A couple of times," Jim said. "They were nice guys, but nothing really changed. One of them told me not to drink so much."

"How much do you drink?"

"I binge. When I really want to let loose, I go out and tie one on. It's an old family tradition. My dad drank a lot. I guess you could say he was an alcoholic. I don't think I'm an alcoholic, but that's what they all say, huh? Anyway, I get these terrible hangovers the next day, so I don't go back to it for a while."

Often people with ADD self-medicate with alcohol or marijuana or cocaine. Cocaine, particularly, is similar to one of the medications used in the pharmacological treatment of ADD.

Jim began to cross and uncross his legs a lot as we talked. "If you're feeling restless, feel free to pace a bit while we talk," I said.

"Really? You don't mind? Thanks a lot." He stood up and began to walk around, conducting his conversation with his arms as he spoke. "This is great. Most people would get unnerved if I did this, but I really think better when I walk. Is that weird? No wonder I had trouble in school. You know, that's half my problem. I'm always so tied up inside. And you can imagine it doesn't go over big at work if I want to pace half the time."

"I don't know," I said. "Maybe you just haven't found the right job."

"You sound like all my bosses. Is there a right job for me?"

ADD comes in many shapes and sizes. In many people, particularly adults, the symptoms of ADD are masked by more obvious problems, such as depression or gambling or drinking, and the underlying ADD is never detected. In other people the symptoms take on a particular cast, congruent with the person's personality as it evolves over time, so that the symptoms are never really noticed the way symptoms of a cold or flu might be but rather are dismissed as being part of "just the way he is," not warranting medical or psychiatric intervention. And within the domain of properly diagnosed ADD there is also much variability. Jim's ADD, I was discovering, was the high-energy, hyperactive type. But there is another kind of ADD that shows no hyperactivity whatsoever. Indeed, these people can be underactive. This is the child, often a girl, who sits at the back of the classroom daydreaming, or the adult who moves serenely within a cloud, never quite present anywhere.

"I don't know if there is a right job for you," I said, coming back to Jim's question. "For now I'd just like to hear more of your story. Have you ever really told it before?"

"No. Nobody can follow me. I go off on too many tangents, they all say."

"Well, you just keep talking, and let me do the organizing. That's what I'm paid for."

Jim talked for a long while, over weeks. He told many stories of misunderstanding, miscommunication, self-reproach, underachievement, missed chances, angry people, and risky behavior. It often seemed, as his mother had told him when he was twelve, that he simply didn't know enough to come in out of the rain. He'd do foolish things, forget, and dilly-dally all the time. But he also told stories of adventure, and kindness, of intuition and charm and energy and enthusiasm. He told stories of big dreams and high hopes and big disappointments as well. Baffled and frustrated, he never blamed anyone but himself. He was a very likable guy, even though he didn't like himself very much.

And this is the case with so many people who have ADD. They are very likable, although they get into the most difficult of patches. They can be exasperating in the extreme—one mother called me about her son, who had ADD and had just inadvertently almost set fire to his school, and asked me if she could run over him in her truck—but they can also be unusually empathic, intuitive, and compassionate, as if in that tangled brain circuitry there is a special capacity to see into people and situations.

Jim's story took us through many twists and turns. There was the time he had a job as a bus driver: one dreamy afternoon doing his regular run he made what he thought was his last stop and headed home for the bus yard only to pull into the lot with a bus half-full of confused and angry customers. He had forgotten to make the actual final stop on the line. "Where are we?" the passengers demanded. "Where have you taken us?" It was Jim's last ride for that bus company. Or there was the time in conversation with a female colleague when he referred to his boss as a "pinhead," only to realize almost as he was saying it that the female colleague was his boss's wife. "I don't do it on purpose," he said. "I just put my foot in my mouth. I don't think about who I'm talking to or where I am. Is it my unconscious wish to fail?"

"It could be," I said. "That sort of thing has been known to happen. On the other hand, it could be something completely different." I began to tell Jim about ADD. "You see, it might be that you're not a screw-up or a loser at all, and that you do not have an unconscious wish to sabotage yourself. It might be, and it is beginning to sound to me as if this is very much the case, that you have a neurological condition called attention deficit disorder. It's no more a thing to be ashamed of than being nearsighted is. In fact, it's sort of like being nearsighted. You don't focus very well. You have to strain to see clearly. People with ADD have trouble attending to one task at a time. You've probably heard of hyperactive children, and that was how this syndrome was originally described—hyperactivity in kids. We now know that the symptoms include more than just hyperactivity and that it affects adults as well as children. The hallmark symptoms of ADD are easy distractibility, impulsivity, and sometimes, but not always, hyperactivity or excess energy. These people are on the go. Type A personalities. Thrill seekers. High-energy–, action-oriented–, bottom-line–, gotta-run–type people. They have lots of projects going simultaneously. They're always scrambling. They procrastinate a lot and they have trouble finishing things. Their moods can be quite unstable, going from high to low in the bat of an eye for no apparent reason. They can be irritable, even rageful, especially when interrupted or when making transitions. Their memories are porous. They daydream a lot. They love high-stimulus situations. They love action and novelty. Just as this kind of problem can get in the way at work, it can also interfere with close relationships. Your girlfriend can get the wrong impression if you're constantly tuning out or going for fast action."

As I explained to Jim what attention deficit disorder was, I watched him. He leaned forward in his chair and looked right at me. He began to nod his head at the mention of each new symptom. An excited look came over the face that had been so harried when we first met. "When I was a kid," he broke in, "it was always 'Earth to Jim!' or 'Where's Jim?' or 'Jim, why don't you just shape up?' My parents and my teachers just thought I was lazy. So I would get punished or yelled at. For a while I yelled back, but then I just sort of began to agree with them. I mean, what can you do? My dad had a way of smacking me across the side of my head if I talked back. It was kind of brutal, come to think of it. So I don't think of it much. I have to wonder, though, what kept me going. I mean, I never lost my spunk. I remember a teacher in the sixth grade making me copy pages out of a geography textbook because I had lost my homework. She said if I would admit I just hadn't done the homework instead of lying and saying I'd lost it, she wouldn't make me copy the pages. Well, I had done the damn homework, so I was not about to say I hadn't. Well, she got ticked off and really lost it. She got into this thing where she kept upping the ante, assuming I would back down. She kept adding on pages for me to copy. When she reached a hundred pages, she stopped. I stayed up all night copying those pages, and I would have reached the hundred pages if my mother hadn't found me in the middle of the night. She made me stop. Plus she went into school the next day and raised a big stink. Old Miss Willmott had to apologize to me. To me! It was the most satisfying moment of my entire educational career, bar none, and I'll always love my mother for it."

"But I wish they had known then what you are telling me now," Jim went on. "There were so many stories. My whole ninth-grade year was like one long war with my parents. They got into the same thing Miss Willmott did, always upping the ante. Their basic idea was that I wasn't trying hard enough, so they kept coming up with more and more punishments, none of which worked. It makes me kind of sick to think back on it. It wasn't my parents' fault. They didn't know what was going on. Why didn't anybody tell me about this before?" Jim finally asked me in exasperation.

"People haven't really known about it very much until fairly recently," I answered.

■ ■ ■

It can't be said when ADD came into existence. The fidgety, overactive child has been around, one may presume, for as long as children have been around. And they have not been treated well.

The treatment of children has been terrible throughout history, one of the consistent but little-mentioned black marks in almost every epoch of human civilization; people have seldom differentiated much when it comes to children who behaved "badly." Too often, it was simply recommended that these children be beaten, or in some cases, killed. There is something in the most inhumane part of human nature that enjoys hurting smaller and weaker beings, particularly if they annoy us or make demands on us. It is beyond the scope of this book to document the abuse of children that mars human history; I bring it up in connection with ADD because it has often been the overactive children, the ADD kids, who have been subjected to the worst abuse. It is only recently that we have conferred upon children rights beyond those of animals and decided to look upon their "misbehavior" as possibly signifying something other than satanic possession or a moral infirmity deserving punishment.

So it is not surprising that although the syndrome we now call ADD has been around for centuries, it was simply lumped together with all other "bad behaviors." It was not until this century that it began to be recognized as a medical condition. Although it is hard to say who first defined the syndrome, credit usually goes to British pediatrician George Frederic Still, who, in a series of lectures to the Royal College of Physicians in 1902, described some children in his medical practice who were difficult to control, showing signs of "lawlessness," lacking "inhibitory volition," and in general being obstreperous, dishonest, and willful. He hypothesized that the condition was not the result of bad parenting or moral turpitude, but rather was biologically inherited or due to injury at birth.

The theme of injury at birth and brain damage continued in the thirties and forties in the idea of the "brain-injured child." Even when no actual evidence of neurological impairment could be found, "brain damage" was invoked to explain uncontrollable behavior. It was during these decades that stimulant medication (amphetamine) was first tried, successfully, to help contain the behavior of some of these children.

Other terms began to appear, some quite descriptive, such as "organic drivenness," others rather amorphous and bleak, like "minimal brain dysfunction." One had to wonder whether the brain itself was minimal or the dysfunction was minimal or perhaps whether the understanding of what was happening in the first place was minimal.

Separating the symptom of hyperactivity from any notion of brain damage, Stella Chess in 1960 and others around the same time began to write about the "hyperactive child syndrome." Chess saw the symptoms as part of a "physiologic hyperactivity," whose causes were rooted in biology rather than the environment.

By the 1970s many major researchers were investigating the syndrome of hyperactivity. Virginia Douglas, in Canada, began to look broadly at the symptoms associated with hyperactivity and found four major traits to account for the clinical picture: (1) deficits in attention and effort, (2) impulsivity, (3) problems in regulating one's level of arousal, and (4) the need for immediate reinforcement. In large part due to her work, in 1980 the syndrome was renamed attention deficit disorder.

In the decade since that time, research has ballooned. Probably the most up-to-date and definitive account of the history and current state of the field is to be found in a book written by one of the great researchers in the area, Russell Barkley; his book is entitled, simply, *Attention Deficit Hyperactivity Disorder*.

■ ■ ■

"So what does it mean, exactly?" Jim asked me. "Does it mean I'm stupid?"

"Not at all. But don't let me tell you. You tell me. Are you stupid?" I asked.

"No, I'm not. I know I'm not," he said emphatically. "I've just had this trouble all my life of getting out what's inside."

"Exactly," I said. "That can be due to a lot of different things in different people, but in your case I think it's due to ADD."

"Is it common?" he asked.

"Probably fifteen million people in this country have it, both children and adults. It affects males more than females, probably in a ratio of about three to one. We don't know what causes it exactly, but the best evidence is genetic. Other factors may contribute, like problems at birth, but genetics is the main cause. Environmental factors can make it a lot worse, but they don't cause it."

"You mean my mother didn't screw me up?" he asked ironically.

"Not in this case. Maybe in other ways, who knows. Do you want to blame her?"

"No, no. But I want to blame someone. Not blame someone, I just want to get mad. It really pisses me off that no one told me about this before. If this is just the way I'm wired—"

"Then," I interrupted, "you don't have to blame yourself."

"Who is, of course, the person I've been blaming all along. But it is my fault, isn't it? I mean it doesn't matter whether I've got ADD or XYZ —if I've messed up, I've messed up and at my age there's no one but me to take the heat. Right?"

"In a way, I guess," I said, rubbing my shoulder as if his words had activated an old ache. "But what's to gain in all the blame? I want to give you a framework to understand yourself in such a way you can forgive yourself and move on."

"OK," Jim said, "I get what you're saying. What's the bottom line, though? Is there anything you can do for this?"

"ADD people love bottom lines," I answered, laughing. "It's always, 'Get to the point'; 'What's the next show?'; 'Where's the beef?' "

"Yeah, you're right," he said. "I'm not big on scenery. I want to get there. Is that bad?"

"I didn't mean to put you on the defensive. I have ADD myself. I know how it feels."

"You have ADD?" Jim asked, apparently taken aback. "You seem so calm."

"Practice," I said, smiling. "Actually, I'm sure for you there are times when you can be quite focused and relaxed. For me, doing this kind of work is one of those times. But the practice part is true also, and we'll get into that."

From this point Jim's treatment began. Actually, it had begun already. Just finding out about the syndrome, finding at last that there is a name for it, constitutes a large part of the treatment for most people.

"What is it with me?" he asked in one session. "I don't mean to be rude. But this guy calls me up and he starts to tell me the materials I sent him were the wrong ones, when I knew perfectly well they were the right ones, he just didn't know why they were the right ones, and so he thought they were the wrong ones, and so immediately that started to annoy me, but it wasn't even that that got to me, it was his tone of voice. Can you believe it? I knew from the first second he started on the phone that I wanted to hang up on him or punch him."

"You had like a rage reaction," I offered.

"Damn straight. And when I think about it now, I get mad all over again. So I tried to do what you said. Pause. Think of the consequences. This was a good customer. I didn't want to lose him and I didn't want him bad-mouthing me to his friends. So I paused. But the more I paused, the more he talked on, in this really slow, dumb voice, on and on, and I wanted to scream at him, '*Get to the point!*' So instead, I just cleared my throat. But then he said to me, 'Don't interrupt me, I'm not finished.' Well, I lost it. I told him I thought we could be on the phone until next Christmas and he still wouldn't be finished and I had better things to do and I hung up. Can you believe that?"

I laughed. "I think you did very well. At least up until you lost it. The guy was pushing your buttons. And let's face it, there are going to be times where you're going to get annoyed and you're going to lose it. Treatment for ADD won't take that away completely, and you wouldn't want it to, would you?"

"I guess not. But is this part of ADD, this rage reaction, as you call it?"

"Yes," I said. "It's part of the impulsivity. If you think of ADD as a basic problem with inhibition, it helps explain how ADD people get angry quicker. They don't inhibit their impulses as well as other people. They lack the little pause between impulse and action that allows most people to be able to stop and think. Treatment helps with that but it doesn't cure it completely."

"You know what the funny thing was?" he asked. "The guy called me back the next day and said he was sorry we had developed a communication problem between us the day before and maybe we could start over. A communication problem, can you believe that? I said sure, only let me start this time. I explained to him in ten seconds why what I had sent him was what he needed, he said he understood and said thank you, I said, 'No, it is me who should thank you, I'm sorry for our communication problem yesterday,' and we said goodbye, best of friends." Jim slapped his knee.

"How do you like that?" I said. "Your guardian angel must have been on duty."

"But where does it come from, this anger?"

"Can you tell me?" I asked.

"I think it's built up over the years. When I was a little kid, I was all over the place, but I wasn't angry. I think it built up, in school. All the failures. All the frustration." Jim clenched his fists without knowing it as he talked about his feelings. "It got so I knew before I started something it wasn't going to work out. So all I had left was tenacity. I wouldn't give up. But, damn, why didn't I, with all the screw-ups I had to show for my efforts?"

■ ■ ■

Jim was beginning to get into what is a large and very important part of ADD, although, strictly speaking, it is not part of the neurological syndrome itself. He was starting to talk about the secondary psychological problems that typically develop in the wake of the primary neurological problem of ADD.

Due to repeated failures, misunderstandings, mislabelings, and all manner of other emotional mishaps, children with ADD usually develop problems with their self-image and self-esteem. Throughout childhood, at home and at school they are told they are defective. They are called dumb, stupid, lazy, stubborn, willful, or obnoxious. They hear terms like "space-shot" or "daydreamer" or "out in left field" all the time. They are blamed for the chaos of family mealtimes or the disaster of family vacations. They are reprimanded for classroom disturbances of all sorts and they are easily scapegoated at school. They are the subject of numerous parent-teacher conferences. Time and again, an exasperated teacher meets a frustrated parent in a meeting that later explodes all over the child who isn't there. He feels the shock waves afterward. "Do you know what your teacher said?

Do you know how embarrassed your mother and I were?" Or, from the teacher, "I understand you have no greater control of yourself at home than you do in school. We must work on this, mustn't we?"

Month after month, year after year, the tapes of negativity play over and over again until they become the voice the child knows best. "You're bad," they say in many different ways. "You're dumb. You just don't get it. You're so out of it. You really are pathetic." This voice pulls the child's self-esteem down and down, out of the reach of the helping hands that might be extended, into the private world of adolescent self-reproach. Liking yourself in adolescence is hard enough work for any child. But for the child with ADD it is especially difficult.

"You kept up your efforts, but it must have been tough," I said to Jim.

"It sure was," he responded with a kind of ruefulness in his voice that said to me, You don't know the half of it."

"Tell me about it," I said.

"It's just that I wouldn't know where to begin. By high school they almost had me convinced I was just plain stupid. I mean, I couldn't figure it out. I could understand the stuff in class. I could follow what was said. I could even jump ahead in my mind. But when it came to writing the papers or getting the assignments organized or taking tests, everything just went out the window. I would try. Believe me, I would try. I got lectures all the time on how I didn't try, but I did try. It's just that the bigger sledge-hammer didn't work. I'd lock myself in my room and before you knew it I was gone. Doing something else. Reading. Listening to music. Then I'd catch myself and try and get to studying again, but goddamn it, it just didn't work." Jim's voice got harsh and his face turned red.

"It all comes back, huh," I said.

"It sure does. They'd tell me to try harder. Over and over again. Try harder. And I'd try harder and it wouldn't work. After a while I figured I didn't have the brain to do it. And at the same time I knew I did. But it just didn't work out."

"So you were frustrated all the time. No wonder you felt angry."

"Do you think that's why I started drinking? I felt better after I had a few pops. But doesn't everybody?"

"Sure," I said. "But it is likely that you had special reasons to drink. You were medicating yourself, as so many people with ADD do. Alcohol, marijuana, cocaine are all common. In different ways each of those drugs calms you down. But only in the short run. In the long run, they can all be disastrous."

"I think I knew that. I think that's why I never let myself develop a regular habit. I thought that would really be the end of the line for me." Jim paused. "Why cocaine? I thought that juiced you up."

"It does for most people. For people with ADD, however, it helps them focus. So, without knowing it, when they use cocaine they are medicating themselves."

"No kidding. Anyway, I'm just glad I found out about this before I let my whole life get away."

"How did it affect your relationships with other people?" I asked.

"I didn't think about it at the time, but all the things we've been talking about got in the way with friends and girls and everyone else. I wouldn't listen—"

"Couldn't listen," I corrected him.

"OK, couldn't. But everybody else thought *wouldn't*. I'd be late for things, or I wouldn't show up at all, having forgot. I wouldn't hear things right, so I wouldn't respond right—you know the story. People thought I was arrogant or I just didn't care. I did have a short fuse, that much was true. When someone would call me on something, I'd just tell them to kiss off. Didn't make me real popular. But still I had friends. Most important of all, Pauline stuck with me. Sometimes I wonder why. I would forget things, not show up, get angry or depressed for no reason. I'd be talking to her, and then I would disappear into some daydream. I'd promise to do something with her, and then I would forget. Somehow, she didn't dump me. But it sure wasn't easy. We always seemed to be in the midst of some potential argument. There's always been a fight waiting to happen. When I would screw up at work, she offered encouragement, but I could tell she was thinking, What is it with this guy? I was thinking the same thing. I don't think I could have survived this long without Pauline. She's incredible. But the relationship has been awful tough on her. I'm just not an easy guy. I know that. I know I'm exasperating. I'm exasperating to myself. I wish to hell I weren't. Believe me, I'm not like this on purpose. I think Pauline believes that, too, deep down. Otherwise how could she have stuck with me?"

"She probably does. But you're a good guy, Jim. People put up with your annoying habits because you made it worth their while in other ways."

An important, and often overlooked part of both learning disabilities and ADD is the social consequence of having them. ADD can interfere with one's interpersonal life just as dramatically as it does with one's academic or job performance. To make friends, you have to be able to pay attention. To get along in a group, you have to be able to follow what is being said in the group. Social cues are often subtle: the narrowing of eyes, the raising of eyebrows, a slight change in tone of voice, a tilting of the head. Often the person with ADD doesn't pick up on these cues. This can lead to real social gaffes or a general sense of being out of it. Particularly in childhood, where social transactions happen so rapidly and the transgressor of norms is dealt with so pitilessly, a lapse in social awareness due to the distractibility or impulsivity of ADD can preclude acceptance by a group or deny understanding from a friend.

"I sometimes wonder how I made it this far without getting killed," Jim laughed. "Must be the luck of the Irish."

"Could be," I said. "But maybe you learned little tricks along the way without even knowing it. In a sense, having ADD was part of your ethnicity, too. It defined how you were, what was in your bones, just as much as your Irish heritage did, but in different ways."

Jim's treatment lasted about a year. It included psychotherapy once a week as well as small doses of medication. The psychotherapy was more like coaching than traditional psychotherapy in that it was educational, informative, directive, and explicitly encouraging. I cheered Jim on from the sidelines. I helped him build a new understanding of himself, taking into account his ADD, and I helped him build ways of organizing and structuring his life so that ADD wouldn't get in the way so much. The medication helped him focus and stay on task. As he put it, it took the static out of the broadcast.

We will discuss treatment in detail in chapter 8, but as an introduction, here is a synopsis of the most effective components of treatment. Note that while the medications used for ADD can provide remarkable help, they are not the whole treatment by any means. A comprehensive program works best.

■

SYNOPSIS OF TREATMENT OF ADD

1. *Diagnosis*: The first step in treatment is making the diagnosis. Often this carries with it considerable relief as the individual feels, "At last there's a name for it!" The therapy begins with the diagnosis.

2. *Education*: The more one can learn about ADD, the more successful the therapy will be. A thorough understanding of what ADD is allows you to better understand where ADD affects your life and what to do about it. It also allows you to take the key step of explaining it to other people.

3. *Structuring*: Structure refers to the external limits and controls people with ADD so urgently need. Such concrete, practical tools as lists, reminders, simple filing systems, appointment books, goals, daily planning, and the like can greatly reduce the inner chaos of an ADD life and improve productivity as well as one's sense of control.

4. *Coaching* and/or *Psychotherapy*: The person with ADD will greatly benefit from having a "coach," someone standing on the sidelines with a whistle around his neck calling out encouragement, instructions, and reminders, and in general helping to keep things going on task. People with ADD thrive with this sort of structured encouragement, and they feel lost without it. Group therapy can provide this most excellently. Traditional psychotherapy may also be indicated if depression, problems with self-esteem, or other internal problems exist.

5. *Medication*: There are several medications that can help correct many of the symptoms of ADD. The medication works like a pair of eyeglasses, helping the individual to focus. It can also reduce the sense of inner turmoil and anxiety that is so common with ADD. The medication works by correcting a chemical imbalance of neurotransmitters that exists in ADD in the parts of

the brain that regulate attention, impulse control, and mood. While medication is not the whole answer, it can provide profound relief, and when it is used properly, it is very safe.

In Jim's case treatment went very well. By the time we parted company, he had changed his life. Within eight months he began to put together his own computer consulting business, specializing in some kind of software manipulation I never did understand, but one that few others could understand and a lot of people wanted, so his business grew. Being his own boss, he didn't have the kinds of troubles with superiors he'd had before. Of course, he did have to relate appropriately with clients, and this was a skill he worked on. He settled into his relationship with Pauline in a way that pleased them both. He had developed a series of techniques for managing himself, as he put it. No longer shooting himself in the foot, he was beginning to make use of the creative brain he'd always had.

Case 2: Carolyn

Carolyn Deauville came to see me one afternoon, "just to chat." When she made the appointment, she told me over the phone, long distance, in her rich southern accent, "Honey, I know what I've got. I just want you to sit there and nod and listen."

Carolyn strode into my office, all five feet ten inches of her, wearing a pastel orange chiffon dress with a white sash and a beige broad-brimmed hat. She wore peach-colored lipstick and smelled of a perfume that immediately filled the room, very pleasantly, but not subtly. Like her perfume, Carolyn filled the room quickly. "You don't mind if I do this?" she asked, lighting up a Vantage. Exhaling smoke, she opened her blue eyes wide and looked right at me. "I feel like we're old friends. I've heard you speak. I've read some of your articles. We both have ADD. I'm a therapist, you're a therapist. Lord, we're practically neighbors. Except I'm from three thousand miles away in California."

"California?" I asked. "I would have guessed—"

"From my accent, you would have guessed somewhere in the South, and you would have been right, since I grew up in New Orleans. But marriage number two took me to the Golden Gate, and I've never been back."

"You said on the phone you just wanted to chat."

"I've been a psychologist for twenty years now and I've been specializing in ADD for the past ten. I've never told anyone my story, and I thought you'd be a good person to start with, since I liked you from the way you talked."

We agreed to have a few appointments. She was in town with her husband at a convention for his business. She'd be here a few days.

As her story unfolded, I had to marvel at her resilience and ingenuity. "I'm an orphan, or at least I used to be. My mother got pregnant and Catholic teenage girls in Louisiana in the thirties didn't have abortions. So here I am. I was adopted when I was two. What a mismatch my mother and I were. She was a wonderful lady and I love her dearly, but she was so ladylike and organized, and I, well, I wasn't. My mama couldn't civilize me, try as she might. I sat with my legs apart, I bit my nails, I let my skirt ride up, I got dirty all the time, I was a real pigpen. My first vivid memory is running away from Summation Bible School at age four. It was so boring. Jimmy Tundooras and I tiptoed out the back door and ran down the dirt road toward the river. After a little while Jimmy got scared and went back, but not me. I wandered all over town until I fell down asleep. They found me late that afternoon in a ditch by the side of the road. Did Mama give me what for. Must've wondered why she ever went to that orphanage.

"My next best memory is sitting on top of the water tower. Must not have been a day over six. Once I learned how to climb up to the top of that tower, I did it all the time. Sometimes, after I learned to read, I'd put a book in my teeth and climb up and sit all afternoon reading. Can you believe it? Whenever I drive past a water tower today, I shiver. They're very high! Back then I remember dangling my feet over the side and looking down and saying, 'O-o-o-o-e-e-e.' "

"Didn't anybody tell you not to go up there?" I asked.

"Nobody knew I did," she answered in a whisper, as if it were supposed to remain secret to this day. "Oh, I was a devil of a kid, or so Mama said, but she loved me, too. It's just that I was always into things. Saturdays. I hated Saturdays. Some inexplicable uneasiness would come over me on Saturdays. I didn't know why then, but looking back I can see that it was because on Saturday all my sins of the week would be discovered. Mama was a schoolteacher and too busy to notice during the week, but come

Saturday she'd inspect my clothes and find that one white cotton glove I needed for church was missing, or was filthy dirty. Or that I'd torn the sash for my dress. Or that a bunch of clothes were missing. I was in the habit of giving away clothes to the kids at the orphanage. I didn't know that I was adopted, so I don't know why I gave my clothes away, but I did. Mama would despair."

"And your father?" I asked.

"Daddy was like the pied piper. He loved children, and he loved me. Which was lucky, because I needed all the love I could get. Especially after I started school and after Warren was born. After all the trouble Mama had getting pregnant, what does she do but produce a menopause baby, Warren, my brother. He was an angel as much as I was a devil. They might as well have put a halo over his head. And school? Well, my first memory of school is getting spanked by Mrs. Kimble for not being able to lie still on my pallet. I never did lie still, or sit still for that matter.

"I was slow to learn how to read, but once I did, I was a voracious reader. *Little Women, The Secret Garden, Hans Brinker*—these were my books. On top of the water tower, under the kitchen table, wherever I could find a spot to be left alone, I'd tug a book out of my pocket and read. Math was a disaster. They had flash cards, and one student would pass them out to all of us. I used to save my dessert to bribe whoever was doing the passing out to give me the easy cards. I especially liked the zero cards, one plus zero equals . . . ? I always despaired when they had a dessert I couldn't sequester in my pocket or under my dress, like pudding. Even pie I got pretty good at hiding."

"You do sound like a happy kid, in spite of it all," I said.

"I was. I've always been happy. I think it's temperament, and it's the luckiest thing in the world. Even when I had every reason not to be, I was happy. I always found a way. Once, in second grade, I was being punished for having smacked Nancy Smitt by being told to stand behind a table away from the other kids. This was on a morning parents were coming through to visit, so it was supposed to be particularly embarrassing and humiliating for me to have to stand off to the side behind this table. Well, what did I do? The table came about up to my midsection, so I just rubbed up against it and let my mind drift away as everybody passed through. I'm sure no one noticed, and I'm sure I hardly even knew that I was masturbating right there in public view in the second-grade classroom.

"I always did talk too much," Carolyn said, as if she thought she still did. But I didn't think so. I loved hearing her story, particularly the way she told it, from incident to incident, all in the thickest and softest southern voice. "The hardest thing about it all was getting teased so much. I was so reactive. All my emotions were on the surface. Someone would make a face at me, and I'd stick my tongue out right back. Someone would whisper something about me, and I'd jump on their back. Also, I cried really easily. Someone would hurt my feelings, and boohoo, the tears would come. Well, you know how kids hone in on that. So I was always getting teased. Daddy would coach me on how to ignore it, but I never could. In third grade I beat up two boys on the playground, and that was at a time when girls simply did not fight, let alone fight boys. Mama was mortified, but Daddy took me aside and told me he was proud.

"Poor Mama, she got mortified a lot. In sixth grade my teacher got so fed up with looking at my messy desk—strewn with bits of paper, balled-up gum, a bent fork, and even old desserts—that she took a few brown paper bags and emptied it all for me to take home to show my mother after school. Mama was mortified once again.

"She tried so hard to make me be a lady. I wanted to peroxide my hair, but she said no. What did I do? I was such a slob. I took lipstick and tried to streak my hair with that instead. It just became a greasy mess. I was forever stuffing my chest with rolled-up socks. Except I didn't do that very skillfully either. One day a sock popped out of my dress in tenth-grade science class. You can imagine the reaction.

"Somehow, though, I got through. All my reading must have paid off, because I scored high on achievement tests and got a scholarship to college. At the time, I was amazed I did so well on the tests, as was everybody else. There were even whispers that I must have cheated. But knowing what I know, I think I did well because I was so motivated I went into one of those hyperfocused states people with ADD can go into. For once Mama wasn't mortified. And I scraped my way through college and got into graduate school, which I did part-time since I was having babies. Then I quit school completely for a few years before going back and finishing my Ph.D. and becoming the woman you see sitting before you now."

"You never knew you had attention deficit disorder?" I asked.

"Never. Not until I diagnosed myself well after graduate school. What do you think? Do I fit the picture?"

"Yes, you surely do," I said. "How did you feel when you discovered you'd had ADD all along?"

"Just this huge relief. At last there was a name for it, especially all the emotional reactivity that got me teased so much. I had thought I was a typical female hysteric or something. Plus everything else. The not sitting still, the going up the water tower, the fights, being a mess, having trouble in school. Things fit into place. The best thing was getting a name for it. I'd pretty much figured out how to handle it by the time I found out I had it."

"Why did you want to see me?" I asked.

"To get a second opinion," she said. "I've only had myself to confirm my diagnosis."

"Well," I said, "it sounds like pretty classic ADD to me. We could get some testing to get further confirmation. But you could have done that already. And I think you know you have ADD. Are you sure there isn't some other reason you came here?" I asked.

Carolyn, who had told her story virtually without missing a beat or coming up for air, paused. She took her hat off, which revealed her whole face from broad forehead to pointed, definite chin, and she shook out her light brown hair. Tall, elegant, secure, she surprised me by what she said next. "I wanted you to tell me I'd done a good job," she said softly. "That sounds infantile, I'm sure, but you can't imagine what an effort it's been. Actually, I thought perhaps you would know how much it's taken, since you see so many people like me."

"Not many people like you," I said. "You never got any help along the way and you've overcome your obstacles just by intuition and persistence. You've done an amazing job, Carolyn. You've done very well. You should feel proud."

"Thank you," she said. "I needed to hear that from someone who really knew."

Carolyn's story is remarkable in some ways and representative in others. As a child, her symptoms were typical: hyperactivity, thrill-seeking, trouble in school, emotional intensity, and impulsivity. She also had many of the positive qualities that are often not mentioned when one hears about ADD: spunk, resilience, persistence, charm, creativity, and hidden intellectual talent. What was remarkable was that she was able to develop her talents without any special help. She did not get buried under the teasing she received; she did not lose her positive sense of who she was, or who she could be. In many ways the most dangerous aspect of undiagnosed and untreated ADD is the assault to self-esteem that usually occurs. Whatever talents these people may have, they often never get to use them because they give up, feeling lost and stupid. Carolyn is a wonderful example of someone who prevailed.

Case 3: Maria

Maria Berlin came to me for a consultation after reading a piece in the newspaper about ADD in adults. "I didn't know there was such a thing," she said, crossing her legs at the calf as she settled back into my overstuffed office couch. "My husband showed me this article in the paper, and I started to wonder."

"Tell me a little about yourself," I said. It is always hard to know where to jump in when I meet a patient for the first time. There is a standard way of taking a history—name, address, presenting problem, and so forth—but that can be overly structured and not give the person the chance to say what they really want to say. So I usually start with something that invites the person to say whatever he or she thinks matters. Of course, this can be misleading as well, because the inevitable jitters associated with the first appointment can lead one far astray.

Maria, however, got right into things. "I don't know what is wrong with me—maybe there's nothing. Whatever it is, I've been like this for a long time. As long as I can remember. Since I'm now forty-one, that's a long time. My main problem is that I don't get around to doing the things I want to do. Maybe that's just the pace of my life. I'm married and I have two children, eleven and eight, and they take up a lot of my time. But I have been working on my Ph.D. for years, and the dissertation keeps sitting there, half-done, winking at me like a sleeping turtle. Sometimes I wish it would walk away and leave me alone."

"Do you have a regular job as well?" I asked.

"Yes. Well, when I want to, that is. I work at the library in town, and they're very flexible about when I come and go. What I've really been trying to do, aside from finishing my dissertation, is start an exercise clinic for women over forty at our local health club. I have a brochure I've been wanting to write for what seems like forever. The management of the place has been very receptive. If I ever get to it, they'll let me run it as my own business and if I pay them a small rent. They think it would be good publicity for the club."

"Your Ph.D. is in—"

"Totally unrelated. English literature. Don't ask me what the connection between that and exercise is. I'm sure there is one somewhere, but I don't know where. My dissertation is supposed to be on Eugene O'Neill. I fell in love with O'Neill when I read *A Long Day's Journey into Night* when I was in high school, and that love continued through graduate school. But in case anyone hasn't told you, the best way to fall out of love with something is to write a Ph.D. thesis about it. I'm so tired of O'Neill I could spit. Isn't that sad? I thought at one time I had something original to say about him, but now I could care less."

"Do you remember what you had set out to say?" I asked.

"Oh, please," she said, "don't make me dredge that up. It had to do with the autobiographical impulse and transforming that into art. Sounds pretty unoriginal, huh. But I had a new twist on it, or at least I thought I did. Maybe it was all just a daydream."

"You got sidetracked?"

"Sidetracked?" she said with a big smile. "My whole life is one long sidetrack. I was supposed to marry Arthur, but instead I met Jim, and now we've been married for sixteen years."

"You haven't been sidetracked from him?"

"No, I haven't. He's my anchor. I don't know why he hasn't been sidetracked from me, but I don't think he has. 'Anchor' is the wrong word, actually. It makes it sound like he's holding me back. What he does is stabilize me. I don't know where I'd be without him."

Maria's energy and openness and her story so far were all typical of ADD, as was her tendency to get sidetracked, both in her life and in her conversation with me. "Tell me more."

"About what? I'm not trying to be a wiseguy, but what do you need to know?"

"Well, tell me something about your childhood. In particular, what was school like for you?"

"School was a real mixed bag. I loved to read from day one, but I was a *very* slow reader. The public school where I grew up was OK, but not very challenging. I got fair grades. They always said I could do better, but I was more interested in looking out the window or at some other kid.

The classroom material was just very dull. It wasn't where the action was, as far as I was concerned."

"You graduated from high school?"

"Barely, but I did. Then in college I did really well. Can you imagine that? Which is why I went to graduate school. But that was probably a big mistake. I should have quit while I was ahead. You see, my problem is I don't know whether I'm smart or if I'm stupid. I've done well, and I've done poorly, and I've been told that I'm gifted and I've been told that I'm slow. I don't know what I am."

"It is not unusual for people with ADD to have erratic, inconsistent educational histories like yours," I said. "Were you hyperactive as a child?" I asked. "Or any kind of discipline problem?"

"Oh, no," Maria said. "I was a good little girl. I wanted to please, whenever I could. I didn't want to please so much that I paid attention in class—my father used to say, 'If you really want to make your dad happy you'll pay attention in class'—but I never disobeyed or acted up or anything like that. I just always had a fantasy world I could go off into."

"You got bored easily?"

"I'll say," Maria answered. "But then, maybe I had dull teachers. I wasn't bored in college."

"What's in your way now?" I asked.

"The same thing that's always been. My erratic nature. One minute I'm there and then the next I'm not. I don't finish things. I get started, and then I drift off to something else, and then I've forgotten about what I had started on in the first place."

"How did you get into exercise?" I asked. Maria was obviously quite fit. She didn't look forty-one—maybe ten years younger. Dark hair, red lipstick, bright cheeks—she looked like she could have played a part onstage. I wasn't surprised that she had taken up exercise. Aside from being one of our culture's preoccupations, it is remarkably good therapy for ADD, both focusing and relaxing the mind.

"Like everything else, it just happened. I had a friend who wanted me to take an aerobics class with her, and I said that sounded like death, but she persuaded me to do it. To my complete amazement I loved it. I'm not a fitness freak; I just loved how the aerobics made me feel. And I liked the social aspects of it. So I began to hang around the club, took extra classes, qualified as an instructor, and came up with this 'over-forty' idea, which I still think is a great idea but one I'll probably never get to."

"How have you dealt with yourself so far?" I asked, thinking as soon as I asked it that it was a dumb question. But Maria seemed to understand what I meant.

"Just by winging it. I thought I had a screw loose somewhere. I went to a shrink once. It was when I was still very invested in trying to get my dissertation done and I thought maybe I had some kind of block he could cure me of. But we really didn't get anywhere, so I stopped going. Now you."

"Yes, now me," I said. "At your husband's urging?"

"No, this was my idea. He just showed me the article. What do you think? Is there any hope for me?" she asked with mock melodrama.

"You're joking," I said, "but I have a hunch this has been more painful for you than you let on."

"Yes, yes it has," Maria said, looking past me out the window. "It's such an insidious thing. I've always known there was something wrong, but I thought it was dyed into me, if you know what I mean. But with two kids, a husband, and a world to keep up with, I don't let myself dwell on it too much. It sure would be nice, though, to begin to finish things at least."

"Yes," I said. "It's been very frustrating for you. How about reading? Can you read OK?" I asked.

"If by OK you mean 'Do the words get in?' then yes. But I'm a very slow reader. Always have been. Plus I get distracted in the middle of a page and there's no telling when I'll come back."

"Maria," I said, "I think you might have ADD. We'll want to do some tests and talk some more about your history, but everything you've said so far makes me think you've had ADD ever since you were a child. The daydreaming, the way you read, the getting sidetracked, your erratic nature, as you call it, your inconsistency, and your general sense of not knowing for sure how bright you are, all these things may be manifestations of ADD. You've compensated well, which is to say you've found ways of getting along, but you haven't done the things you've wanted to do."

"What does that mean? Can my life be different?"

"It is always difficult to answer that question in advance," I said. "You just don't know how the treatment for ADD will work before you try it. But, yes, things can be different if the treatment works."

It turned out that Maria did not respond to medication. While about 85 percent of adults will benefit from one of the several medications that are used for ADD, about 15 percent do not, for one reason or another. Some people have side effects to the medication they cannot tolerate. Some people simply find they do not like the way it makes them feel. Some people do not want to try medication at all. And for some people, like Maria, the medication just does not do anything.

However, as we have mentioned, there is more to the treatment for ADD than just medication. Education, behavioral modification, and psychotherapy all can help. Maria derived benefit from all of these.

In the first phase of her treatment we focused on developing an understanding of ADD. As Maria learned about the syndrome, she was able to rethink many of her long-held views about herself: that she had "a screw loose," that she was not competent, that she was defective.

As she began to see how many of her problems related to her being unusually distractible, we began to set up ways of restructuring her time to help her focus. She began to employ traits she knew about herself but had not used to best advantage: that she worked best in short spurts; that exercise helped her focus; that she benefited from lists, reminders, schedules, and rituals; that large, seemingly overwhelming tasks could actually get done if she broke them down into a series of small, manageable tasks; that she needed frequent feedback and encouragement; that it helped her to have someone, in this instance me, act as a kind of coach, keeping her on track.

This was not traditional psychotherapy, but a variant of therapy that I call "coaching" to stress the active, encouraging role played by the therapist or "coach." I would not tell Maria what to do, but rather I would ask her what she wanted to do; then I would remind her of what she had told me, regularly and repeatedly. One might say that at the beginning of her treatment we agreed upon a "game plan," and that my role as coach was to remind her of her goals and objectives in an encouraging way, always with an eye toward keeping her on track. People with ADD can get off course so easily, they can so frequently get "sidetracked," to use Maria's term, that it can be very helpful to have an outside person keep them engaged.

Done this way, the therapy can act as a structuring force in the person's life, bringing her back, time and again, to where she wants to be but has trouble staying on her own. This is not psychoanalytically oriented psychotherapy, in that it does not depend upon the development and interpretation of transference, but the therapist does stand ready to receive and discuss the individual's hopes, fears, fantasies, and dreams. And such coaching therapy does encourage the development of insight. Indeed, insight is one of the most powerfully transforming factors in working with people with ADD.

We should add that both authors of this book respect the value of psychoanalysis, both in treating patients and in researching and understanding human nature. Psychoanalysis remains the definitive and most thorough treatment available for what is commonly called neurotic conflict or pain. We do not recommend it as a specific therapy for ADD—indeed, psychoanalyzing someone with undiagnosed ADD can be frustratingly ineffective—but once the ADD has been diagnosed and treated, the psychoanalysis can proceed apace. Certainly, the kinds of neurotic conflicts for which psychoanalysis is the definitive treatment can occur in people who have ADD, and the treatment for ADD will not resolve those conflicts. Such people can benefit greatly from psychoanalysis as long as their ADD is understood as well.

Maria rearranged her view of herself and her way of running her life. In our work together the combination of education, encouragement, "coaching," and insight led Maria to a new place. She completed her brochure for the health club and opened her business. It did very well. She decided she did not want to write her dissertation, that, really, she had never wanted to. She had been keeping it alive, as many people with ADD do, as an organizing principle in her life, something that although it regularly and predictably emanated pain and anxiety, still provided an axis around which she could organize. She replaced her daily mantra of "I haven't done my thesis, I must do my thesis" with more useful self-directions. As she began to achieve success at something she really wanted to do, that activity became her new, and far more healthy, organizing principle. Most of all, she developed an awareness of how to work within herself, making the most of her abilities, while learning how to work around her limitations.

Case 4: Penny

Penny McBride's parents came to see me after Penny's fifth-grade teacher suggested she get a psychiatric evaluation. "I don't know what to think," her mother said at our first appointment. Her hands were interlocked at the tips of her fingers and she was looking down at them as she spoke. "I hate to think that we've done anything wrong."

"Coming to see me doesn't mean that you've done something wrong," I said, noting to myself that it is still the case, although much less so than it was twenty or thirty years ago, that consulting a psychiatrist about your child carries a stigma in many people's minds. "What is going on with Penny?"

"She's falling behind," her father said. "That's all. She's a good girl. Never any trouble."

"She just daydreams all the time," her mother picked up. "Ever since I can remember, she's been my little dreamer, my faraway child—"

"Tell him about the stories," the father interrupted.

"She's my youngest, my baby," Mrs. McBride continued, holding one finger up to her husband as if to say, Just one minute. "We had four children two years apart and then six years later Penny appeared. I had more time for her than I did for the others. She was easier because she was quieter, more like me, I guess, than the four boys. I loved the boys." She paused and looked out my third-floor window at the trees beyond, seeming for a moment to be lost in remembrance of her sons. Then she clicked back into the room. "But Penny and I were more tuned in to each other from the start, I think. When you've had four boys and never had a girl, well, you forget what being a girl is all about almost, and when Penny arrived, nothing against you, Joe, or the boys, but it was as if a compatriot had joined my life. I do not mean that we were enmeshed or entangled or whatever the psychological term is for an overinvolved mother, because we were not— believe me, we weren't. But in a house full of males, it was good to balance things for me a bit. Anyway, the stories Joe was referring to are stories Penny and I made up. We called them the Faraway Stories, about children who lived in Faraway Land. The name came to me when I was telling Penny a story when she was three and the look in her eyes was so faraway. I wanted to come join her wherever she was, so I said let's go to a faraway land. And that's where the stories started."

"She liked the stories?" I asked.

"Oh, she loved them. I could calm her down almost anytime with a story. Not that she got upset very often."

"Could she add to the stories?" I asked. "Make things up?" A crude assessment of imaginative and linguistic ability is the capacity to add on to a story line.

"She was better at listening," her mother said. "I could tell story after story and she would sit next to me rocking and smiling. If I asked her a question, it would become clear some of the story had passed right by her. Because she was so faraway, I'd tell myself. But I didn't know what I meant by that. It was just a feeling I had."

"It sounds like you were well attuned to her," I said.

"But now I think she wasn't getting it at all. She did love to listen, though." Regret began to fill Mrs. McBride's voice. "Why didn't I get some help sooner?"

Joe McBride, a ruddy-faced man smartly dressed in a business suit and a muted purple and turquoise tie, put his arm around his wife as she started to cry. Sitting together on my office couch, they looked frightened and embarrassed. "What Polly means," Joe said, "is that we had no idea anything was wrong. Penny was a quiet little girl, that's all."

"I understand," I said. "Try to go easy on yourselves. You're obviously concerned parents. It was hard for you to come here at all. Let's see if I can't make it worth your while."

Wearing a red wool sweater, jeans, and her slightly graying blond hair up in a bandanna, Polly looked like she'd come directly from a hike with her children. She was a casual contrast to her more packaged-for-the-public husband. "It's a bit of a shock to the system to hear your daughter needs to see a psychiatrist," she said, wiping her eyes not with the handkerchief her husband offered her but with the first knuckle of each hand.

As we began to get more history—and the key to making a diagnosis in this complicated field is through the story of the child's life, rather than through complicated tests—what emerged was a picture of an intelligent girl who had some language and attentional problems.

Problems in the development of language can occur at a number of levels and in a number of ways. One can have difficulty with input or with output. Input problems, or what are called receptive language problems, can affect both what you take in and what you are able to put out, because what you put out is dependent on what you were able to take in. Output problems, or what are called expressive language problems, can affect what you are able to write or speak as well as what you are able to conceptualize within your brain.

Although a full discussion of learning and language problems, including dyslexia, is well beyond the scope of this book, we cannot discuss ADD without some mention of language problems—and learning disabilities in general—since they so often coexist with ADD, each usually making the other worse. In addition, we will have to touch on other neurological problems that can mimic or exacerbate ADD, from the obvious, such as hearing impairment, nearsightedness, or a nerve problem that affects articulation, to the more subtle aphasias and memory problems and seizure disorders.

I asked Polly if Penny were late in learning to talk. Although developmental milestones, as these moments of specific achievement are referred to, are not etched in stone, they do give a quick reference point as to whether it is a developmental delay worth investigating. You also have to be sure you and the parent have the same definition of "early" or "late." Some parents consider their child late if he or she cannot recite Shakespeare by ten months, while others consider no language at all until age three just fine, if not a relief.

"Yes, she was," Polly said. "Her first words didn't come until about twenty-two months, and little sentences didn't come until she was three. Our pediatrician suggested that I read to her a lot and make up stories together. That's where the Faraway Stories came from."

"She liked them?" I asked.

"She loved them. That's what was so touching. Even though I knew she wasn't getting it all, she'd sit still and ask to hear more stories. And if I stopped in the middle, she'd pull on my arm and say, 'I want more!' "

"Could she play with words at all?" I asked.

"What do you mean?" Polly responded.

"You know, make rhymes, repeat rhymes, make up nonsense words—"

Polly, who was leaning forward eagerly, interrupted to answer. "She couldn't do rhymes exactly. But she made up words all the time. She couldn't think of the right word, so she'd make one up. Instead of saying we're going to the airport, she'd say we're going to the plane place. Or instead of birthday present, she'd say box-day thing."

"You remember these well," I said. "What would you do when she said them?"

"I would correct her. Shouldn't I have?"

"No, it doesn't matter at all. I'm just trying to get a sense of what this was like for her emotionally."

"She would say the new phrase I told her. I didn't want her to think she was stupid."

"Did you think she was stupid?" I asked.

"No, not at all," Polly said emphatically. "If I'd thought she was stupid, I probably wouldn't have corrected her so easily. But I knew she was smart and would want to get the right word. Plus, I thought her ability to improvise and make words up proved she was smart."

"You're right," I said. "It sounds like her problem was in finding the right word in her storage bin, so to speak. Or in finding the right storage bin. Or in remembering the word. Or in transporting the word from the storage bin to her mouth."

"This sounds pretty complicated," Polly said.

"Well, it is," I said. "But that's really good news that it's complicated, and that we know that it's complicated. Not so long ago we seemed to think all this was very simple. You were either smart or you were stupid. Oh, we had some ultra categories like genius and moron, but it was all based on a really simpleminded notion of intelligence. Smart versus stupid. And that was the basic ball game. But lately we've been finding out how complicated intelligence and learning really are. For example, Mel Levine, one of the great figures in the world of learning problems, talks about seven kinds of memory, and you can have a problem with any one of them that can interfere with learning. That's what I was referring to when I was talking about getting words out of the storage bins. I just wanted to think of some analogy. You get what I mean?"

"Yes, I do, and it's exciting," Polly said.

"What about in school?" I asked. "What happened then?"

"She fell behind in reading from the start," Joe said a little glumly.

"That's not quite true, honey," Polly said, gently containing her annoyance with his performance-appraisal approach. "She was more interested in books than any of the kids. She just couldn't comprehend them all. But she always wanted me to read to her and she still likes to hear the Faraway Stories even to this day."

"What about the daydreaming?" I asked.

Polly handed me a stack of papers. "These are teacher reports going back to first grade. You'll see they all say about the same thing. 'Tunes out.' 'Seems shy.' 'Can't pay attention without frequent reminders.' One of the teachers even wondered if she might be depressed, she seemed so quiet all the time. But it wasn't until this year that Becky Truesdale—"

"Who?" I interrupted.

"Becky Truesdale, her fifth-grade teacher. She was the first to bring up the possibility of ADD or a learning disorder. I have to admit I'd never even heard of ADD. I only knew about hyperactivity in boys. But Becky says girls can get it and sometimes there's no hyperactivity, just tuning out."

"Becky's right," I said. "Girls can have ADD as well as boys. Hyperactivity is the old name for the syndrome. More recently, the label ADD was invented to focus on the symptom of attention inconsistency these kids have. A lot of girls who have it never get diagnosed. Instead, they're just thought of as shy or quiet or even depressed, like Penny." In giving the McBrides an overview of the ADD syndrome, I stressed that ADD was often found in particularly creative, intuitive children. "Lots of kids who have ADD also have something else, something we don't have a name for, something good. They can be highly imaginative and empathic, closely attuned to the moods and thoughts of the people around them, even as they are missing most of the words that are being said. The key is to make the diagnosis early before these kids start getting stuck in school with all kinds of pejorative labels. With some help, they can really blossom."

I took a few minutes to read through the teacher comments which, as Polly had told me, were full of descriptions of absentmindedness or daydreaminess or unfinished work. The comments reminded me of a term Priscilla Vail uses in reference to children who don't quite fit any mold exactly: conundrum kids.

"Would you like to meet Penny?" Polly asked.

"Of course," I said. "But why don't I go to her. Often kids with ADD can focus very well in the one-on-one situation of the doctor's office. In here there is structure, and novelty, both of which drastically reduce ADD symptoms. Even the fear a child sometimes feels in a doctor's office can increase concentration, and so mask the ADD symptoms. That's why it can be so easy for a pediatrician to miss the diagnosis. The symptoms just aren't there in the office. In a classroom you get a truer picture. So may I visit?"

Polly and Joe McBride enthusiastically agreed and made arrangements with Becky Truesdale. Schools are usually quite receptive to this kind of visit. They are eager to share what they know. What they have to say is usually of great value.

I slipped quietly into the classroom during what looked like math period and took an empty chair along the bookshelves in one corner of the room. Another teacher who had guided me to the classroom pointed Penny out before she left. I watched her, trying not to stare. She was a cute little brown-haired girl with a ponytail, wearing a yellow dress and Nike sneakers. Her desk was where I'm sure she wanted it to be: at the back of the room, right next to a window.

Now I should put in a word here about windows and schools and ADD. One can easily get the idea from a school that it thinks windows are the devil's own work, placed in schoolrooms as a means of temptation, pure and simple. The good children look away from windows, while the bad cannot resist their transparent allure, free passage to the sky and trees and daydreams beyond.

People with ADD do look out windows. They do not stay on track. They stray. But they also see new things or find new ways to see old things. They are not just the tuned-out of this world; they are also tuned in, often to the fresh and the new. They are often the inventors and the innovators, the movers and the doers. Good Do-Bees they may not always be, but we should be wise enough not to force them into a mold they'll never fit.

But what of these devilish windows? Is it so bad—a sure mark of educational decline—to look out them? I wonder instead if it isn't the duller child who does not look out windows.

Penny's eye certainly found its way there. As she sat, her right cheek comfortably contained in the palm of her right hand, the fingers of her left hand tapped soundlessly on the wooden desk while she gazed out the window. I looked to see what she saw, but I could only see sky and an ascending branch of a nearby tree. That's one thing about window-staring: you can never really tell what the other person is seeing out there.

Every now and then, usually in response to a noise of some sort, Penny would look toward the blackboard and the numbers that were accumulating. Today's board was sprouting fractions by the minute. Penny must have seen something in them because she'd wrinkle her brow now and again when she'd look at them. She didn't seem troubled, just serenely uncomprehending. Then she'd brush back her hair, and, as if following the trail of a speck of dust, slowly turn her head back to the window. She made no noise. She caused no disturbance whatever. If anything, her serenity lent a calming influence to the classroom. It was easy to imagine how she could go unnoticed over the years.

I introduced myself to her after class, as there was a break for recess. Her parents had told her I'd be coming. "Hello, Dr. Hallowell," she said with a big smile. "My mom said you're a nice man."

"Well, you have a nice mom," I said. "Did she tell you anything else?"

"I don't think so," Penny said, her face contorting into a there's-something-I'm-supposed-to-remember-but-I-can't look.

"That's OK," I said. "Do you want to get outside for recess?"

"Mom said you might want to talk to me," Penny said.

"Just for a second. Your mom and dad came to see me to ask if I could help out with how things go for you in school and stuff. Do you like school?"

"Oh, yes," Penny said enthusiastically.

"What do you like about it?" I asked.

"I like the teacher and I like the other kids, and I like the walk to get here from home and I like the time to sit and listen—"

"What do you listen to?" I asked.

"Oh, to anything," Penny said. "Mostly my own thoughts. I like to make up stories in my head. Mom and I have a kind of game—"

"She told me about it," I said. "Sounds like fun. Is that what you were doing during math class this morning?"

"Yes," she said. "I was making one up about fat old men who looked like sixes and funny old women who looked like nines and they went dancing together and turned into eights."

"That's great, Penny," I said. "Do you think the eights will get back to sixes and nines?"

"Maybe," she said, pulling at the yellow-spangled stretch band around her ponytail. "I was actually going to have them lie down and become binoculars that could see very far away."

"All the way to Faraway Land," I said.

"Yes," she said, blushing a little bit that I knew the name of the place in the stories.

"Is there anything you don't like about school?" I asked.

Penny looked down at her sneakers. "I'm behind all the time. I don't get the homework."

"Maybe we can find you some help with that," I said. "Recess is almost over, I bet. Maybe we could meet sometime later when you're not in school."

"Sure," Penny said. "But you'll have to speak to my mom. She makes all my appointments."

"Of course," I said. "Great meeting you, Penny. See you later."

Becky Truesdale was a young teacher just out of a teaching internship at a private school near Boston. She knew a lot about ADD and learning disabilities. "I'm so glad you could come," she said to me. "I didn't want to call on Penny in class so you could see how she is when she's left alone. She's really smart, you know."

"Mmm," I said, "and she seems happy, at least today." I thought I heard a trace of a southern accent in Becky's words. "Are you from the South?" I asked, the impulsivity of my own ADD overcoming the tact and sequentiality I should have given the exchange.

"Why, yes," Becky said, not annoyed by my change of subject. "I grew up in Charleston until my family moved to Maine."

"Quite a change."

"That's for sure. And you?"

"I actually lived for a few years in Charleston myself," I said. "As a kid." We paused. "How long have you known Penny?" I asked.

"Just since the beginning of the school year. Six weeks. Not long enough to know her well, but long enough to like her. She reminds me of a young artist or something, sitting in the back daydreaming."

"Do you think she's depressed?" I asked.

"No," Becky said with a laugh. "Far from it. She brightens right up whenever you talk to her. The other kids like her. Even when she stands off, they don't pick on her. It's as if they accept that that's just her way."

"What is your main concern about her?" I asked.

"That she really isn't with us," Becky said without hesitation. "And I'm afraid that the further she goes in school the more of a problem that will become. Even in this class she misses a lot, but somehow she compensates. Still, I know she could be learning more."

Becky and I talked until the end of recess. I thanked her for her help and said goodbye, promising to stay in touch.

There was a list of conditions in my mind that could explain Penny's situation. After I met with Penny in person again, met with her parents once more, and got some neuropsychological testing done, that list had narrowed to two: attention deficit disorder without hyperactivity and both expressive and receptive language disabilities.

ADD exacerbates learning problems in the same way that nearsightedness does: you can't focus as well as you should, so you are not able to use the talents you have to the fullest. The first step in treatment is to get glasses, or treat the ADD, and then reassess the extent of the residual learning disability.

Just making the diagnosis, giving a medical name with a rational treatment to what Penny's parents had thought was an immutable quirk of temperament, helped a lot. Once everybody understood what was going on, we started medication. While the medication by itself would not be sufficient treatment, the results in this instance were dramatic and quick.

There are several medications used in the treatment of ADD. They all help the individual to focus better. In a sense, they act like internal eyeglasses, increasing the brain's ability to focus on one task over time while filtering out competing stimuli or distractions.

Of the various medications available, we chose Norpramin for Penny. Norpramin is in the class of medications referred to as the tricyclic anti-depressants. Although medications in this group are called antidepressants, they have many other uses than for the treatment of depression, including the treatment of ADD, both in children and adults. The most common other group of medications used to treat ADD are the stimulants, which include Ritalin and Dexedrine. Used properly, both groups are extremely safe and effective. We chose Norpramin for Penny because it can be taken just once a day, instead of the two or three times a day required for the stimulants.

Within a few days of Penny's starting medication, her parents as well as Becky were on the phone to me. They were all amazed. She was tuned in in class, focused on the work at hand, participating actively and creatively. Most of all, she was really enjoying school, and in ways she had not enjoyed it before. She was enjoying learning. The medication's only side effect in Penny's case was mild dry mouth, caused by the anticholinergic property of the tricyclics (that is, they block the neurotransmitter acetylcholine, which mediates various bodily functions, including salivation) as happens with many over-the-counter cold remedies. This is tolerable and may be counteracted with a Life Saver or other lozenge. The medication did not take anything away from Penny; she could still daydream when she wanted to.

While this was only the beginning of the treatment, it was in many ways the most moving part for everyone, including me. As Penny's mother put it to me in one of our follow-up visits, "It's as if a veil has been lifted from Penny's eyes. She can see us and we can see her. She's still my dreamer, but now it's on purpose that she dreams."

▪ 2 ▪

"I Sang in My Chains Like the Sea"

THE CHILD WITH ADD

Our first knowledge of attention deficit disorder came from children, before we knew that the syndrome continued into adulthood. ADD is now one of the conditions within the field of childhood development about which we know a great deal. A conservative estimate would be that 5 percent of school-age children have ADD, and yet it remains poorly understood by the general public, often going unrecognized or misdiagnosed. The hallmark symptoms of ADD—distractibility, impulsivity, and high activity—are so commonly associated with children in general that the diagnosis is often not considered. A child with undiagnosed ADD is thought to be "just being a child," only more so. It wouldn't occur to anyone that the "more so" was a tip-off to a medical diagnosis unless they knew something about that diagnosis in advance.

Where does the "more so" leave off and the neurological syndrome of ADD begin? How can we tell a spoiled child from an ADD child? How can we tell a child with emotional problems from a child with ADD? One must look carefully at the child's individual history. The diagnosis rests primarily upon the history.

There are also psychological tests that can provide additional evidence in making a diagnosis. Certain subtests of the WISC (Wechsler Intelligence

Scale for Children)—a standard test for children—may suggest ADD. Typically, the subscores for digit span, arithmetic, and coding are low in ADD. Additionally, there is often a wide split between what is called the verbal subscore and what is called the performance subscore. There are other tests that attempt to assess attention and impulsivity, but it should be stressed there is no one definitive "test" for ADD. The most reliable diagnostic tool is the individual's history as elicited from the child, from parents, and, very importantly, from teacher reports.

There is no clear line of demarcation between ADD and normal behavior. Rather, one must make a judgment based on a comparison of the individual child to his or her peer group. If he or she stands out as markedly more distractible, impulsive, and restless, and if there is no other apparent cause for this behavior, such as a disruption of the family or substance abuse or depression or other medical condition, then the diagnosis of ADD can be entertained. However, only a professional who has experience in working with ADD should make the diagnosis.

The two most common errors in the diagnostic process are missing the diagnosis or making the diagnosis too often.

The most common reason for missing the diagnosis is not knowing about ADD in the first place. Not every teacher, not every psychologist, not every medical doctor knows about ADD.

Even professionals who know about ADD can miss the diagnosis if they rely too heavily on psychological testing. While psychological testing can be very helpful, it is *not definitive*. Children who have ADD can appear not to have it when psychologically tested. This is because the structure, novelty, and motivation associated with the testing procedure can effectively, for the moment, "treat" the child's ADD. The child may be focused by the one-on-one structure of the testing, focused by the novelty of the situation, and be so motivated to "do well" that the motivation overrides the ADD. For these reasons, the clinical data—the teachers' reports, the parents' reports, the evidence of human eyes and ears over time—must take precedence over the data garnered through psychological testing.

The second-most-common error in the diagnostic process is the reverse of the first. It is overcalling ADD, seeing it everywhere. A careful evaluation must take into account a number of conditions that can look just like ADD. Some of these, like hyperthyroidism, require testing by a physician in order to be ruled out.

In addition to making sure that no other medical condition is causing the symptoms, one must recognize that ADD is a comparative diagnosis. It depends not just upon the presence of symptoms but upon the intensity and duration of those symptoms. Most children are distractible, impulsive, and restless some of the time. The vast majority of children do not have ADD, and one must be very careful not to make the diagnosis so easily that it loses meaning or becomes a fad.

For those children who do, in fact, have ADD, it is of great importance that the diagnosis be made as early as possible so as to minimize the damage to self-esteem that usually occurs when these children are misunderstood and labeled lazy or defiant or odd or bad. The life of a child, and his or her family, with undiagnosed ADD is a life full of unnecessary struggle, accusation, guilt, recrimination, underachievement, and sadness. The sooner the diagnosis can be made, the sooner this unnecessary pain can cease. While diagnosis and treatment do not put an end to the difficulties ADD creates in the child's life, at least they allow for those difficulties to be known for what they are.

We all want our children to develop confidence, a solid sense of self-esteem that can sustain them over time. It is an invisible but decisive process, the weaving of self-esteem, drawing in threads of experience every day, threads that will last a lifetime. If those threads are made of humiliation, failure, and embarrassment, then the cloth will not be worn with much comfort. We should do everything we can to see to it that the threads are made of success, confidence, and a sense of the fairness of things. Understanding early on that a child has a learning disorder, such as ADD, is one way to help reach that goal.

Throughout history there have been many great men and women who have had various learning disabilities that they managed to overcome. Although it can't be proved he had it, Mozart would be a good example of a person with ADD: impatient, impulsive, distractible, energetic, emotionally needy, creative, innovative, irreverent, and a maverick. Structure is one of the hallmarks of the treatment of ADD, and the tight forms within which Mozart worked show how beautifully structure can capture the dart-here, dart-there genius of the ADD mind. In fact, there is a powerfully positive aspect to ADD, and learning disorders in general, a positive aspect that is as yet ill defined. You might describe many with ADD as having a "special something," a hard-to-pin-down yet undeniable potential. If that potential can be tapped, the results can be spectacular. Albert Einstein, Edgar Allan Poe, George Bernard Shaw, and Salvador Dali were all expelled from school, and Thomas Edison was at the bottom of his class. Abraham Lincoln and Henry Ford were pronounced by their teachers to show no promise. The novelist John Irving nearly flunked out of high school because of an undiagnosed learning disability. There is a long, long list of people who achieved greatness in adult life after performing abysmally in school due to undiagnosed learning disabilities. Unfortunately, there is a longer list of those people whose spirits were broken in school, who therefore never got the chance to realize their potential.

With that as introduction, let me take you now into the world of Maxwell McCarthy.

■ ■ ■

When Maxwell was born, his mother held him in her arms and cried tears of joy. He was the son Sylvia and Patrick McCarthy had wished for after their two daughters. Maxwell stared up at his mom as his dad leaned across the pillows and drew little circles with his forefinger on Maxwell's wrinkled forehead.

"He looks like my father," Patrick said.

"You can't tell this soon, silly."

"I just have a feeling," Patrick replied. His father, Maxwell McCarthy, after whom this new Maxwell was named, had been a prominent Boston lawyer, the rod and staff of Patrick's life, his hero and his guide. The values of intellectual achievement and rock-solid integrity combined with a hard-drinking, convivial bonhomie made the senior Maxwell an almost legendary figure. As Patrick looked down at his son now, he saw some of his old man in him. The large head size he concluded meant brains. The twinkle in the baby's eyes meant *joie de vivre*. And the integrity would come from a disciplined upbringing. A gurgling, swaddled package now, Maxwell McCarthy was destined for great things.

Sylvia's fantasies drifted more toward the simple but boundless joy of holding this little baby. Oh, she had thought about his future before he was born. She hoped for him what she hoped for her other children, that he could have the advantages she hadn't had when she was growing up. Her family had been torn apart by mental illness, depression, and alcoholism. She had worked her way through law school, where she met Patrick, and she was now juggling part-time legal work with being a mother of—now —three. In the process, she'd lost all contact with her family, and she was never far from the sadness of that. As she looked down at Maxwell, she thought, We will be good to you, beautiful one.

As an infant and toddler, Max never liked to be left alone. He was gregarious and active. When he learned how to walk, it was almost impossible to childproof the house, Max was so fast. Cute as he was, it was exhausting to take care of him. As one of his baby-sitters said, somewhat vengefully, after a long night with Max, "You have a very high-maintenance baby."

By the time he was four, young Max had a nickname, "Mad Max." "How shall I put it to you?" said Max's day-care provider to Sylvia and Patrick. "He is very enthusiastic."

"You can be straight with us," Patrick said sternly, for the moment forgetting he was surrounded by teddy bears, little bunnies, and storybooks, not leather-bound tomes.

"Well, it's just that he likes to do so many things, he's all over the place. The minute he starts one thing he's into another. He's a bundle of joy, but he also can be very disruptive in the group."

In the car on the way home Patrick said, "What Miss Rebecca of Sunnybrook Farm was trying to tell us is that Max is a brat."

"She was not," said Sylvia. "He's just rambunctious, like you used to be."

"I was not. I had discipline. Standards. Max has no standards."

"He's only four, for crying out loud," Sylvia said. "Can't you let him be a little boy?"

"Sure. Just not a spoiled little boy."

"Oh. And I suppose his behavior is all my fault," said Sylvia.

"I didn't say that," Patrick replied.

"No, you didn't say that, but since I'm home twice as much as you, you've made it pretty clear to me who has primary responsibility for the kids. But Pat, boys need dads."

"Oh, so it's my fault now. Clever way of turning it around." They drove on in silence.

At age six Max entered the first grade at Meadow Glen, a coed private school. Things went all right at first, but then one day, as the kids were on the floor doing projects in pairs, Max suddenly took his jar of paint, smashed it on the floor, kicked the project he and his partner were making across the room, and started punching himself in the face. His teacher took him outside to calm down while the co-teacher stayed with the other children. "What happened in there?" his teacher asked Max.

"Everything I make breaks," he said, tears beading down his cheeks.

"That's not true," his teacher said. "Your project was looking very good."

"It was not," Max said. "It sucked."

"Max, you know we can't talk like that here."

"I know," Max said sadly. "I need more discipline and better standards."

Later, at the request of the teacher, some testing was done on Max, but as it turned out it was only intelligence-testing. Max had a full-scale IQ of 145, with a ten-point split between performance and verbal. "You see? He's plenty smart," Max's dad would say. "What he needs is to buckle down."

Through the early years Max's grades were fine. The comments on his report cards, however, were upsetting, comments such as "Despite my best efforts, I cannot persuade Max to pay attention consistently," or "Although he doesn't mean to be, Max is a constant disruption in class," or "His social adjustment lags behind," or "He is so obviously bright—but he is a born daydreamer."

As for Max himself, he felt confused. He tried to do what he was told, like sit still or pay attention or keep his hands to himself, but he found that in spite of his best efforts he couldn't do these things. So he kept getting into trouble. He hated his nickname at home, Mad Max, but whenever he complained about it, his sisters teased him, and when they teased him, he hit them, and when he hit them, he got in trouble. He didn't know what to do.

"I don't know what to do with you," his father said one day.

"Why don't you send me back to the dealership like you did with the Fiat? Maybe they have a lemon law for kids." He had learned about the lemon law through listening to many conversations between his parents.

"Oh, Max," his father said, trying to give him a hug, "we wouldn't trade you for anything. We love you."

"Then how come," Max asked, pulling away, "how come you said to Mom that all the problems in this family are because of me?"

"I never said that, Max."

"Yes, Dad, you did," Max said softly.

"Well, I didn't mean it if I did. It's just that we need a game plan for you, like when we watch the Patriots I tell you about the game plan. What kind of game plan can we come up with to keep you out of trouble?"

"Well, Dad, you say it's up to the coach to come up with a game plan that works, and if he can't do that they should fire the coach. You're the coach around here, aren't you Dad, you and Mom?"

"Yes, son, we are. But we can't be fired. And we need your help."

"I'll try harder," Max said. He was nine years old at the time. That night he wrote on a piece of paper, "I wish I was dead," then crumpled it up and threw it in the wastebasket.

His life, however, was not all gloom. For one thing, he was, as his second-grade teacher put it, "chock full of spunk." And, as that same teacher said, he was cute as a button. He was smart, no doubt about that, and he did love to get into things. He could turn a telephone booth into a playground and a telephone book into a novel. His father thought Max was more creative than just about anyone he'd ever met; he just wished he could help Max contain it.

What Max couldn't do was behave. Conform. Sit still. Raise his hand. And he didn't know why he couldn't. Because there was no explanation, he began to believe the worst: that he was bad, a spaceshot, a dingbat, a functional retard, all names he'd been called. When he asked his mother what a functional retard meant, she asked him where he'd heard the term.

"I read it in a book," Max said, lying.

"What book?" his mother asked.

"Just a book. What does it matter what book? Do you think I keep records?"

"No, Max, I just wondered if maybe someone called you that and you don't want to tell me who." As soon as she said it, his mother realized her mistake, but the words were out and irretrievable. "Max, it doesn't mean anything," his mother hurried to add as she tried to hug him.

"Let me go," he said.

"Max, it means nothing. Whoever said it is stupid."

"Like Dad?" Max said, staring into his mother's eyes through tears.

By the sixth grade, Max's grades became erratic, ranging from the best in the class to barely passing. "How is it," one of his teachers asked him, "that one week you can be one of the best students I've ever had and the next week act as if you weren't even in the room?"

"I don't know," said Max glumly, by now getting used to this line of questioning. "I guess I've got a funny brain."

"You've got a very good brain," the teacher responded.

"A brain is only a brain," said Max philosophically, "but a good person is hard to find."

The teacher looked astonished at this precocious remark, astonished and perplexed, which Max picked up on. "Don't try and figure me out," Max said with resignation in his voice. "I just need more discipline. I'll try harder."

Later, at a parent-teacher conference one of the teachers offered this description: "Watching Max sit at his desk in class is like watching a kind of ballet. A leg will come up, then an arm will arch around it, and then a foot will appear as the head disappears from sight. This is often followed by a crash. Then, often, a swear. You know, he's so hard on himself it's hard for me to come down on him."

Max's parents listened, felt guilty, and sighed.

Although Max thought quite poorly of himself by now, his spunk and pride kept him from talking with anyone about it. However, he did have conversations with himself. Sometimes he would beat up on himself. "You're bad, bad, bad," he would say. "Why don't you change?" Then he would make a list of resolutions. "Study harder. Sit still. Get homework done on time. Don't do things that make Mom and Dad worry. Keep your hands to yourself."

Brought up Catholic, sometimes he talked to God. "Why did you make me so different?" he would ask.

And other times, the best times, he would wander unperturbed with his thoughts, from one image or idea to the next, so that big chunks of time could pass without his even noticing it. Often this happened when he was reading a book. He would start on page 1, and by the time he was in the middle of page 3, he would be off in fantasy on a moonwalk or winning a football game with a rushing touchdown in the last minute. The daydream could go on for a half hour or so as Max sat staring at page 3. This was one of his greatest pleasures, but also a real obstacle to getting his homework in on time.

Although Max had friends, he at times annoyed them by what they took to be his selfishness. As he got older, he found it hard to follow the conversation in a group of friends and so he stared off, blankly. "Hey, what's with you, McCarthy?" his friends said. "You on drugs or something?"

But because of his basically cheerful personality—he had learned how to put up a good front—and because his raw intelligence could carry him academically, Max avoided social or academic catastrophe.

By ninth grade his family had grown accustomed to him as Mad Max; instead of fighting back, he took the teasing and added to it by making fun of himself, tripping over his feet intentionally or pointing to his head and saying, "Crazy." His mother moved his room to the basement. "At least the mess can be contained in one place out of sight," she said. "Since you're constitutionally incapable of straightening your room, at least we can move you to the least offensive spot." That suited Max just fine.

In contrast to the time he drew circles on his son's forehead when he looked at him as a baby in the hospital, Max's father now just hoped and prayed that Max could survive in this cruel world, that he would find some niche for himself where his creativity and good nature were rewarded and his gargantuan carelessness and irresponsibility not get him fired. When his mother looked at him now, she thought of him as her lovable genius-goof. At times she felt very guilty at not having been able to straighten Max out, but after three children and more professional compromises than she cared to think of, she was trying to learn to go easy on herself. Indeed, she felt relief that the family had not been destroyed by the problems Max had caused earlier on.

This period of relative calm and accommodation ended as Max encountered the greater stimulations the world of high school offered. He felt an internal restlessness that could only be soothed by engaging in some external situation of equally high energy.

He began to find release in athletics, becoming a fanatical long-distance runner and wrestler. He talked about "the pleasure in the pain of the long-distance run" and the mental relief, the feeling of "absolute psychic clarity" in the last half mile. He was also an excellent wrestler. He was especially good at the move at the start of a period when you explode out of your opponent's grasp. Here at last was a place where he could legitimately go crazy, where at last he could release all the energy he had stored in his cells and slash through the bonds of good behavior as if escaping from a briar patch. In wrestling Max could break free. He also loved the agony of getting down to the proper weight for a meet. "I hate it, of course," he would say, "but I also love it. It focuses my mind on one thing, one goal."

But, as relatively adaptive as his sports were, he also began to flirt with danger. He began experimenting with drugs, particularly cocaine, which he noticed calmed him and helped him focus. He was always on the go. He had more girlfriends than he could keep straight. All this left him little time for studying. He continued to play a game he called "chicken," walking into exams totally unprepared and seeing if he could fake his way through. He began to discover that he couldn't do this as well as he had in grade school.

In a part of his being, he knew he was courting disaster. On his way out the door one day, he casually said to his mother, "You know, Mom, I'm a walking time bomb."

Thinking he was joking, she answered with a laugh, "At least you're not a dud." The family had learned long ago to turn Max's self-deprecatory remarks into jokes. They weren't unfeeling; they just didn't know what else to do.

What happened next could have happened in many different ways. Or, it might not have happened at all. There are many adult Maxes out there who have managed not to trip and fall. They simply live frenetic lives, a whirligig of high stimulation and often high achievement, with an abiding sense that their world is on the brink of collapse.

But Max, fortunately, did trip and fall. It could have been academic failure or drugs or alcohol or some high-risk prank. In Max's case, though, it was the unusual route of wrestling. In an effort to make weight, he violated all the rules; he was found comatose and thoroughly dehydrated in his basement room. When he was hospitalized, his family doctor was sensitive enough to see this episode as a signal of some pretty serious psychological problems.

In the course of Max's evaluation, neuropsychological testing revealed, in addition to Max's already documented high IQ, a number of other issues. There was good evidence that he had attention deficit disorder. Second, projective testing revealed extremely low self-esteem as well as recurring depressive themes and images. In marked contrast to his cheerful exterior, Max's inner life was, in the words of the psychologist, "full of chaos and impulse surrounded by a fog of depression, heated by desperation."

At a parent-child meeting with the psychologist, Max's mother broke down in tears. "It's not your fault," Max said softly. His father cleared his throat defensively. "It's not your fault either, Dad."

"It's nobody's fault," the psychologist interrupted, and began to explain to Max and his parents what they had been living with for these many years.

"But if it's this attention deficit thing," his mother said, "why didn't we pick it up earlier? I feel so guilty."

"It often goes undiagnosed," the psychologist said, "particularly in bright children."

The more Max listened, the more things began to fit together and make sense to him. What he had known about himself, dimly, intuitively, for a long while finally had a name. "Just giving it a name really helps," Max said.

"Better than calling you Mad Max," his father said. "I guess we all have some guilt to deal with."

"But the good news is that there are some corrective steps we can take now," the psychologist said. "It won't be an easy process, but life will be a lot better than it has been."

■ ■ ■

There are a few points from Max's story worth highlighting. He came from a relatively stable family. It is important to dispel any notion that ADD is someone's fault. While inadequate parenting can exacerbate the situation, it does not cause it. We don't know for sure what causes it—as stated earlier, our best evidence says it's genetic—but we do know it is not the result of bad mothering or fathering.

Max's high IQ delayed the diagnosis of ADD. When a child is obviously bright and gets good grades, one often fails to consider ADD as a possibility. This is a mistake. Many very bright children have ADD. Missing the diagnosis in these bright children can lead them to use their intelligence and creativity in the service of getting into interesting mischief but to miss out on making the most of school.

A corollary to this point is that the diagnosis of ADD should not carry with it the perception of an educational death sentence. After all the testing and psychiatric interviews children and their parents go through en route to the diagnosis, many a parent and child leaves the consulting room where the diagnosis of ADD has just been pronounced thinking they have been told, in very fancy language, that the child is stupid. A frequent though hidden component of the emotional experience of ADD is the feeling of being defective or retarded. It is very important that parents and teachers reassure the child about this matter. While one doesn't rejoice at the diagnosis of ADD, neither need one despair. With help, children with ADD can draw on their emotional and intellectual strengths.

Max's story also brings out the crucial difference between the primary and secondary symptoms of ADD. Primary symptoms are the symptoms of the syndrome itself: distractibility, impulsivity, restlessness, and so forth. The secondary symptoms, and the ones that are most difficult to treat, are the symptoms that develop in the wake of the primary syndrome not being recognized: low self-esteem, depression, boredom and frustration with school, fear of learning new things, impaired peer relations, sometimes drug or alcohol abuse, stealing, or even violent behavior due to mounting frustration. The longer the diagnosis of ADD is delayed, the greater the secondary problems may become. There are a great many adults out there in the world with undiagnosed ADD who think of themselves in all sorts of unnecessary negative terms. They may have fast-track hyperkinetic personalities, be impatient, restless, impulsive, often intuitive and creative but unable to follow through, frequently unable to linger long enough to develop a stable intimate relationship. Usually, they have self-esteem problems that began in childhood. The earlier the diagnosis can be made, the better these secondary problems can be managed, the sooner one can begin the creative process of learning to live with one's brain without the obstacles of moralistic or taunting labels.

Max's story is also meant to illustrate how ADD occurs within a developmental framework. That is to say, it evolves over time, just as a child's personality and cognitive ability evolve over time. It is not a stagnant phenomenon but a dynamic one, and its influence changes over time. The tasks of each stage of development may be unnecessarily difficult as long as the ADD remains undiagnosed. Even with a proper diagnosis, ADD will pose problems along the way, but at least the problems will be recognized.

Although we tend to focus on the cognitive aspects of ADD, it is equally important to pay attention to how this disorder affects relations between people. Max's friends thought he was egocentric or on drugs, that these possibilities explained his spacing out or failing to connect with them; many adults also misinterpret the emotional style of the ADD child. People with ADD often do not pick up on the subtle social cues and messages that are crucial in getting along with others. They may appear to be blasé or indifferent or self-centered or even hostile when they are simply confused or unaware of what is going on around them. As they become more confused, they may get angry or they may withdraw, both responses causing interpersonal damage. Bear in mind that just as the child may have trouble focusing on his math assignment, so he may also have a hard time listening to an account of what his friend did over the summer. These problems with people can be just as damaging over the long run to one's ability to get on in the world as the cognitive problems.

The family problems alluded to in Max's story can be severe indeed and contribute heavily to the painful experience of ADD. Children with ADD are often the source of family squabbles or marital discord. Parents get so angry and frustrated that they lash out, not only at the child but at each other. Soon full-scale battles erupt as the child becomes the scapegoat for everything that's wrong in the family. This same process can happen in the classroom. Two or three children with undiagnosed ADD can turn a happy classroom into a war zone and a kind and competent teacher into a burned-out wreck. ADD is almost never a one-person problem. It affects whole classrooms and entire families.

The next example centers on a family.

Theresa and Matt were married without children when Theresa met David and Danny, a set of twins. She was working as a pediatric nurse in a hospital in Providence. "David and Danny were three years old," Theresa explained. "They were patients of the pediatrics ward. That was the first contact I had ever had with them. They were admitted to the hospital for social reasons. They had severe failure to thrive but really were admitted for social reasons.

"It was very apparent in the emergency room that their mother was mentally unable to take care of the children. They were in the hospital for three-and-a-half months. I would see them every day because they were sick children, but they were also running wild throughout the ward every day. I would go down there and they would be just starving for attention, and anybody who gave them attention they loved. I would go down there every day and they would be sort of all over me, running around, throwing things, climbing on me. That's how I got to know them."

The prevalence of ADD is higher among foster children and adopted children than it is among the general population. It has been suggested that this is due to higher rates of parental risk factors associated with ADD, such as drug abuse and mental illness, among the people who give their children up for adoption or have children removed from the home. In any case, the state placed Danny and David with Theresa and Matt. After various negotiations with the Department of Social Services (DSS), Theresa and Matt were allowed to adopt the twins. But there were many problems along the way. Danny and David were wild, out-of-control kids. They were in constant motion, eating erratically, unable to carry on what would be considered normal conversations for their age. It was clear to Theresa from the moment she met them that there was something wrong. The only question was what. Certainly, one part of the problem was that for the first three years of their lives they had not had a stable home or adequate shelter or sufficient nourishment. How much neurological damage was done during those years remains unclear.

But even after they had been nourished properly and stabilized in the home of Theresa and Matt, severe difficulties persisted. Theresa said, "There were behavior problems. At day care they were on the verge of being dismissed because the day-care center could not handle them—their activity level, their impulsiveness, the fact that they couldn't lay down and sleep when everybody else did, that they would want something and then get it without asking. If they wanted something, they just went after it. If they wanted to do something, then they did it. If they were outside and felt like climbing up six feet on a pole and jumping off, at the age of four, they would do it! They had no control over their behavior at all. So when we took them to the psychiatrist, the recommendation was that they go to a special school that could handle their 'emotional problems.' "

For the next couple of years the boys were treated in a special therapeutic nursery school. It was thought by the school that their disruptive behavior was due to unconscious, repressed feelings they harbored about being adopted, about being "abandoned" by their biological mother. Theresa vigorously disagreed with this assessment but went along with the treatment because she had been told by the Department of Social Services to do so. Since at that time she did not have legal custody of the children, she was compelled to do what the DSS told her or face losing the children.

The situation did not improve as treatment at the special school went on. As Theresa put it, "Both Danny and David had several teachers in the groups [in the therapeutic day school]. I had to hire them a tutor because I realized that they were not learning anything. Now they were seven, going on eight, and they still didn't know how to read numbers, they didn't know anything. I thought they were learning things at the school, but I came to find out they weren't learning reading and writing and arithmetic. They spent fifteen minutes a day on these things and the rest of the day was spent on therapy. Therapy was getting together and sitting in a group with the other little children and discussing what your problems were. And if you didn't discuss your problems, you were timed out. If you wouldn't talk, you were timed out. Timed out meant that you went and you sat on somebody's lap in the group; time out from group was that. If you fought them, to get off their lap, you were then held to the ground by two of them until you 'gained control of yourself.' "

"Well, Danny and David did not gain control of themselves. They just fought all the more. They would come home and tell me that so and so had a bloody nose today because they were held on the floor and the person banged their face against the floor when they were holding them down. Frequently, Danny and David were held to the floor by two people, one on the arms, one on the legs. Danny and David were able, by the end of the year, to display to me—me, who had worked in pediatrics for years—how to control a child who was out of control, better than I could ever, ever have done myself. They knew exactly. There is no doubt in my mind that this kind of physical restraint was done to them frequently because they knew exactly how to restrain a child so that he could not move."

I asked whether the school restrained them this way because they wouldn't talk about their problems.

"It was because they wouldn't talk or wouldn't participate in some group. Or Danny and David would start doing cartwheels during group therapy, or they would be looking out the window or get up and walk around in circles. Danny was always the one who was more active and he would be the one who would be more disruptive, not in the manner that he would talk out, but in the manner that he would be going off on his own or doing something or standing on his head. He went through several years of standing on his head continually.

"So that's how the school would handle the problem. They continually badgered Danny and David about their biological mother, about why Danny and David wouldn't talk about her, about how it was OK to talk about her, about how it was OK to talk about the fact that she left them. Her leaving them was continually put into their heads. What Matt and I had been telling Danny and David all along was the truth of the matter: their biological mother was mentally unfit. But that's not the way we would put it. We would tell them that their biological mother was unable to take care of them because she had problems. She loved them, she wanted them, she fought for them, but she just could not manage having children with her. And the school would continually contradict that message with their message about a mother who had abandoned her children. I would fight with the school and tell the school that it was wrong for them to tell the kids bad things, untrue things, about their mother. I told the school the kids were not to be told that their biological mother left them. She did not leave them. They were taken away from her. Instead, the school insisted on telling Danny and David that she left them and they should talk about it, talk about it, talk about it. If they didn't, they would be, you know, reprimanded."

The school felt that the boys needed more intensive treatment. Theresa said, "Their recommendation, based on all their psychological testing, was to put Danny into a Point Four program in the local public school system. A Point Four program is the most restrictive program that you can have in a public school system. And they recommended that David go to a Point Five program, which is a step before a residential program, a step before placing him as an inpatient at a psychiatric hospital. There was still no diagnosis except for the diagnosis of emotional problems. Basically, we were told by the school that Danny and David would never really be anything. They had low IQs, according to the school, and with their history, they said, would never amount to anything."

The parents did not believe this assessment. After extensive haggling with the DSS, they got permission to take Danny and David out of the special school and place them in the local public school. This school happened to have an excellent learning specialist who suggested that the diagnosis of ADD might be worth looking into. This points up the importance of a second opinion. For years the special school, staffed by top-notch professionals, had believed in one working diagnosis, namely behavioral problems due to emotional conflict. And, indeed, that diagnosis was accurate as far as it went. As is so often the case, once one diagnosis is made, it is terribly difficult for those who made it to revise that diagnosis. In this case a second opinion was needed from someone outside the school, someone not limited by adherence to a single precept.

When Theresa and Matt got the opinion of the learning specialist at the new school, they found out that Danny and David had severe ADD as well. The treatment they had received at the special school, not aimed at ADD but rather at uncovering unconscious conflict, might have caused the children great harm had it not been stopped.

Theresa finished the story as follows: "This was September-October when we first brought them to you. I had decided I could not control their behavior at home anymore—it was so unsafe, and so many accidents had happened. I remember someone came to my house one day and Danny had been doing cartwheels for one and a half hours in the room we were in. I didn't pay attention to it because it was always the way life was for us. The person visiting me was a nurse and she said, 'Theresa, you know, I don't mean to say anything about Danny, but don't you think it's a little strange that he has not stopped doing cartwheels for the last one and a half hours?' And I said, 'Yeah, but that's the way he is, you know, he's just very active.'

"But it did get unsafe. They were being unsafe with each other and somebody was going to get hurt. I had decided that it was time to try something different. I had given Danny and David that year to be free, to see where they were going. . . .

"I came to see you and you started them on medication. And over a period of two weeks to a month their response to Ritalin was phenomenal. The teachers were amazed at the fact that these children, who had been so disruptive to the classroom, now could sit in their seats. David, who could not sit at his desk for longer than five minutes without flipping the desk over, well, all this sort of thing stopped. It all stopped.

"They were both mainstreamed, with a resource room available to them just in case something happened.

"They've had their problems, like any other child has problems in school. Their behavior is not always appropriate, it is not age-appropriate still, and my assessment is that their behavior will never be age-appropriate, that there will always be a lag—a lag physically, a lag mentally—there will always be a lag time because they lost too much time the first three years of their life. But we can handle that.

"They are now in fourth grade. In a matter of two years they have accomplished four years of school. They went from being told they would never get out of a Point Four classroom, they went from being told they would never amount to anything, to doing four grades in two years. On their most recent report cards nothing is unsatisfactory with their work. David has had some problems this semester, occasional fighting and those issues, but both kids are considered very bright by their teachers and are very well liked by most of their peers. They get along. It's a tough school. The teachers have told us that it is a tough school and Danny and David are the only new children there. All the other kids have been together for four years, four to six years.

"Danny and David started taking piano lessons about a year and a half ago. The assessment by their piano teacher is that Danny is playing at the level of a high-school student and they are both at least six years beyond where she would expect them to be. Danny and David play and listen to Bach, Beethoven, Mozart, Tchaikovsky, all the great composers. That's who they listen to, that is what they play. They are exceptionally talented on the piano. They also take karate. They have taken it for three or four years. Last year both of them won awards in sparring. They have done exceptionally well. Karate has really taught them a lot about focusing and discipline and all the things they have needed to learn.

"They are fantastically athletic. They can basically pick up any sport that they want to and do well at it. They both take ballet and have been in a recital already. They both take tap, too. They've had their recital and are the only two boys in the entire school to have done that. Matt and I do not push them to do these things. We have had a lot of conversations where we have sat down and said, 'Listen, this is too much . . .' Because besides doing these things they also work out three to four hours a day in karate and they take gymnastics. They are considered natural gymnasts. In addition, they play soccer, which I actually took them out of last year. That was a very big disappointment to their coach because they were the stars of the team. We've sat down and said, 'You guys, this is too much, you have too much homework to do, you have too much working out to do—you cannot do everything every day of the week.' They cried. They didn't want to take anything out of the schedules. I mean, financially, we are in ruins because of them! But they won't give anything up; they want to stay in everything. Danny thought that ballet was for girls but he loves it now and is waiting for his recital. Both of them are stars of the ballet recital that is going to be coming up, because again, they have a natural ability. And what they have done in karate helps them in ballet because they are as flexible as can be.

"I've had a lot of concern. . . . I've worried a lot that we were pushing them, asking too much of them, that they were doing these things only for me. But they won't drop anything. I would like them to stop some of these things! (Laughs.) Because I would like to not have to spend so much money! It costs a thousand dollars per month for their activities and that doesn't include tournaments and all the things they go to, and costumes.

"But it is worth it. With their ADD, they have to put all that energy somewhere. We want them to be ready for adolescence. And so we are trying our hardest to make sure that they do not get with a wrong group of children. I worry. I worry because Danny especially continues to be very, very impulsive, and you just don't know.

"These children are . . . I mean, had we had these children in the appropriate place when we first got them, they probably would have been child prodigies in something. Instead, we were led to believe we had adopted severely disturbed children. We thought, Oh my God, what have we got ourselves into? Here are two kids who we are going to have to support when they are thirty-five. That was what we were told back then. Our belief now is that these kids have the world open to them. They could do anything that they want to do.

"And let me say something else. I want to say something about the issue of a parent who goes through this experience and finds out later on that the child has been misdiagnosed and could have been treated years before.

"The guilt is incredible, as a parent. Especially as a professional who works with children every day and has let this go on. You feel like you have . . . I mean, I feel responsible for the fact that for three, four, however many years, I let Danny and David down, that I didn't give them the proper care that they should have been given. They could be much further ahead than they are now—although I don't know how much further ahead these two could get!

"The guilt that you feel—all I can say is that it is incredible. Matt feels it, too, but not as strongly as I do."

I asked Theresa how it had affected their marriage.

"This is a general statement about children with ADD, particularly ADD with hyperactivity like Danny and David have, and, in my case, coupled with the experience of going through the therapeutic-school problem and dealing with DSS. Beyond being destructive to a marriage, and it probably destroys a lot of marriages, it creates issues that will never, ever be able to be resolved. There were too many people hurt. There were too many fights, too many hard feelings between husband and wife about what happened and what didn't happen, what should have happened and what should not have happened. In our case our marriage will never, never be the same. Had we not had Danny and David, if we had not made the commitment to stick with them, Matt and I would not be with each other now."

The story of Danny and David teaches many lessons, but one of the most important is just how significant diagnosis really is in psychiatry. How dangerous and damaging it would have been had these boys never been treated for the right condition.

Theresa and Matt are both strong, devoted parents who lived through a nightmare and are now finding ways of steadying their lives. As the interview with Theresa points up, the problems did not end once the diagnosis of ADD was made and treatment begun. The management of ADD is really a lifetime undertaking.

If there were ever poster children for ADD, Danny and David would be good candidates. It is hard to believe how well they have done, considering what they were up against. I see them now about once a month. They come bounding into my office, usually in full, colorful karate regalia, and start playing games right away—asking permission first, of course. They are involved in all the activities Theresa spoke of, and to listen to these crew-cut, karate-robed "tough" kids talk about Mozart (pronounced *mo*-zaht) and Bach is to appreciate the marvelous.

■ ■ ■

While Danny and David had relatively severe cases of ADD, there are many moderate cases that frequently are not diagnosed until adolescence. The following case concerns a boy who came from a very stable, loving family. Will had all of the advantages in his early life that Danny and David did not have—including the attention of excellent teachers in two fine schools. Yet his ADD was not diagnosed until after he graduated from high school. Here are actual excerpts from his teachers' comments beginning in nursery school and moving through the twelfth grade.

Notice in the comments what the teachers couldn't recognize because they were unaware of the existence of such a syndrome: the thread of ADD running throughout. Listen in the comments for signs in Will of distractibility and impulsivity, high energy and creativity, enthusiasm and inconsistency. Look for signs of risk-taking, for erratic academic performance, for underachievement. Note how many times reference is made to Will's not paying attention or to his being disorganized. Hear how much the teachers like Will, how imaginative they think he is, but how exasperated they become over time at his difficulty in getting on track:

NURSERY SCHOOL, 1975: Will is an active, imaginative, and friendly boy. He enjoys people and school. Most of his time is spent in dramatic play with his best friend—usually acting out some superhero escapade. This involves imaginary, daring physical feats.

KINDERGARTEN: Will enjoys an enviable position in kindergarten. He is loved by everyone.

Will has a real flair for imagination, fantasy, and dramatic playacting. This skill can be used to advantage; it can also be a distraction for him.

FIRST GRADE: Will's ability seems to exceed his performance in terms of the amount of work he produces. He is a good reader, writes interesting, usually humorous stories, and has good reading comprehension. However, he dawdles over simple board work and work sheets and takes longer than expected to complete questions on his books. While his expression of ideas is sophisticated, his speech is immature.

At times Will can work well independently, while at other times his conversations with friends interfere with his work. He gets into long discussions that distract others as well as himself from work. He is not careful with his materials or the appearance of his work. He needs to learn to more accurately follow directions.

THIRD GRADE: Will has been unable to take full advantage of the opportunities offered in workshop, as social relationships have occupied a good deal of his time and energy this term. He has had some difficulty organizing his ideas, and needs to develop a step-by-step approach. Will would gain greater satisfaction from results if he were more committed to his work.

FOURTH GRADE: Will started out the year doing lovely work based on the concept of the straight line. He came up with an original solution. This together with previous experiences made me aware that Will has artistic potential.

On the other hand, all his other work has been sloppily executed and his general behavior very poor. His mind cannot focus on his work, and he does not give his talent a chance to come out. I would like to see Will make an effort to settle down in class.

SIXTH GRADE: Will has not yet completed many projects. . . .

Will seems to bring a sense of fun with him to the learning environment.

His [lack of] organizational skills continue[s] to slow down his academic progress.

■ ■ ■

At this point Will moved from one school to another, entering the new school in the seventh grade.

SEVENTH GRADE: Will is a satisfactory to excellent student. With more consistent effort, he could probably do very well in all subjects. He must try to minimize the times when he lets himself become distracted during class.

Will could be doing much better work in Latin if he would only establish a regular routine of home study. . . . It is up to Will whether or not he is satisfied with just passing work or whether he settles down to achieve good results.

EIGHTH GRADE (January): This has been a year of improvement and development for Will. His biggest problem now will be to maintain the level of intensity needed to carry on this good record and not to rest on his laurels or get careless. During the last few weeks he has begun to enjoy himself more in his classes, which is good if he doesn't let this relaxed attitude keep him from paying close attention.

NINTH GRADE (February) Ecology: Will is selling himself short in this course. He is not keeping up with his note-taking, does not take advantage of opportunities to make up poor tests, and did not maintain his test average on the exam with a grade of only 67. This laziness has been much more apparent in the latter half of the term. Will could be doing better! Grade C+

(April) English: His writing doesn't show his good insight because it is underdeveloped—urge him to take care with it: his ideas are worth the effort! Grade: C+

(April) Ecology: Will must take his work more seriously and use the good ability he has. Grade: D

TENTH GRADE (November) French: Will's knowledge of France and his sense of humor make great contributions. He just needs to focus his mind a little more. . . . Grade: B

(November) Biology: Will has the ability to do as well as he pleases in biology. To date, he has seldom put forth a full effort. He is the first to admit that with more effort he could be doing better, yet he is often the first to conduct himself poorly in class. I get very frustrated with someone like Will who has the ability to do very well and only does average work. Grade: C

(January) Biology: The improvement in Will's attitude and effort has been absolutely amazing. At midterm I mentioned that Will seldom put forth full effort. This statement is no longer true. . . . A little extra concentration will be beneficial. Grade: B

(April) French: This may be a long spring for Will. A 20 on a quiz is typical of the type of nosedive that plagues him. I am also troubled by the difficulty he sometimes has paying attention in class. All this is offset by his good humor. . . . Of course, his innate ability can help him too, if he applies it a little more. Grade: C+

(April) Biology: Will is the type of student that you very much enjoy having in the classroom because he is always energetic and keeps the class alive with interesting questions. Will is also the type of student that can frustrate the heck out of a teacher because at times he is just not into what he is doing and does not work to his potential. Grade: B

(April) Math: Wow! A student emerges! As of late, Will's work has been excellent. I hope success will breed success and Will will finish the year with a flourish! Grade: B+

(June) Math: The student disappeared. I don't know why Will worked hard at times and at times did *nothing*. The last month he spent more time worrying about the dress code than doing math. Grade: C

(June) English: I very much enjoyed teaching him—he's bright and enthusiastic. And with his Klinger version of civil disobedience [relating to the dress code], he showed that he knows how to apply abstract knowledge in the moral world. I was pleased.

ELEVENTH GRADE (January) English: Will's exam was the best in the class, and a recent story he wrote was also outstanding. Perhaps as he continues to mature, he will achieve consistency. He obviously has intelligence and skill. Grade: Exam, A−; Semester, B−

(January) Science: Will seems to have academic moods that show a wide variation of productiveness. There were times when he literally held out and then he would show a burst of energy and do some fine work. This stop-and-go approach to learning greatly dilutes Will's learning. Grade: B

(June) English: . . . I was greatly impressed with his articulate discussion of how what we do does not discount the basic goodness of who we are. Grade: B–

TWELFTH GRADE (January) Physics: Will remains extremely unpredictable, yet managed to squeeze his average forward slightly with a recent makeup exam on the dynamics of motion. Will must continuously overcome chronic tardiness, missed classes, haphazard organization, and lapses of attention during class, and still manage to concentrate on the specific topics at hand. Unfortunately he will not receive as many chances for redemption in the future. . . . Grade C–

(January) Philosophy: Will is an eloquent and often impassioned participant in our discussions in class. His essay on the imprisonment of Japanese-Americans was insightful, although very late. Grade: C

(April) Physics: I have only praise for Will's improved overall efforts in physics thus far. His punctuality and consistent attentiveness have improved, and he is handling himself responsibly.

(April) French: Will is not making any perceptible effort. I don't want to put him on the defensive, and he may be making some effort that I can't see. . . .

(April) Good and Evil: Will is an eloquent and impassioned participant in our class discussions . . . but I hope to see more consistency. . . .

(April) Ceramics: Will is capable of producing nice work when he wants to but often becomes distracted by friends.

Varsity Squash: Will had a good season. Despite injuries and having to play our best player every day in practice, Will maintained a very positive attitude. As in soccer, what Will lacks in talent he more than makes up for in spirit.

■ ■ ■

Will's story is, unfortunately, very common. The picture of a young child who starts out well and then gradually sees his school performance tail off while teachers grow increasingly moralistic in their explanations should always suggest the possibility of ADD.

I let Will's teachers' comments tell his story because they do it so well. They show us the cute, creative little boy who as early as kindergarten was getting distracted easily and distracting others. They show us the exasperation of teachers who knew Will could do better if only he would try harder, as they said in so many different ways. They show us the boy that "you very much enjoy having in the classroom," who at the same time can "frustrate the heck out of a teacher because at times he is just not into what he is doing." They show us the Will who can be impassioned, articulate, committed to some cause we hear about involving civil disobedience and the dress code, and they show us the Will who can seem not to care at all. They show us Will the inconsistent. As one teacher put it, "I get very frustrated with someone like Will who has the ability to do very well and only does average work." Just as one teacher is giving up on him, stating almost biblically, "Unfortunately, he will not have as many chances for redemption in the future," Will comes through, leading the same teacher months later to state, "I have only praise for Will's overall efforts." But then, as another teacher is praising him, cheering, "Wow! A student emerges!" Will's performance deteriorates, leading the same teacher to comment, months later, "The student disappeared."

The themes of ADD run throughout: inconsistency, and inconsistency again, creativity, provocative behavior, winning personality, varying motivation, exasperating forgetfulness, disorganization and indifference, underachievement, impulsivity, and the search for excitement rather than discipline.

I put Will's story in this book not to chide the school or the teachers or parents for missing the diagnosis of ADD. Nobody picked up on it, nobody, from parents to pediatrician, to school, to anybody else, because nobody knew what to look for. When Will was in school, not many people were that conversant with ADD. Nobody is to blame for the diagnosis being missed. If anything, the teachers and parents should be praised for their continuing, patient effort to help Will work to his potential. The damage they did, although real, was inadvertent.

Without knowing about ADD, one looks at Will's reports and simply sees a boy who is terribly inconsistent and probably needs to buckle down. But when you know there is such a thing as attention deficit disorder, and what the symptoms are, then it is astonishing how all Will's teachers' comments fall into place, describing various manifestations of Will's ADD.

The situation is like one of those trick photographs: when you're shown it the first time, you see nothing but a black and white blotchy mess. Then, when you are told it is actually a photograph of the face of a cow, the cow's face jumps out at you, clear as can be, and you can never look at the photograph again without seeing the face of that cow.

How much happier and more productive Will's school years could have been if people had known he had ADD all along. The moral condemnation that seeps into so many of the comments could have been excised, the inconsistency of Will's academic work could have been understood in terms other than those of laziness or selfishness or irresponsibility. His intermittent poor performance could have found remedies more effective than exhortation or disapprobation, and, in short, Will could have gotten more out of school.

Another reason for including Will's story is to stress that the child with ADD need not be flunking out of school, or have a specific learning disability, or be so hyperactive as to be disruptive, or a major discipline problem. He, or she, can be like Will: an attractive, well-liked student, given to periods of high achievement as well as periods of low, moving along from grade to grade without anybody thinking anything much was wrong that a little growing up or a kick in the pants wouldn't cure.

By the time a solid diagnosis of ADD had been made for Will he was about to flunk out of college. By then his self-image had solidified around such ideas as "I'm lazy"; "I'm a born B.S. artist"; "I never really come through when I should"; and "I'm talented, but I don't dare to give it my best shot in case I might fail."

As Will learned about ADD, he had mixed reactions, reactions that are not uncommon, particularly among young men. On the one hand, Will felt a sense of relief. He was excited to know there was a name for his problem other than laziness, a cause for his trouble other than "badness" of character. And he was excited that there was treatment available. On the other hand, Will was skeptical. A part of him did not believe in the diagnosis. It was too perfect to be true. A part of him felt much more comfortable with calling himself lazy than with accepting the idea of ADD.

Will felt more at home seeing his life in terms of a sort of macho struggle, a struggle he was losing, a struggle to "buckle down" or to "shape up," than in seeing himself as not totally in control, the victim of a syndrome called ADD.

In addition to resisting the diagnosis, Will also resisted the treatment, which included medication. He didn't want to rely on a pill, as he put it, to think straight. In fact, the medication, which in Will's case was Ritalin, worked very well to help him focus. However, Will would only take it erratically. When he took it, his grades improved; when he stopped it, they went back down. This linear correspondence between school performance and taking the medication, if anything, impressed Will too much. It left him feeling that it was the medication, not himself, that was getting the good grades. So he would discontinue the medication in an effort to prove he could make it on his own. This cycle of Will's taking the medication followed by improved grades followed by stopping the medication followed by falling grades repeated itself a dozen times during Will's college career. He never reached the point where he could see the medication as a legitimate treatment, like eyeglasses, instead of a crutch or even a form of cheating. Will subjected his life to a rigorous, if idiosyncratic, code of honor. And taking medication sometimes went against his code of honor.

This kind of deep-seated self-reliance is not uncommon among young males diagnosed with ADD. It was preferable to Will to go it on his own, albeit with great difficulty in focusing and concentrating, than to rely on a medication, however helpful it may have been. It was easier for him to make use of coaching—tips from family, therapist, and others who knew about ADD.

With this combination of insight, support, intermittent medication, and intermittent hard work, Will eventually put together a fairly good college career, after a near-disastrous start. He continues to wrestle with the diagnosis of ADD. He also continues to be warm, gregarious, friendly, creative—and often depressed, due to his underachieving. He fiercely resists using the diagnosis of ADD as a crutch. At the same time, he continues to be brought up short by the limitations ADD places upon him.

Not surprisingly, Will's ADD took a toll on his parents. They are no-nonsense Yankee types who all along thought Will was a creative, talented kid who just couldn't get his act together. They tried all the tactics parents of adolescents try: they yelled at him, they grounded him, they ignored him, they fought with him, they negotiated with him, they sent him to a psychotherapist, they hovered over him, they bribed him, they scolded him, they pleaded with him, they hugged him. They always loved him, and they never gave up on him, but they felt endlessly exasperated at his inconsistency and apparent lack of effort. They wanted the best for him, and they ached for him while helplessly watching him apparently let so much promise slip away.

After the diagnosis of ADD was made, and after Will had spent a couple of years in college, he said something to his mom which prompted a letter, which I excerpt here.

Dear Will,

We know so well how much you care—about us, about the family, about doing well, about honesty and pride and compassion. You are an incredible person and have been ever since you were a little boy. I've always said that you were born smiling. You were. People looked at you when you were a baby, and they smiled back. You had an innate something that just made people happy—and you were happy.

It killed me to watch that happy little boy fade into a frustrated adolescent. Where did Will go? Dad and I tried to understand. We hadn't a clue that there was even such a thing as ADD, and neither did you. So, what do you do when you watch a kid not do his work, but then try, and then not try, and then be sad, etc., etc. I yelled at you and tried to wake you up. Wrong tactic. Dad talked soberly and grounded you. Again, wrong tactic. We were trying to reach you on the only levels we knew. And all that time, we knew we were missing the boat. We knew that we hadn't found the key. [Once the diagnosis was made], Dad and I knew we had blown it with you.

So, Will. What do we say? Sorry? We are. I hope you know that. We are so damned sorry. Part of it wasn't our fault because no one knew what ADD was, etc. But a lot of it was our fault, because we knew something was wrong and we didn't find out what it was. That is what parents are supposed to do. We were trying, but we screwed up. It's not because we didn't care about you. We cared.

Do you believe that? I could see that you might not. But actually, I know that you know just how much we cared, and care. . . . We look on you as a really terrific person who we love to have be around us. I think of you as one of my best friends as well as my little kid (no longer). Who do I call when something goes wrong with one of the other kids? How much do I ask for your advice? You must see how much I value your judgment. . . .

But I also think you are struggling to figure out who you are and what you want out of life. Any kid your age worth anything is in the same situation. Some don't show it obviously, but most kids are worried and wondering. There's a lot to worry about. On top of this, you are trying to figure out how to deal with ADD. You are right when you say that Dad and I don't really understand it. We don't, but we are trying. We want to. And we want to help you get a handle on it. I think that you beat it last year—although you are still fighting it and will always have to—last spring you won. It was great! I think you are making tremendous progress dealing with a disability that is so insidiously difficult that it's amazing you don't just quit. But that isn't you and never has been.

Frustration! We do understand frustration. When you have a little kid you absolutely adore, you will understand better how frustrated Dad and I have been. At you, sure—but on your behalf even more. We wanted you to feel successful and happy. You might not think that we do, but we do. We understand—we hate it that you have to deal with ADD—and we can't fix it. Dad wants to fix it. But we can't. Only you can do that, and it is an ongoing process. What we can do is tell you that we understand and care very, very much. We want to help in any way that we can, but it is up to you now to let us know how. . . .

Always, always we loved you and were solidly behind you no matter what scrape you got yourself into. Always. I think that is one of the few things you can count on in your life. Your parents think you are *great*. And there is nothing that, as a team, we can't beat. You'll figure out ADD. I think you are well on your way. . . .

Love,

Mom

■ 3 ■

"Sequence Ravelled Out of Sound"

ADULT ADD

> I felt a Cleaving in my Mind—
> As if my Brain had split—
> I tried to match it—Seam by Seam—
> But could not make them fit.
>
> The thought behind, I strove to join
> Unto the thought before—
> But Sequence ravelled out of Sound—
> Like Balls—upon a Floor.
> —Emily Dickinson (1864)

Emily Dickinson captures with her customary startling simplicity the distress of the ADD mind. Although of course not written explicitly about ADD, this lyric poem gives a wonderfully apt description of the subjective experience of ADD. "I felt a Cleaving in my Mind— / As if my Brain had split." Not a cleft, but a cleaving; the use of the gerund just adds to the activity of the description. How many of us with ADD have felt, as we whirl around from one project to the next, trying to stay abreast of the mounting mass of details, that our brains were about to split? And then we look down to find our projects rolling around, like balls upon the floor. Most adults with ADD are struggling to express a part of themselves that often seems unraveled as they strive to join the thought behind unto the thought before.

As we are learning more and more about ADD in adults, we are realizing how far-reaching its impact can be. It is only fairly recently that research has begun at all into ADD in adults.*

* Paul Wender, Joseph Biederman, Rachel Gittleman-Klein, Gabrielle Weiss, Leopold Bellak, Russell Barkley, Kevin Murphy, and Bennett and Sally Shaywitz, to name a few, have now all written about ADD as it occurs in adults.

70

In 1978 Leopold Bellak chaired a conference on what was then called minimal brain dysfunction (now ADD) in adults. The collected papers from this conference were published in 1979 and comprise a remarkable book —accurate, ahead of its time, full of new and exciting data. The presenters at that conference, including Hans Huessy, Dennis Cantwell, Paul Wender, Donald Klein, and others, were onto something new and important. They were reporting on their finding that MBD (or ADD) does not just go away in childhood. Instead, it persists into adulthood and can be as vexing for adults as it can be for children. Unfortunately, it took another decade before people began to recognize the clinical significance of Bellak's book—how widespread ADD is in adults and what a human toll it exacts when it is not diagnosed.

Bellak's book, which is now out of print, was written for a professional audience and was published under the dour title, *Psychiatric Aspects of Minimal Brain Dysfunction in Adults*. In the popular press there is still very little. Paul Wender's book, *The Hyperactive Child, Adolescent, and Adult*, is an excellent text for the layperson that includes a brief section on adults. Lynn Weiss, a psychologist from Texas, has written a book entitled *Attention Deficit Disorder in Adults* that includes a great deal of useful information. But our knowledge of ADD as it appears in adults is still young, and 'the field is still finding itself.

Interestingly enough, one of the landmark studies in the entire ADD area, a study which really marked a turning point in establishing a biological basis for ADD, was done not on children but on adults by Dr. Alan Zametkin, at the National Institutes of Mental Health. We will discuss this study in detail in chapter 9, whose subject is the biology of ADD. In brief, what Zametkin proved was that there is a difference at the cellular level, in energy consumption, between the parts of the brain that regulate attention, emotion, and impulse control in subjects with ADD as compared with subjects without ADD. The study was published in 1990 in one of the most highly respected, rigorously edited of all medical journals, the *New England Journal of Medicine*. While there had been other studies that suggested a biological basis for ADD before, this study was the best designed and the most convincing.

Subsequent to that study, David Hauser and Alan Zametkin published another study in 1993, again in the *New England Journal of Medicine*, which added evidence to the biological basis for ADD. Hauser and Zametkin found a strong correlation between a rare form of thyroid dysfunction, called generalized resistance to thyroid hormone (GRTH), and attention deficit disorder. It was interesting enough to find a correlation between a certain kind of thyroid disease and ADD. But to find the kind of correlation they reported—70 percent of people studied who had GRTH also had ADD—added strong evidence to the growing data demonstrating a biological, likely genetic, basis for ADD.

Since the publication of Zametkin's study, and then Hauser and Zametkin's study, and with the ongoing excitement that surrounds research in this field in general, many investigators have become interested in adult ADD. We are only beginning to discover how extensive ADD is—probably over 10 million American adults have it—and we are only beginning to appreciate how dramatically effective treatment for it can be.

As we have begun to understand the biological basis for it, we are also beginning to know ADD in human terms: how it influences a life, what shape it takes, how it can get in the way, how it can actually help, and how it can best be managed.

Based on our experience with hundreds of patients, we have compiled the following set of symptoms as being the most frequently reported. The symptoms below are only "suggested" criteria, suggested by us, based upon our experience with adults with ADD. As yet, we do not have any criteria that have been tested and validated by field trials as we do for children. These suggested criteria summarize the symptoms we have seen most commonly in adults with ADD. Other practitioners may well amend them according to their own clinical experience.

As one reads down the list, certain themes emerge. There is the classic triad of symptoms from childhood: distractibility, impulsivity, and hyperactivity or restlessness. In addition, one sees problems with moods, depression, self-esteem, and self-image. In general, the symptoms are the logical outgrowth of what is encountered in childhood.

■

SUGGESTED DIAGNOSTIC CRITERIA
FOR ATTENTION DEFICIT DISORDER
IN ADULTS

NOTE: Consider a criterion met only if the behavior is considerably more frequent than that of most people of the same mental age.

A. A chronic disturbance in which at least fifteen of the following are present:

1. A sense of underachievement, of not meeting one's goals (regardless of how much one has actually accomplished).

We put this symptom first because it is the most common reason an adult seeks help. "I just can't get my act together" is the frequent refrain. The person may be highly accomplished by objective standards, or may be floundering, stuck with a sense of being lost in a maze, unable to capitalize on innate potential.

2. Difficulty getting organized.

A major problem for most adults with ADD. Without the structure of school, without parents around to get things organized for him or her, the adult may stagger under the organizational demands of everyday life. The supposed "little things" may mount up to create huge obstacles. For the want of a proverbial nail—a missed appointment, a lost check, a forgotten deadline—their kingdom may be lost.

3. Chronic procrastination or trouble getting started.

Adults with ADD associate so much anxiety with beginning a task, due to their fears that they won't do it right, that they put it off, and off, which, of course, only adds to the anxiety around the task.

4. Many projects going simultaneously; trouble with follow-through.

A corollary of number 3. As one task is put off, another is taken up. By the end of the day, or week, or year, countless projects have been undertaken, while few have found completion.

5. Tendency to say what comes to mind without necessarily considering the timing or appropriateness of the remark.

Like the child with ADD in the classroom, the adult with ADD gets carried away in enthusiasm. An idea comes and it must be spoken—tact or guile yielding to childlike exuberance.

6. A frequent search for high stimulation.

The adult with ADD is always on the lookout for something novel, something engaging, something in the outside world that can catch up with the whirlwind that's rushing inside.

7. An intolerance of boredom.

A corollary of number 6. Actually, the person with ADD seldom feels bored. This is because the millisecond he senses boredom, he swings into action and finds something new; he changes the channel.

8. Easy distractibility, trouble focusing attention, tendency to tune out or drift away in the middle of a page or a conversation, often coupled with an ability to hyperfocus at times.

The hallmark symptom of ADD. The "tuning out" is quite involuntary. It happens when the person isn't looking, so to speak, and the next thing you know, he or she isn't there. The often extraordinary ability to hyperfocus is also usually present, emphasizing the fact that this is a syndrome not of attention deficit but of attention inconsistency.

9. Often creative, intuitive, highly intelligent.

Not a symptom, but a trait deserving of mention. Adults with ADD often have unusually creative minds. In the midst of their disorganization and distractibility, they show flashes of brilliance. Capturing this "special something" is one of the goals of treatment.

10. Trouble in going through established channels, following "proper" procedure.

Contrary to what one might think, this is not due to some unresolved problem with authority figures. Rather, it is a manifestation of boredom and frustration: boredom with routine ways of doing things and excitement around novel approaches, and frustration with being unable to do things the way they're "supposed" to be done.

11. Impatient; low tolerance for frustration.

Frustration of any sort reminds the adult with ADD of all the failures in the past. "Oh, no," he thinks, "here we go again." So he gets angry or withdraws. The impatience derives from the need for constant stimulation and can lead others to think of the individual as immature or insatiable.

12. Impulsive, either verbally or in action, as in impulsive spending of money, changing plans, enacting new schemes or career plans, and the like.

This is one of the more dangerous of the adult symptoms, or, depending on the impulse, one of the more advantageous.

13. Tendency to worry needlessly, endlessly; tendency to scan the horizon looking for something to worry about, alternating with in-attention to or disregard for actual dangers.

Worry becomes what attention turns into when it isn't focused on some task.

14. Sense of insecurity.

Many adults with ADD feel chronically insecure, no matter how stable their life situation may be. They often feel as if their world could collapse around them.

15. Mood swings, mood lability, especially when disengaged from a person or a project. The person with ADD can suddenly go into a bad mood, then into a good mood, then into a bad mood all in the space of a few hours and for no apparent reasons. These mood swings are not as pronounced as those associated with manic-depressive illness or depression.

Adults with ADD, more than children, are given to unstable moods. Much of this is due to their experience of frustration and/or failure, while some of it is due to the biology of the disorder.

16. Restlessness.

One usually does not see, in an adult, the full-blown hyperactivity one may see in a child. Instead, one sees what looks like "nervous energy": pacing, drumming of fingers, shifting position while sitting, leaving a table or room frequently, feeling edgy while at rest.

17. Tendency toward addictive behavior.

The addiction may be to a substance such as alcohol or cocaine, or to an activity, such as gambling, or shopping, or eating, or overwork.

18. Chronic problems with self-esteem.

These problems are the direct and unhappy result of years of frustration, failure, or of just not getting it right. Even the person with ADD who has achieved a great deal usually feels in some way defective. What is impressive is how resilient most adults are, despite all the setbacks.

19. Inaccurate self-observation.

People with ADD are poor self-observers. They do not accurately gauge the impact they have on other people. They usually see themselves as less effective or powerful than other people do.

20. Family history of ADD or manic-depressive illness or depression or substance abuse or other disorders of impulse control or mood.

Since ADD is probably genetically transmitted and related to the other conditions mentioned, it is not uncommon (but not necessary) to find such a family history.

B. Childhood history of ADD. (It may not have been formally diagnosed, but in reviewing the history, the signs and symptoms must have been there.)

C. Situation not explained by other medical or psychiatric condition.

The criteria above are based on our clinical experience. They emphasize the full range of symptoms associated with adult ADD. Paul Wender has proposed another set of criteria for the diagnosis of ADD adults that has been used by many practitioners and researchers in the field. These criteria focus on the core symptoms of adult ADD without going into associated symptoms or findings, such as substance abuse or family history. These are commonly referred to as the "Utah Criteria," because Wender, a pioneer in the field of ADD, is a professor of psychiatry at the University of Utah School of Medicine.

■

UTAH CRITERIA FOR ADULT ADD

I. A childhood history of ADD with both attentional deficits and motor hyperactivity, together with at least one of the following characteristics: behavior problems in school, impulsivity, overexcitability, and temper outbursts.

II. An adult history of persistent attentional problems and motor hyperactivity together with two of the following five symptoms: affective lability, hot temper, stress intolerance, disorganization, and impulsivity.

While there are many points of agreement between our criteria and the Utah criteria, the main difference between the two is that we do recognize a syndrome of ADD without hyperactivity while the Utah criteria do not. Wender himself recognizes that ADD without hyperactivity exists as a clinical syndrome. However, his Utah criteria do not include it because they, having been developed for research purposes, select a more homogenous set of patients by excluding those without a history of hyperactivity.

In our experience (and in the experience of many others) we have seen a host of individuals, particularly women, who fit the clinical picture of ADD perfectly, by both sets of criteria, except that they do not have a history of hyperactivity. They do respond well to treatment with stimulant medication or other standard medications used for ADD. Their symptoms cannot be explained by any condition other than ADD, and they do not respond as well to any medical treatment other than the treatment for ADD. Therefore, we include this nonhyperactive group as meeting our diagnostic criteria for adult ADD.

Whatever diagnostic criteria one refers to, it cannot be stressed too firmly in this book how important it is not to diagnose oneself. An evaluation by a physician to confirm the diagnosis and to rule out other conditions is essential.

■ ■ ■

Having laid out some diagnostic criteria, what does this syndrome look like in real life? What is the typical picture of the adult with ADD? There is no one defining portrait because the syndrome includes so many subtypes. However, to get a further feel for ADD in adults, let's look at a few snapshots of different people with ADD:

■ Elizabeth is a forty-six-year-old woman who has struggled with dyslexia since she was a child. What she didn't realize until recently was that she also has ADD. "I always knew I couldn't read. Well, I could read, but not very well. What I didn't understand was why I lived in such a disorganized state all the time. I thought I was just spacey, you know, the 'dizzy dame' stereotype. I really bought into that. I thought I was simply inept. Then I went to this women's group and I found out about ADD and everything makes sense for the first time. Why I procrastinate. Why I have no confidence. Why I space out in the middle of conversations. Why I can never seem to get it together. I just wish I had found out about this earlier."

■ Now a successful businessman and an upstanding member of his community, Harry sheepishly brought me a folder an inch-and-a-half thick from his first twelve years of school. Although he was a very bright boy who scored well on aptitude tests, in his file there were approximately sixty letters home to Harry's parents from the rabbi who was head of the school. The letters all seemed to begin with words like, "We regret to inform you . . ." Harry said his main memory of school was sitting in the rabbi's office watching him pick up an old-fashioned Dictaphone into which he would always utter the same forbidding words: "To be added to the cumulative file of Harry . . ." Harry dreaded the cumulative file. "It is full of the misery of my youth. I want you to expunge it for me," he said. Although it could not be expunged, it could be explained through the lens of ADD. It at last gave Harry an answer to why he could never "do school," as he put it. "It has gnawed at my self-respect all these years. I've always hid from people the fact I had so much difficulty finishing my degree. Now I know why."

■ Jack works as an editor for a magazine. He does well, although he has a reputation for being rude. He leaves meetings abruptly, without warning, fails to return telephone calls, insults writers without knowing that he's doing it, makes no attempt to hide it when he's bored, changes the subject almost in mid-sentence, and in general lacks tact. "He's brilliant," an associate says, "but he's so unpredictable. You'll be talking to him, and you'll look away for a moment, and when you look back, he won't be there anymore. You'll be thinking you're having this really interesting conversation, then poof!—he's gone. It's annoying, to say the least. On the other hand, he's great to have around because he's so full of ideas and energy."

■ George does his work from his car. "I don't know why I have an office. I can't sit in it for more than a few minutes before I get this really creepy feeling. It's like I'm being interred. Then I get in my car, go out on the highway, pick up my car phone, and I'm in business. I've got to be moving in order to think—that's all there is to it."

■ "I like the way I am," says Grace, who works in the movie business. "I don't know if anybody else does, but I'd be bored being any other way. It's a good thing I'm the boss or I'd get fired. Come and go as I please, take on new work before the old is done, make spot decisions and undo them an hour later. I don't know how most people live their lives, so predictable. That's their bag, I guess, but it sure ain't mine. L.A. is probably the only city I'd survive in. Maybe Manhattan, but the weather's bad. Finding out about ADD at least gives me a name for it, but I don't want to change anything. Half this city has ADD, you know. Probably can't survive in this business without it."

■ Peter's study looks like—well, let him describe it. "I have my piles," he says. "Everything I do goes into a pile. There are little piles and big piles, stacks of papers, stacks of magazines, stacks of books, stacks of bills. Some stacks are mixed. It's like a field, little piles with white tops scattered everywhere like mushrooms. There's no real organization to any of it. I'll just think that pile looks a little small, I can add something to it, or this space needs a new pile, or these things I'll move over to this other pile. Somehow or other, I survive. The piles and I must be in some kind of unconscious synchrony, I guess."

These examples reflect the stuff adult ADD is made of. Peter's piles are particularly emblematic. So many adults with ADD have piles, little mess-piles, big mess-piles, piles everywhere. They are like a by-product of the brain's work. What other people somehow put away, people with ADD put into piles.

People with ADD also love cars. ADD loves movement. Many adults with ADD report that their best thinking is done while driving. And people with ADD love big cities, all big cities but particularly New York, Las Vegas, and, especially, Los Angeles. ADD might as well have been invented in Los Angeles.

It is not always as obvious as the examples above. For many adults ADD is a subtle but definite part of who they are, like a red thread sewn into a pinstripe suit, changing its look but only visible upon close inspection. The red thread may be a thread of distractibility, or of impulsivity, or of disorganization, sewn into a stripe of creativity or gregariousness or industry. And the treatment may not be to remove the red thread but rather to change its hue only slightly so that it enhances rather than clashes with its surroundings.

One woman, for example, found that she needed help only with technical writing. Since that was a major part of her job, it was important that she do it well. Prior to her discovering she had ADD, it was an excruciating chore for her. She could not focus on it, and the more she tried to focus, the more anxious she became, thus becoming further distracted. She tried tranquilizers, but they only sedated her. Coffee helped some, but it also made her jangly. Once the diagnosis of ADD was made, she tried stimulant medication. It helped her focus quite definitely, and it had no side effects. She found that by taking medication a half hour prior to doing her writing it went much more smoothly for her. She didn't need the medication for anything else.

To give another brief example: A man was having problems getting along with other people. It was nothing blatant, but he could sense that people pulled away from him. He could feel it even as it happened, as he was talking to someone and the conversation went bland. Although he felt it happening, he was not aware of what specifically he was doing. It turned out that he had mild ADD, the most problematic manifestation of which was an inability to observe his own behavior and to gauge correctly the responses of other people. This made him appear quite self-centered or indifferent. In fact, his problem was in paying attention, in noticing the subtle cues social fluency depends upon and in regulating his own responses. Before leaping into the psychodynamic realm to explain such "self-centered" behavior, it is worthwhile to check at the doorway of attention. Are the lights on? Is the individual neurologically able to notice the particulars of human interaction, from voice tone to body language, to timing, to irony, and so forth? In this man's case he needed some coaching and role-playing to learn how to tune into what he was missing. In treating his hidden ADD, his interpersonal life improved greatly.

These are a few of the areas in which mild ADD may interfere with an adult's life: underachievement; reading one's interpersonal world accurately; getting started on a creative project, or finishing it; staying with emotions long enough to work them out; getting organized; getting rid of perseverative, negative thinking; slowing down; finding the time to do what one has always wanted to do; or getting a handle on certain compulsive types of behavior.

■ ■ ■

Taking stock of oneself in terms of attention and cognitive style is not the aim of most adult introspection. We are more geared to think in terms of who likes whom, or who dislikes who else, or why did our families do this or that, or how can we deal with this fear or that. We analyze ourselves through stories and we quickly jump into the plot. We think of this person or that and we have bits of conversation and we move ourselves along in the scene, from one scene to the next, often quite painfully, but usually as part of a story with a plot. But ADD precedes the plot. It adjusts the lighting and sets the stage. If the lighting is too low or significant props are missing from the stage, the story cannot be fully comprehended. Before getting the story going, before developing the plot lines of one's ongoing narrative of introspection, it is worthwhile to have a lighting specialist and a propman check the stage out.

Finding out that you have ADD in adulthood is a bit startling. These kinds of conditions, one supposes, are supposed to be sorted out during childhood. After that, you make do with the brain you have, with the lighting you've been wired with. You don't expect at, say, age forty, to be told you have a learning disorder or that you have ADD. You don't expect to get therapy to help you read and study better, to learn your way around the stage.

The diagnosis gets made by circuitous routes. With children school should act as a kind of diagnostic screening center for the various learning problems. But adults have no such center. Rare is the workplace that would consider an evaluation for ADD in an employee who was erratic, underachieving, and inattentive. Rare is the spouse who would counter her husband's flight into distraction by saying, "Honey, have you ever considered you might have ADD?" Adults, by and large, have to stumble into the diagnosis, by word of mouth, by reading a chance article, or by hearing about it through a child.

A common scenario in my office goes as follows. A set of parents makes an appointment for an evaluation for their son or daughter. After I complete the evaluation, while I'm meeting with the child and parents together to go over the findings, one parent, usually the father, clears his throat and asks, in as businesslike a tone as possible, "Umm, doctor, tell me, do you ever see ADD in, uh, adults? I mean, can that ever happen?" Since ADD is genetically carried, it is not unusual for one parent to have it as well as the child.

But when there is no direct connection through a child to a clinician treating ADD, adults are on their own. In the medical community and the mental-health fields, knowledge of adult ADD is not widespread. As our awareness of the disorder increases, this will change. But for now, looking for help, as an adult, can be a frustrating and time-consuming process. At the end of this book we will list some places where reliable help can be found.

The people who come to see me are usually referred by other mental-health professionals. I have seen hundreds of patients over the past years and have come to appreciate the wide variety that exists within the one term, adult ADD. The syndrome is even more heterogeneous in adults than it is in children. Probably a half dozen clinical syndromes are camouflaged under the one diagnostic umbrella term, ADD.

■ ■ ■

Let us take up some more examples. Laura came to see me for the most common reason anybody goes to see a psychiatrist: she was unhappy. There was no acute problem, and she was not bitterly unhappy. She did feel chronically anxious, and she complained of a vague feeling of despair. "Despair isn't usually vague," I said.

"It's not in me yet," she answered, "but it's out there building, a big

cloud. So I thought I'd come see you first. Before it hits." Laura was thirty-
two, a minister in a Christian church, married to a baker. They had two
young children. We looked at the most obvious things first. How was her
marriage? Was being a minister too draining? How did she get along with
her congregation? Were the demands of being a mother weighing too
heavily? Were there spiritual problems she'd been pushing aside? None of
these questions turned up much to worry about. She loved her husband.
They started each day in the bakeshop talking and drinking coffee after the
kids had gone off to school. She loved her work and had a loyal congregation. Yes, the work was draining, but she enjoyed feeling so useful. As
for spiritual matters, her faith in God was strong; it was her faith in herself
that was shaky.

"Well," I said, "let's look at the cloud you mentioned when you came
in. Can you describe it? What's it made of? How did it get there?"

"It's a feeling," she said. "I don't know how to put it, exactly. It's a
feeling that my world could collapse. Just fall down all around me. Sort of
like the cartoon character who's run out over the cliff and his legs are still
pumping, but he's only standing on air and he's about to fall a long, long
way down. I don't know how I've done as much as I have, and I don't
know how long I can keep it up. I ascribe my success to the grace of God,
but I'm still left with this feeling that it could all be taken away."

"Is there any reason you can think of that it should?" I asked. "Is
there something you feel particularly guilty about?"

"No more than my everyday crimes," she answered with a smile. "No,
it's not guilt. It's insecurity. A feeling of being a fraud. Not a fraud, really,
because I know I'm not deliberately faking anything. It's as if I woke up
one day and I was at this grand ball, but I don't know how I got there,
and I don't know how I'll carry it off."

Laura and I spent several sessions looking at this feeling of insecurity
from many different angles—from her childhood history, from her religious
perspective, from dreams and fantasies and whatever other unconscious
material we could garner, and we came up with a lot of interesting information but nothing that seemed to explain the cloud she felt on her horizon.

But then we started to look into her educational history and her
struggles with academic achievement. She always did very well, was always
at or near the top of her class through high school, college, and seminary.
That was why she didn't mention anything about it in our first interviews;

she had done so well she thought there was no problem there. But now she told me academics had always been a struggle for her. Just thinking about it brought back fears, fears of failing, of not getting things in on time, of being rejected. Each paper had been an ordeal. She wouldn't start until the last minute, and she wouldn't finish until the deadline. She had an abiding sense of having to strain to get it, whatever it was, as if she were nearsighted and had to strain to see the blackboard. "I began to worry about everything," she said. "That's where the insecurity started."

"When?" I asked.

"College. No, high school. Senior year, junior year, maybe. Whenever things got hard."

Without the perspective of ADD, Laura's history would make one think of a perfectionist personality, which indeed she did have, and a diagnosis of obsessive-compulsive disorder or some kind of anxiety state. But if she had ADD as the starting point of these problems, with the anxiety and perfectionism occurring in the wake of ADD, that would cast a new light on things.

After she graduated from seminary and found a congregation and got married, she thought the troubling years had been put to rest. But the feelings came back in other ways. Organizing the family became a major task. Her husband helped, but she always fretted she was going to forget something or overlook an important detail. Old feelings of incompetence and insecurity surrounded her. She developed a habit of anxiety that she could not let go of.

"I want to let go of it," she said, "but I don't dare. I pray to let go of it, to feel bold and confident, but I don't dare. I have an image of letting go of it, my worry, as if I were leaning over the stern of a rowboat and watching a big heavy weight sink slowly to the bottom, out of sight."

"Back into the unconscious," I said.

"No," she said. "Gone forever. When I lean over that boat, kneeling on the seat in the stern, I let go of the weight and it is gone forever. I can see it sinking away from me and it feels wonderful. I can let go of it in my fantasy—why can't I do it in real life?"

"Well," I said, "maybe you literally can't. Maybe your brain won't let you because of the way it's wired."

We explored the subject of ADD, and then we got some testing done. While there is no definitive "test" for ADD, what testing can do is help confirm the diagnosis and/or elucidate any associated learning disabilities or other hidden emotional issues. The testing itself involved a few hours of paper-and-pencil tests—tests of cognitive style, attention span, memory, organizational style, specific aptitudes, mood, and a neurological examination. Although testing is not always necessary, when it is done, it usually adds solid information to the often ambiguous diagnostic process.

Based upon her history and the results of the testing, Laura did indeed have adult ADD. "I think what you've been doing, Laura, is working so hard most of your life to stave off chaos that you've developed a habit of doing it with worry. You use one toxic state to stave off another. You're right when you say you can't let go of the worry, of the weight. In a way, it's been your lifeline. Your brain won't let it go."

With treatment for ADD, Laura gradually began to gain a surer sense of who she was. She began to believe that she didn't wake up at the ball one day, that there was some continuity and logic to her being where she was. The treatment, which included both medication and psychotherapy, did not eradicate the threat posed by the cloud, but it did give Laura greater control over it.

We also worked on letting go of the weight, leaning over the rowboat, in fantasy, in psychotherapy, letting the weight go, watching it fall. Laura would watch, and describe it to me as it grew smaller to her eyes before disappearing into the depth of the water. She practiced being rid of the weight. At first it was scary. We talked through the fantasy over and over again, dozens of times, but gradually the weight did subside and take on proportions that most people carry every day.

■ ■ ■

The next example involves a man who didn't think he was seeking help for himself. Douglas and his wife Melanie came to see me for an evaluation of their son, a marvelously imaginative first-grader who had been seriously ill the year before. I thought their son was doing fine, but during the course of the evaluation some problems emerged in Douglas and Melanie's marriage that they wanted to talk about.

Most of the problems in the marriage, at least as initially expressed, centered around Douglas. He had bothersome mood swings. He drank a lot, perhaps a bottle of wine a day. He worked, as a stockbroker, with great intensity, and achieved significant financial success, making well into the six-figure realm every year. He had trouble with bosses, but he was so good at his job that his bosses let him work pretty much on his own. Before becoming a broker, he was a jazz musician, and he still took to composing with an attitude little short of rapture. He also loved to cook, and would give dinner parties every chance he could. The father of two children, he tried to be as involved as possible with his kids. The time he had left for Melanie wasn't much, but it would have been enough, she felt, if he were really there during that time. Instead, at any moment, he could disappear, literally. In the time it took to turn one's head, he'd be gone, gone off in pursuit of some new project, some new idea, some greater stimulation.

Melanie felt that Douglas had a problem with intimacy and was using alcohol to treat his malaise. Douglas felt that he just wanted some space and some freedom to be himself, to compose his music, drink his wine, cook his food, and think his thoughts. He acknowledged he could be difficult, but he said he was working on this.

In going back and taking more history from Douglas, it became clear that, whatever else he had, he surely did have ADD. All the symptoms of ADD of the intensity-seeking type were there: creative male, high energy, restless, distractible, impulsive, seeking stimulation in many ways, engaging at times, at times evanescent, moody, independent, and anxious when left without structure and routine.

After I explained to Douglas and Melanie what ADD was, there was a pause in the room. The couple looked at each other, then broke out in laughter. "That's me!" Douglas said. "You have me down to a T!"

Melanie leaned over and patted her husband's knee. "You mean there's a name for all the stuff you pull? Honey, there's hope?" Then she looked at me. "There is something we can do for this?"

"Yes, I think so," I said. "But first, let's talk some more."

Such was their curiosity and excitement, the appointment took the time of two sessions. Afterward, Douglas wrote me a letter, which I excerpt here. "A theory of behavior," he began,

> is only a good metaphor as long as it allows you to explain a whole raft of activities as stemming from the theory. I have to tell you that your description of me as "classic" ADD has been a particularly useful metaphor for me. In fact, coming upon it has provided me with one of the most singular experiences of my entire life, because all of a

sudden there are an enormous (on the order of 1,000+ instances) number of moments in my life which make sense to me now, and didn't before, as a consequence of your providing me with this metaphor.

He then went on to write of some of these problems.

I had always done well in English, but I remember realizing one day that I couldn't "comprehend" what I was reading in one of the lessons well enough to be able to answer any of the questions. I remember going over and over the same bit and not having it stick any better the fifth time than the first. So, for really the only time in my life, I cheated and found the answer sheet. . . . I can now recall the feeling of complete confusion I felt with the assignments. I have continued to feel that way at various other times in my life. Even now I have an inordinately hard time reading, especially for someone who makes his living absorbing written documents. I have had my glasses and contact lens prescriptions changed at least three times apiece in the last three years in an attempt to "fix" my reading problem, which essentially involves starting to read a page, getting through about three lines with comprehension, then all of a sudden finding myself at the bottom of the page not recalling any of the words I just read.

At the end of my junior year in high school, having never really attended study hall or anything of the sort, and following my third straight year of A+ grades, I made a conscious decision that "if they thought *that* was good, getting my grades, wait until I really turn on the after burners in my senior year." I decided to attend study halls and *really* apply myself in order to insure my acceptance into Harvard. I really did work harder that year than I ever had before, but I got, for example, a 50 percent on my midyear exam in math, having never got less than a 90 percent in my life. I also completely blew history and couldn't remember anything from any of my lessons, and essentially screwed up the entire year in every course except creative writing. Even now I have dreams which involve finding myself in prep school, and all of a sudden realizing I hadn't graduated because I had blown all those courses so badly.

I had a similar experience in graduate school in music, where I wrote a lot of music for other students and dedicated the pieces to them. I was asked by a French horn player if I could write a piece for her recital in seven or eight months' time. In all previous cases *I did it on my own time*, and invariably got the thing done in less than a month. But in this case the pressure associated with her commission totally froze me. I was never able even to begin to write the piece, much less finish it.

These examples of what I would term "random failure" were incredibly unnerving to me and contributed to a sense I had of myself (and probably still do have) that every success I had prior to that moment was proven, *by that moment*, to have been a sham, and a fake, and a hoax on everyone including me, which led me to the inevitable question, "Why don't you just admit that you are of limited intelligence, even less vision, and give up?" For some reason, I didn't.

I have had any number of subsequent occurrences where, under some sort of pressure, I have, for varying periods of time, lost the ability to concentrate completely, and fallen into fairly significant depressions whose main characteristic is this self-flagellation. My wife, Melanie, finds this behavior the toughest of all my "foibles" to deal with because there is essentially no answer she has been able to find to get me out. I always feel as if describing how I feel and think about myself is too complicated; it's as if I can hear the whole conversation in advance and I know all of the twists and turns it will take before they happen, so why bother? The effort just isn't worth it. So, when Melanie asks me in these moods if there is anything she can say or do, she is met with an impatient "Thanks, but no thanks." As a consequence, she has felt totally disconnected from me for sustained periods of time. I will, in those periods, come home and sit down in front of the TV and watch the news or listen to music late into the night, unable to speak more than monosyllabically with anyone in my family. I always thought my attention to that TV was the result of my intense interest in current events, but it's pretty clear to me now that when I was feeling overwhelmed, going to sit in my favorite chair in my habitual spot in our living room had a salutary effect on my state of mind—it helped break the state of negative hyperfocus I'd fallen into—regardless of the content of the news that night.

And when I haven't been depressed during these periods, I have become a stimulation hound. When I was down, I started smoking again, I went out to hear a lot of loud electric blues several nights a week, I drank more, etc. Melanie thought this was all the behavior of a basically decadent person who had sort of lost it, but for me it was very clearly a need to achieve some centeredness by "going for the gusto."

More recently, I was working as an analyst for a particularly difficult man in New York, and one afternoon, before Melanie and I and the kids were supposed to go off for the weekend, this man, Bob, and I had a very difficult argument, which was simply the latest of a series of serious disagreements. I found this conversation so unnerving that when Melanie came to pick me up I was essentially unable to talk for the entire ride up in the car and for the rest of the evening. That obviously didn't go over very well with Melanie, who thought that I should just "snap out of it." The next morning I woke up and we were supposed to go skiing with some friends, and just as I was about to get on the ski lift, I turned to Melanie and said that I had to leave. I didn't just *want* to leave; I *had* to leave. I couldn't really explain to her or to myself why I had to leave, but I just knew I couldn't stay there anymore. As usual, she found my behavior completely unacceptable, but also knew there was nothing she could do to stop me. I found a car-rental agency thirty miles away and told the people at the lodge where we were staying that I had a medical emergency back in Boston so they would have one of their young employees drive me to this gas station where they had one car left. I drove back to Boston listening to reports of the developments in the Iraq-Kuwait war and promptly went to my office, which had all of the things I needed to get myself back in a "crisp" or "clear" frame of mind—my computers, my card files, my IN-box, my calendar, etc. As a consequence, I was able to find the peace of mind to think about what I couldn't think about in the midst of my wife and children and friends.

It was clear to me when I got back to the office having driven all of that way, that that was what I needed, but I couldn't articulate it. As a matter of fact, I was embarrassed to articulate it, because both my friends and Melanie have always made disparaging remarks about how I work on weekends. But since I have been an adult, first as a composer, then as a professional in the money business, I have always needed to be 'at my post,' so to speak, for at least some portion of

every day. It keeps me in focus to have a routine to plug myself into.
But since none of my friends or wife or children have such a need,
they have long regarded such behavior as changeable, that if I would
just relax a little bit, I wouldn't need to go to the office, I would see
more of my kids, and everything would be great. Although I love to
see my family and do things together, being a father in the same way
someone without ADD is just isn't possible because it is very clear to
me I get into panic situations if I don't have a pretty strict routine
built into my life, which involves a good deal of alone time, not
necessarily quiet, but alone time.

Many of Douglas's symptoms could be explained by other
diagnoses—anxiety disorder, alcohol abuse, phobic personality, depressive
disorder, obsessive-compulsive disorder—but no single diagnosis explains
all the symptoms as well as ADD does. His reading problem in school is
quite typical of ADD. He may have had dyslexia as well, but his tuning
out a few lines into a page is exactly what you see with ADD. His independence, needing to do things on his own time, on his own schedule, is
also typical of ADD, as is his frustration intolerance and his sense of being
a fraud. His cognitive failures invalidated all his successes, in his own mind,
and his self-esteem plummeted.

We see the same difficulty in tolerating tension interpersonally in his
description of not being able to explain himself to Melanie. "I always feel
as if describing how I feel and think about myself is too complicated—it's
as if I can hear the whole conversation in advance, and I know all of the
twists and turns it will take before they happen, so why bother? The effort
just isn't worth it." It was not that he couldn't think it through. He certainly
could do that. It was bearing with the tension of explaining himself that
so upset him. The tension of constructing an explanation, from A to B to
C to D, apparently so simple a task, irritates many people with ADD. While
they can hold the information in mind, they do not have the patience to
sequentially put it out. That is too tedious. They would like to dump the
information in a heap on the floor all at once and have it be comprehended
instantly. Otherwise, as Douglas says, it's just not worth the effort. It's too
boring.

Other symptoms are worth noticing. He used intense living and alcohol to treat depressive moods, and he used structure to relieve anxiety.

His flight home from the skiing trip to the structure of his office, which in one individual may have represented a problem with intimacy or in another person a kind of agoraphobia, in Douglas was a way of quelling the anxiety the unstructured activity at the ski lodge created.

What of Douglas's need for structure? In chapter 8, on treatment, we will stress how important structure can be, and how upsetting its absence is in children and adults with ADD. Douglas sought structure regularly, and desperately missed it on his skiing trip. While we all need external structure in our lives—some degree of predictability, routine, organization—those with ADD need it much more than most people. They need external structure so much because they so lack internal structure. They carry with them a frightening sense that their world might cave in at any moment. They often feel on the brink of disaster, as if they were juggling a few more balls than they're able to. Their inner world begs for reassurance, for signposts and guidelines. They need the devices Douglas reached for in his moment of misery—in his words, "my computers, my card files, my IN box, my calendar"—because they feel overwhelmed by chaos without them. What differentiates their need for structure from everybody's ordinary need for it is a matter of degree. They need it a lot, and they need it often. While someone else might bolt from the ski slope and rush home to take a medication, or make a deadline, Douglas rushed home to find his computers and calendars, to find the signposts he had set up to give himself organization and control. Without these structures, when challenged by open-ended time, he felt he was coming unhinged. Intuitively, desperately, he sought out what he needed; he found his best treatment. One can almost see him settling into his office, reaching for his calendar, turning on his computer, checking through his IN box, and imagine him heaving a sigh of relief as the anxiety subsides from within and he is calmed by an old friend.

Douglas shows us how he used structure to "treat" himself, but how does a therapist work structure into an actual treatment regimen?

The therapist must become active and directive in helping the patient reorganize his life. Contrary to the practice of psychoanalytic psychotherapists, the ADD therapist must offer concrete suggestions concerning ways of getting organized, staying focused, making plans, keeping to schedules, prioritizing tasks to be done, and, in general, dealing with the chaos of everyday life. The therapist should not do this *for* the patient, but *with* the patient, so that the patient can learn to do it for himself.

The therapist might, for example, suggest that the patient buy a daily organizer, and then go over with the patient how to set it up. Or the therapist might suggest ways of finding a financial planner, and then remind the patient to do it until it gets done. This is anathema to most traditional therapy, but with people with ADD it is essential. They need direction. They need structure. The therapist should not tell the patient whom to marry, but the therapist most certainly should coach the patient on how to get organized for a date.

Douglas knew intuitively about the importance of structure. I can use myself as another example of someone who knew intuitively that he needed structure more than most people do. Long before I knew I had ADD, I realized that I needed special kinds of organizational aids. In medical school, for example, I relied heavily upon flash cards to help me master the huge amount of information one must assimilate during those four years. Particularly during the first two years of medical school when the basic medical sciences are presented, I broke down each course into hundreds of index cards. Each card would contain one or two facts I had to remember. Each card was manageable, and by focusing on one card at a time, I never had to deal with the seemingly unmanageable entirety of any one course. This structuring technique of breaking down large tasks into small ones—in my case a large course into a series of small index cards—is a valuable technique for anyone to learn to use, but it is particularly valuable for those of us who have ADD, because we can quickly feel overwhelmed by big projects or complex undertakings. When I learned what ADD was, I realized that I had been effectively "treating" my ADD throughout my education with various structuring techniques.

As Douglas learned more about ADD, he also became articulate in describing his feelings associated with the condition. One of his best descriptions was the recounting of a dream he had:

> Melanie and I were sitting in a chemistry classroom with twenty or so other students and a fifty-six-year-old professor. He was furiously writing on the blackboard. He was putting down a long series of equations, and he was defining the constants, represented by x, y, and z. He was thinking carefully.
>
> After a few minutes he turned around and began to engage all of us, telling us this was about the development of Cizimar. But he

didn't tell us what Cizimar was, what it was used for, or why you would want to know how to "develop" it.

He then began to "solve" the series of equations, plugging in the constants as he went, and in a very short time he arrived at the answer—zero—and he turned around proudly. Everyone else in the class looked proud, too.

He then began to talk about the process of solving this equation, and I asked in a relatively quiet voice, because it was clear I was the only one who didn't understand what the point of all this was, "What is Cizimar and why do we want to develop it?" But he didn't hear me because he was quite worked up about the explanation of everything following the solution of the equation. I asked again, this time in a louder voice which got his attention, and he stopped and looked at me, as did everyone else in the class. He said, "It is used to balance macadam," and proceeded down whatever course he was pursuing. I paused for a second, presuming I could apply this piece of knowledge and everything would become clear, but even though I knew what macadam was, I had no idea why one would want to "balance" it. So I asked, "Why do you want to balance macadam, or *when* do you want to balance macadam?"

It was now clear I was interrupting his train of thought, along with everyone else's. But I needed to know what was going on because it was very frustrating to listen to the discussion with no idea what it was about. The professor came over to me, having picked up a spoonlike object from his desk which was filled with something that looked like oily, black salt, clearly measured with some precision, and he began to talk to me—he was standing and I was sitting—in a fairly severe fashion about how this ladle full of Cizimar, which is an example of the result of everything he has just explained, is used in some sort of circumstance to balance macadam. All the while I was straining to understand what he was going on about, but it was hopeless. He and everyone else understood, but I didn't. So I got up, threw my hands in the air, and said, "This is stupid, I'm out of here!" and I left the classroom, knowing that everyone in the room (with the probable exception of Melanie) thought I was a dunce.

But somewhere in my brain I knew I was not a dunce, even though right at that moment I felt like one. I thought to leave the situation for a moment and get some fresh air would solve the problem.

And the fact is that often in my life it has.

Douglas's dream is one of the most vivid examples I've heard of the feeling of just not getting it that bedevils so many people with ADD. In fact, Douglas was very good at math and chemistry, but sometimes there were moments, as in the dream, when he didn't get it at all—because of his ADD. The sense of growing panic, the feeling that gibberish is being passed off as coherent conversation, the fear that the world is engaged in meaningless discourse masquerading as meaningful exchange—these are the blurry states individuals with ADD negotiate each day.

While Douglas continued to need his individual therapy—treatment for ADD does not remove all psychological conflict or pain—the treatment for his ADD helped both Melanie and him reach a new place in their lives. Using a combination of couples therapy, medication, and structure, Douglas learned how to bear with some tension, how to talk to Melanie about his feelings and how to listen to Melanie talk to him, and how to plan and anticipate his emotional needs rather than reacting impulsively to them. As Melanie grew able to understand much of Douglas's behavior in the context of ADD, she became less resentful of him. As Douglas became a better listener and communicator, someone who could "be there" more, he also found that he drank less. This was in part due to an effort initially to please Melanie in recompense for all the hard times he'd caused her, but more and more it was due to a reduced desire to drink. Melanie and Douglas are now both doing well.

■ ■ ■

The next case takes us into the life of a woman who was told from an early age by her father that she "had no more sense than a jaybird" and that her main problem was that she was "lazy." Although a part of her bristled at these remarks, knowing they were untrue, another part of her accepted them, took them in, and incorporated them into her self-image. Now fifty years old, married with grown children, Sarah has a career as a potter. She came in from out of town for a consultation because her husband had discovered he had ADD and Sarah thought many of her symptoms might be understood in a similar light.

She and her husband, Jeff, arrived, sat down, and immediately Sarah smiled back tears. "I don't want to cry. I told myself I wouldn't cry," she said.

"It's OK to cry in here," I said. "Maybe you can try to tell me what the tears are about?"

"It's been so many years living like this, thinking I'm stupid, but knowing I'm not. I brought along this list," she added, holding up some papers. "I wrote down everything I could so you could read it." She handed me the papers, bunched up like a scarf.

The first item on the list referred to a cough drop. As I read it, I asked her about it.

"Oh," she answered, "that is about a cough drop someone left on the dashboard of our car. The other day I saw the cough drop and thought, I'll have to throw that away. When I arrived at my first stop, I forgot to take the cough drop to a trash can. When I got back into the car, I saw it and thought, I'll throw it away at the gas station. The gas station came and went and I hadn't thrown the cough drop away. Well, the whole day went like that, the cough drop still sitting on the dashboard. When I got home, I thought, I'll take it inside with me and throw it out. In the time it took me to open the car door, I forgot about the cough drop. It was there to greet me when I got in the car the next morning. Jeff was with me. I looked at the cough drop and burst into tears. Jeff asked me why I was crying, and I told him it was because of the cough drop. He thought I was losing my mind. 'But you don't understand,' I said, 'my whole life is like that. I see something that I mean to do and then I don't do it. It's not only trivial things like the cough drop; it's big things, too.' That's why I cried."

It was such a classic ADD story that I've come to call it the "cough-drop sign" when a person habitually has trouble following through on plans on a minute-to-minute, even second-to-second, basis. This is not due to procrastination per se as much as it is due to the busyness of the moment interrupting or interfering with one's memory circuits. You can get up from your chair, go into the kitchen to get a glass of water, and then in the kitchen forget the reason for your being there. Or, on a larger scale, the most important item on your agenda for a given day might be to make a certain telephone call, a call that, say, has crucial business consequences. You mean to do it, you want to do it, you are not afraid of doing it, indeed you are eager to make the call and feel confident about doing it. And yet, as the day progresses, you never get around to making the call. An invisible shield of procrastination seems to separate you from the task. You sharpen your pencil instead, talk to an associate, pay some bills, have lunch, get interrupted by a minor problem, return some other calls to clear your desk so you can make the important call, only to find that the end of the day has come and the call still has not been made. Or, on an interpersonal level, you may mean to bring home flowers to your spouse, have it in mind to do it all day, really want to do it, in fact on the subway home envision just which florist shop you will stop at, only to find yourself standing in front of your spouse, saying "Hi, honey" with no flowers in hand. Sometimes this is due to unconsciously not wanting to buy the flowers. But sometimes, far more often than most people realize, it is due to ADD. Wanting to do something, meaning to do something, but just not doing it: this is the "cough drop sign" and it is common among adults with ADD.

The rest of Sarah's list of symptoms read as if lifted from a text on ADD:

Daydreamed a lot in class as a child.

Called "lazy" and "no more sense than a jaybird" by my father.

Got 730 on the verbal college boards but couldn't get my papers in on time so got C's in English.

Like novelty, lots of changing interests.

Have lots of ideas but have a hard time structuring things so they actually happen.

Desk cluttered.

Forgetful.

Often have a hard time finding the right word so impulsively say any word or just stay silent and feel stupid.

Work best in a framework: things need to fit into the whole picture. Feel like I'm always looking for a structure.

Difficult to walk a straight line—tend to veer into things or people.

Have always felt that I think differently from most people.

Unless I'm very involved, usually get sleepy during lectures.

Handwriting: sometimes I write things I don't mean to; skip letters or form them wrong.

Bathroom cleaning on Sat.: look at job, feel overwhelmed. Turn on radio to get me going. Find the music irritating later and turn it off. Remember the job and tackle it, then it goes all right. Often I feel like I have to push through a wall to get into a job.

No matter how organized I try to be, I always mess up!

Stream-of-consciousness way of doing housework—hop from this to that with no apparent logic, just a schedule.

Always trying to organize things, but it doesn't come easily. If I don't organize them, I won't know where they are.

Lose what's in my head very easily.

Organize my life around projects. They give me something to think about.

Feel that I have to push myself all the time, especially getting *into* things.

Like things simple—early music, not romantic.

Weed the garden, remove the clutter. I like to do that.

Problem with lateness. Even when there is plenty of time, I fill it up and then cut things too close or lose track of the time. I don't have a sense of the passing of time.

Inwardly feel desperate. Reassurances from other people don't help. There is something inside that needs to change.

Doors and drawers—never close them after myself, then come back and see them and close them.

Inside, I feel like I'm saying, "I'm not stupid!"

Easily hurt and rejected.

Don't clean up after myself well. Get overwhelmed by a large confused mess.

General problems with distractibility and disorganization.

Most at peace when I'm doing something with my hands like gardening or pottery.

After I read through Sarah's list, I asked her how she composed it. "Jeff took notes and I just spoke it out. What do you think?"

"I think," I said, "that your list could serve as a pamphlet on adult ADD. Running through it, just about everything here fits the picture. But there's more, of course."

There is always more. The problem is almost never just ADD, especially in adults. Sarah's problems—her sense of being desperate and different, her feeling that "there is something inside that needs to change"—these problems were caused by more than just ADD. However, the most successful treatment of them must take ADD into account. Sarah needed to address her issues of insecurity, her feelings about the cruel treatment she received from her father, and her sense of being different. In addressing those issues, she would do best by also understanding how ADD was complicating the picture.

We started medication, but Sarah did not benefit from it at first. She did, however, benefit a great deal just from getting the diagnosis and the knowledge of what ADD is and how it explained many of her symptoms. She also benefited from the practical tips I gave her on the nonmedication management of the disorder. A complete list of these tips is included in chapter 8, but I will mention here some that particularly helped Sarah:

1. Consider joining or starting a support group.

2. Try to get rid of the negativity that has infested your system.

3. Make copious use of external structure: lists, reminders, files, daily rituals, and the like.

4. When it comes to paperwork, use the principle of O.H.I.O.: Only Handle It Once.

5. Make deadlines.

6. Do what you are good at, instead of spending all your time trying to get good at what you're bad at.

7. Understand mood changes and ways to manage these.

8. Expect depression after success.

9. Learn how to advocate for yourself. Adults with ADD are so used to being criticized that they are often unnecessarily defensive in putting their own case forward.

10. Learn to joke with yourself and others about your various symptoms. If you can learn to be relaxed enough about the whole syndrome to be able to joke about it, others will forgive you much more easily.

In addition to making the diagnosis and offering education and practical tips, I also referred Sarah to a psychotherapist in her part of the country and agreed to serve as a consultant via the telephone should the need arise. After she went home, I made an adjustment to her medication in search of the right regimen. I had originally started her on the antidepressant desipramine because, unlike the stimulants, it only needs to be taken once a day creating an effect that is often more even than that of the stimulants, which have to be taken several times a day. I started her on a very low dose, 20 milligrams (mg) per day, but that had little effect. There is some controversy as to what dosage of desipramine one should give. The usual dosage for depression is between 100 and 300 mg per day. However, I have found that considerably lower doses are often effective for ADD. Since lower doses produce fewer side effects, I usually start at a low dose—10 to 20 mg per day. I raise the dose gradually. When I increased Sarah's dose to 40 mg per day, she noticed considerable improvement, which she discusses below. Once the medication was set and Sarah had been in counseling for a while, I got the following letter.

Dear Dr. Hallowell,

I would like to fill you in on how the medication has been helping me.

The adjustment you made with the medication has produced much more noticeable results: In general, I feel much more relaxed, more positive, and more on an even keel emotionally. I am also less confused. I didn't know that I was confused before, but I think that that was one of the reasons that I avoided conflict and have been tense in social situations. I couldn't think or respond quickly under stress. I feel now that it is more possible to engage with people, and that in conflict situations, I have more of a chance to know and say how I feel. This is not to say that I am great at it, but it is definitely better.

I am less threatened by erratic and unpredictable people.

My desk and work areas are not as messy, and it is easier for me to put things in order. They still are not what they should be, but at least I'm making some progress. . . .

I have more energy in the evenings and am able to think more clearly. In general, I am having more fun.

My husband says that I am more steady, less jumpy and controlling, and more involved in general conversation.

The only side effect that I have noticed is that I don't sleep as soundly. I don't stay awake, though, so I can live with it.

The tips on nonmedication management have been very helpful in keeping me on track. I reread them every so often.

I have been thinking more about the issue of my father: the last I wrote to you was that I couldn't imagine wanting a relationship with a father. Since then I have noticed that I have a desire to relate to some of the older "father figures" in my life, ones that are somewhat of a kindred spirit to me. And, probably, as I rethink it, my father, his sister, and my sister have ADD or something like it.

A while back I dreamed I was in the house I grew up in. I was furiously angry at a woman who has been somewhat like an older sister to me. She is a very efficient person who can keep track of ten things at once. I think that she represented my mother, who cared for me but didn't understand me.

Perhaps the greatest benefit that has come since discovering that my husband and I have ADD is that we can understand each other. Previously, I felt that my friends understood me much more than he did. Since finding out about ADD and getting treatment, he is much happier, more productive, more accepting of himself, and easier to talk to. He used to be like a machine that tried to give answers; now I feel that he is the person who understands me the most.

As in children, ADD in adults occurs on a wide spectrum. There are severe cases of adult ADD, where the individual can barely function at all due to rampant disorganization, or uncontrollable impulsivity, or a complete inability to follow through on anything. In addition, the person may be disabled by secondary symptoms of low self-esteem or depression. On the other hand, there are very mild cases of ADD where the symptoms are hardly noticeable at all.

Mild cases can go undetected even by people who know of the disorder. The symptoms can be quite subtle, or they can be masked, as we will discuss in the chapter on diagnosis, by other symptoms, or the individual can have adapted so well that there appears to be no problem.

I have treated a number of cases of adult ADD where I only discovered the disorder late in the treatment of some other problem. For instance, I had been seeing a highly successful businessman for five years in supportive psychotherapy before realizing that he had mild ADD. Bernie had been seeing me once a month or so to discuss worries and concerns that would come up in his busy life. He used me as a confidant, bringing up concerns with me that he wanted kept confidential but lay outside the purview of a business consultant. The matters had to do with his perceptions of his competitors, how he sized them up, how they treated him, what his thoughts were about the business world in general, and what his fears were in particular. Our work together seemed to have nothing to do with ADD, nothing to do with focusing attention, or regulating impulses, or containing restlessness, or dealing with procrastination or disorganization or any of the other usual concerns one hears from people with ADD. What we had set up was an unusual, but in Bernie's case effective, model for getting some psychological support. It was only when we were talking about one of his children, some five years into our relationship, that I mentioned what the symptoms of ADD are. We looked at each other for a moment and had the same thought: Have we been missing something?

Although he was not disabled by ADD, Bernie did indeed have symptoms of distractibility, impulsivity, and moodiness that bothered him. He would frequently tune out at meetings, find himself unable to listen to a telephone conversation even when he wanted to, tangle himself up with patterns of procrastination and overcommitment, and find himself getting angry and irascible without provocation. Once he got started on stimulant medication—Ritalin, 10 mg, three times per day—these symptoms abated. His level of productivity soared, leaving him shaking his head in amazement. "I get more done in a morning now than I used to in a week," he said. Since he was an intuitive and resourceful man, he had been treating his ADD without knowing it by the strategic use of structure and by delegating to others what he hated to do, or could not do. "But," he said, "now with the medication I feel more focused and organized than ever before."

I felt rather foolish, a specialist in ADD, not noticing the symptoms of ADD in a man I saw once a month for five years. My problem was that I had closed my diagnostic book, so to speak, on Bernie. As we settled into our regular conversations, I stopped thinking diagnostically. Only the mention of the symptoms of his child luckily reopened the book. It was a striking lesson to me of how what we see depends so much upon the context. Here I was, a professional highly and specifically trained to notice the symptoms of attention deficit disorder, sitting with a man for years who had many of those symptoms, and I didn't see them. It was because I wasn't ready to notice. The context in which I saw Bernie defined him as someone who did not have ADD. So, even though the symptoms were staring me in the face, I didn't see them. I wager that I wouldn't see them in a close friend, or even my wife, again due to the context.

Most adults with ADD need the fresh look I withheld from Bernie for so long because I'd already made up my mind about him. That's the problem with being an adult: people have already made up their minds about us; we've even made up our minds about ourselves. That makes it terribly difficult to get the radical reappraisal that something like making the diagnosis of ADD requires.

Most cases are more severe than Bernie's. But at the same time, most people who have adult ADD aren't floundering. Many successful people have it. It is particularly common among creative people—artists, actors, writers—scientists, people in high-energy or high-risk jobs, and people who work on their own.

I recently treated a physician, let's call him Joshua, who came to see me for the treatment of depression. He was a man in his fifties, a tall, burly gentleman with a salt-and-pepper beard and a hills-of-Tennessee accent. I didn't know what that was, until he told me. "You sound southern," I had said.

"Hills of Tennessee," he said. "One of the many southern dialects."

He was a warm, friendly man, trained as a general surgeon, but now practicing as a consultant. "When medicine stopped being medicine and became paperwork, I got out," he said. "I'm doing fine professionally. And my marriage is good. I'm just not living the life I know I could. I'm not on top of things. I'm not being as creative as I want to be. Maybe I have no right to be, but I think there's more to me than has come out so far. I don't know if you can help me or not. I'm depressed, but then I've been depressed on and off my whole life. I was alcoholic for a long time, but I quit twenty-one years ago."

"How did you quit?" I asked.

He smiled, as if humoring all the various movements that purport to help people with addictions. "The only way that would work for me. Cold turkey. I just stopped one day. I could see it was going to kill me—or worse, kill one of my patients. Can't say I don't miss it, but I'll never drink again. Anyway, the depression got a little better after I stopped drinking, but I still have these moods. Black, interminable moods where all I can think of is what a rotten, worthless man I am."

"You start in on yourself," I said.

"Boy, do I ever. I'll just have at me, call myself every name in the book and then some, go over and over all my failings, and show no mercy. You know, I can talk about it now like I'm talking about a symptom, but when I'm in it, I'm death. I'll just brood for hours, even a day. I can still function, I can still work, but there's this relentless voice carping away at me inside. My wife can't make it stop, nobody can. I've seen a number of psychiatrists, and I've taken just about every antidepressant medication there is, but nothing works. Maybe it's just my Southern Baptist roots come back to haunt me and I'll have to live with it." He raised an eyebrow as if to put a question mark at the end of his sentence, where his tone of voice had left a period.

"I don't know," I said. "Let's try and find out more about these moods."

After taking a lengthy history, I realized there was more to the story than just the problem with bad moods. Joshua's dark periods were not typical of depression; they were not full of listlessness, hopelessness, and pessimism. He did not lose sleep or stop working or withdraw from the world as so many depressed people do. Rather, he actively brooded within himself, carrying on an internal monologue like a preacher from the pulpit about the extent of his sins. He never thought of suicide, nor, even, did he lose hope for the future.

On the other hand, he gave ample evidence of ADD from childhood on, compensated for with structure and determination. "You know," I said, "I think it might be useful to look at your depression from another vantage point. Let's consider it as a kind of pernicious variation in your way of paying attention. You lose perspective. Instead of paying attention evenly, you hyperfocus on everything negative. This happens subtly, but profoundly. The next thing you know some mad preacher within you has started to harangue at you and you can't stop listening. What this adds up to in terms of a diagnosis, combined with everything else you've told me, is that I think you may have the adult version of attention deficit disorder."

"You mean what hyperactive kids get?" he asked skeptically.

"Yes," I said. "But you have the kind that especially affects mood. You organize around a bad mood and you don't let go. You hold on to it for dear life. You don't dare give it up for fear that chaos will replace it."

Something I said caught his attention. His eyes focused on an upper corner of my ceiling, and he mused, "I organize around a bad mood. Interesting idea. Say more."

While the earlier example of Laura centered around anxiety as the chief symptom, in Joshua what was most troubling was the perseverative, negative thinking. I explained to him about ADD with anxiety and depression. It made sense to him. "You mean," he said, "my mind may fall into one of these ruminative cycles, as you call them, like a muskrat walking into a trap? Snap! The trap shuts, and the muskrat can't get free. That's how it feels to me, because I'm struggling all the time. I've been calling it depression because it hurts so much, but it's more of a fight than a depression, now that you mention it."

"Exactly," I said. "Usually, you organize around a task or a schedule or some other logical schema. But when you happen into one of these traps, you organize around worry and self-contempt. If you can ignore the content of the ruminations, hard as that may be to do, and look instead at the process of ruminating, it may become easier to wriggle free of the trap. Instead of engaging in the argument, instead of answering back to the preacher in the pulpit, you need to ignore him. And the only way you can do that is by leaving his church. Go for a run. Call someone on the telephone. Write a letter. Turn on loud music. Whatever works to shift your focus off of this sermon of self-hatred and onto something else, do that. When you're in one of those moods, it is not the time for introspection. Beware the preacher because he is beguiling. Because you're intelligent and you like words, and you grew up in a strict moral framework, when you hear arguments mounted against you you can hardly resist answering back. But once you join in, the preacher has you. You cannot win. The preacher will always have the last word. In those moods, you can never stare him down."

"You're right," my patient said, then added with a wry smile, "you speak so convincingly about it that you sound like you've been there yourself."

"Well," I said, "let's just say I've heard an awful lot of people talk about it."

"And the other symptoms, what are they?"

"Well, you mentioned your history of drinking, and you talked about how much you procrastinate, how you usually have too much going on, how you can't get organized, how you overwork as a way of getting stimulated, how much you are putting off, your writing for example, because you can't get started—these could all be due to ADD."

Once we had the diagnosis confirmed, we agreed upon a course of treatment. After we started medication—Ritalin—and had a few more sessions to develop insight into his situation, he improved remarkably. He found that he started to really like his work. He noticed what was going on. Most of all, the black moods ceased. He could still feel unhappy, but not in the bone-crushing way as before. "I've learned how to walk out of that preacher's way," he said. "I can see the scowl on his face and I laugh." He used the concept of organizing around depression and anxiety as a means of fighting his tendency to do so. The medication helped both with focusing and with his moods. As focusing and organization became less of a chore, he found that work became more settled, freeing him up to start some projects he had been putting off. Like many people who discover in adulthood that they have ADD, he became excited about this new understanding of himself, and about the effectiveness of the treatment. "You know, I came in here not expecting much. But what has happened is amazing. I'm a new man. My wife is overjoyed. The world really should know about ADD."

While I share Joshua's enthusiasm, I should temper it. The initial phase of treatment for ADD, the time of discovering that you have it, of making use of the insight this brings, of finding out that the medication really works, this phase of treatment is exciting. It can indeed transform one's life. New realms open up to the individual. For some it is as dramatic as suddenly being able to speak a foreign language they'd never been able to understand before, or swing the tennis racquet that had always felt like a pickax in their hands before, or get the books and papers and projects filed and organized that had mounted like heaps of refuse in their minds before.

On the other hand, after the initial phase of treatment, the struggle usually does not end. For some lucky people it does, but for most people ADD continues to pose problems daily. While the treatment helps with the symptoms, it does not eradicate them. The ADD does not go away. It cannot be surgically removed. If one has it as an adult, one has it for life.

People in treatment for ADD usually still struggle with issues of organization, impulse control, and distractibility. But more difficult than that, they struggle with the secondary symptoms that years of living with undiagnosed ADD created. These are symptoms such as impaired self-image, low self-esteem, depression, fearfulness of others, mistrust of self, skittishness in relationships, and anger over the past. These wounds heal very slowly.

■ 4 ■

Living and Loving with ADD

ADD IN COUPLES

In couples where one or both partners have ADD, life can list and yaw from day to day. As one member of a couple said to me, "I never know what to expect. I can't rely on him for anything. It's really a circus." The syndrome can disrupt intimate relationships and leave each partner exhausted. However, if the situation is subtly regulated, both people can work together, instead of being at odds.

When ADD is at the root of a marriage in stress, the diagnosis is often overlooked because the couple's problems can look like those of any couple. A husband comes home and immediately starts reading the newspaper, has trouble paying attention especially when talking about feelings, drinks too much, and struggles with self-esteem while ignoring his wife's repeated attempts to get close to him. Or a wife daydreams chronically, feels depressed, complains of never having reached her potential, and feels trapped at home. These symptoms, in both instances, are consistent with ADD, but few people would think of ADD because the complaints are so commonplace.

Often the symptoms can bring a couple to the brink of divorce. Sam and Mary Rothman, for example, were referred to me by Sam's therapist, whom Sam had been seeing because Mary felt it was the only alternative to separation. Now both in their early forties, they had been married eight years, and they had one child, a boy, David, age five.

They arrived fifteen minutes late for their first appointment. Sam blamed the traffic. "The traffic wouldn't have mattered if we had left on time," Mary quickly added.

"She's right," Sam said. "But that's the way I am. I'm late everywhere."

"What kind of work do you do?" I asked.

"I'm an emergency-room physician," he answered. "But I haven't practiced in a few years. I was a cartoonist for a while, and right now I'm trying to make it as a freelance writer."

"How's it going?" I asked.

"It's tough, but I'm getting work. So far, at least."

"Sam, let's tell him why we're here," Mary interjected.

"Do you want me to, or do you want to?" Sam asked, looking at Mary. They had seated themselves at opposite ends of my couch. Both looked younger than they were—Sam, tall, trim, with thick curly black hair, and Mary, shorter, black hair parted down the middle, tortoiseshell glasses, and a notebook in her hands.

"We're here because . . ." Mary began, then paused, as if gathering many thoughts. "We're here because quite frankly this man is making my life into a living hell. No, he doesn't beat me or cheat on me, or drink, or gamble. He just behaves like an irresponsible little boy. I don't mind that he changes jobs because he finds being a doctor isn't interesting enough. I don't mind that he gets up in the middle of the night because he's bored and wants to go flying; I don't mind that he makes plane reservations for Australia for all of us without asking me about it and then calls me a wet blanket for not being overjoyed; I don't mind that he travels more than he's at home; I don't mind that our life insurance is so expensive it's not worth having because of his flying and gliding and skydiving; I don't mind that Sam is incapable of picking things up or remembering where anything is or keeping track of anybody's birthday or anniversary; I don't mind that he can't watch one TV show for more than five minutes without needing to see what else is on even if he's liking the show he's watching—I don't mind any of that so much. But what I do mind is that he doesn't know that I exist. He is so wrapped up in himself that I might as well be a robot. He has no conception of what my inner life is. He doesn't even know that I have an inner life. He doesn't know who I am. After eight years of marriage, the man I'm married to doesn't know me. And he doesn't know that he doesn't know me. That's what makes it hell. None of this bothers him. He's so oblivious. That is why we're here, doctor. That is why we're here. At least that's my side of it. Would you like to tell yours, honey?"

We both looked at Sam. Sam took a deep breath and let it out slowly. "You always did have a way with words. What can I say? She's right. But I don't do it on purpose. The stuff about your inner life isn't fair. I know you have an inner life. I think I know what's on your mind most of the time, in fact."

"Oh, really?" Mary said. "Then tell me."

"Well, I'm on your mind for one thing—" Sam began.

"There, you see," Mary interrupted, "he's so self-centered he thinks he's the only thing on my mind."

"May I cut in here for a minute?" I asked. "There was a reason you came to see me, as opposed to some other psychiatrist, am I right?"

"Yes," Sam said. "At my wife's insistence, I started psychotherapy a few months ago." Mary sighed at that remark and rolled her eyes, but she let Sam talk on. "My shrink—you don't mind if I call them, or you, a shrink, do you?—anyway Harry, which is actually what I call my shrink, I like him, you know I wasn't sure I would, no offense but psychiatry isn't one of the fields of medicine I trust all that much, anyway, Harry said he thought maybe I had ADD, and if we were to get couples therapy, maybe it would make sense to kill two birds with one stone, so to speak, and do it with someone who knows about ADD. Make sense?"

"That's another thing," Mary put in. "After he rambles on, he says, 'Make sense?' You nod reflexively, but you're thinking, No, that didn't make sense at all."

"Actually, I did understand this time," I said. "As I think Harry told you, he called me before you came here to tell me his concerns."

"OK, great," Sam said. "Harry's on the job."

As we reviewed Sam's history, the evidence mounted for a diagnosis of ADD. "But," Mary asked, "how do you tell ADD from being selfish? I mean, I'm not a psychiatrist, but isn't there such a thing as pathological narcissism? That's what I think Sam has. He's only aware of himself."

"Maybe we could look at it a bit differently," I suggested. "He seems only to be aware of himself because he's constantly being distracted, or he's being drawn to some form of intense stimulation to avert boredom."

"So he finds me boring," Mary said.

"No, it's not you. It's everyday life. He hasn't learned how to focus in on everyday life and be there. Instead, he needs the emergency room, speaking concretely as well as metaphorically, to get his attention."

"I don't find you boring, Mary. Really, I do not," Sam said emphatically.

"But if I matter to you, why don't you pay attention to me, why don't you remember things? Even if you don't care about them, if you cared about me, you'd remember, because you'd know how much they matter to me."

"But you see," I interrupted, "it might be that he can't remember, at least not the way other people do."

"He got through medical school," Mary said.

"It was a struggle," Sam quickly added. "You don't know. All the cram sessions. My friends would coach me before exams. It wasn't easy."

"Plus there was the high intensity of the situation to motivate and focus you," I added.

"So our marriage is too low-intensity to keep his attention, is that what you're saying?" Mary responded.

"Not exactly, but I doubt you'd want your marriage to be under the gun the way medical school is," I said.

"That's my whole problem," Mary said. "It seems like the only way I can get any of his attention at all is to put everything under the gun. And I'm tired of living that way. I want him to take some of the responsibility. I don't care whether you call it ADD or selfishness, or just being a jerk, I'm tired of it. I want him to get to know me. I want him to worry with me about where David's going to school instead of just nodding. I don't want to feel like I have to squeeze everything I have to say into the five seconds of attention he gives me a day. I don't want to feel like I'm married to an immature person who's still trying to find himself. Can't he just grow up?"

"If I told you that the kinds of things you are saying are precisely the kinds of things that usually get said to people with adult ADD, what would you think?" I asked.

"I'd say, 'So what?' I still want a life."

■ ■ ■

Mary and Sam found a life, it is fair to say. It took some time, because, in addition to making the diagnosis of ADD, other work had to be done, much of which was facilitated by Harry in his individual sessions with Sam, and some of which was done in our couples therapy.

Once Sam's ADD was diagnosed, he started on Ritalin at a dosage of 10 mg three times a day, and it worked well in helping him focus and reducing his mood swings. He experienced no side effects, and the medication allowed him to sustain focus in a way he never had been able to before. The medication took him out of the self-centered, fast-paced, stimulation-seeking, always-distracted cloud he'd come to live in and deposited him in the ordinary here and now. It allowed him to get to know his own feelings, to get to know his wife, and to be present wherever he actually was.

The struggle didn't end with the diagnosis, however. Sam and Mary had to work hard to make their marriage last. It took persistence and a daily, habitual tending to each other. Sam had to unlearn a number of habits, and Mary had to get past a backlog of anger and resentment. They loved each other and wanted to be together, and they worked to stay together. But it was by no means easy.

ADD does not occur in a vacuum. The partner of an individual with ADD can benefit from a receptive forum as much as the person with ADD can. The stresses on the partner can mount as he or she tries to hold things together, keep the family from sinking, either financially or emotionally, and generally try to bring order out of the chaos. In Mary's case the single most useful tool was knowing about ADD. Before she knew what ADD was and that Sam had it, she was left with explanations like "selfish" or "narcissistic" to explain what she didn't like about Sam. Once she understood what ADD was, and once she understood that it was a neurological condition, she was much better able to forgive Sam his shortcomings and work on finding solutions.

In addition to rethinking Sam's behavior in terms of ADD, Mary also needed Sam to pay attention to *her* life. Being the spouse of an adult with ADD can be exasperating, as Mary could attest. The spouse often feels enraged and unheard. The more angry the spouse becomes, the more devaluing she becomes, and the more devaluing she becomes, the more her partner withdraws.

We often see the following cycle in couples where one member has ADD:

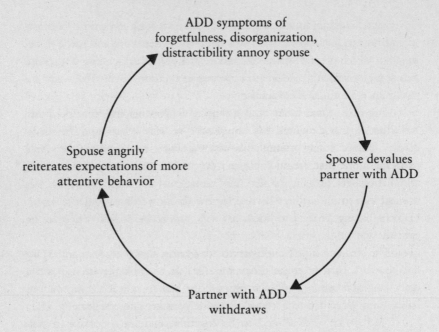

ADD symptoms of forgetfulness, disorganization, distractibility annoy spouse

Spouse devalues partner with ADD

Partner with ADD withdraws

Spouse angrily reiterates expectations of more attentive behavior

In order to interrupt the cycle, one needs not only to treat the ADD but also to address the feelings of anger the non-ADD spouse harbors. Those angry feelings may have built up quite a head of pressure over the years and it may take more than a few weeks or months for them to subside. If the non-ADD spouse has been running the ship for years, feeling unsupported and overlooked all the while, then that person is bound to feel angry. Simply saying "Well, I have ADD" will not make the anger go away. In fact, it may make it worse. The spouse may feel doubly angry finding out, after all these years, that there was a reason for the disorganization and distractibility, a medical condition that was going untreated. "You mean all this suffering has been unnecessary?" one spouse exclaimed. "Now I really want to kill him."

The anger is entirely understandable. It must be acknowledged, expressed, and, finally, put into perspective. It was important for Mary to feel validated and heard. It was important that Sam acknowledge how difficult he had been, whether it was his "fault" or not. It was not that Mary needed to blame Sam, but rather that she needed for Sam to know how much pain she had been in due to Sam's ADD. Just as Sam needed Mary to understand what ADD was and how it affected his behavior, Mary also needed for Sam to understand what living with a spouse with untreated ADD was like, and how that had affected Mary's behavior. It is essential in treating a couple where one partner has ADD that the feelings of *both* partners be heard and taken up with equal seriousness.

Sometimes one member of a couple will present himself as the "identified patient" and request that the spouse be left out of the treatment. A patient named Edgar brought his wife with him, but he wanted to speak with me alone first, he said. Edgar came to see me because he had been thrown out of the family system. His extended family decided they had had enough of him. Since they owned the car business Edgar worked for, they had the power to fire him. One day they called him in and told him that because he was so irresponsible they could no longer employ him. They would see to it that he didn't starve, but he was no longer welcome in the business or at their homes. They were fed up with him, tired of his shenanigans, and they felt the only way to deal with him was to put him out. They thought he was a born loser, and an annoying one at that.

"What can I tell you, Doc?" he said, looking at me through thick glasses, chewing a piece of gum, his forehead wrinkled in worry. "I am obnoxious. I'm extremely obnoxious. My family couldn't stand me anymore so they threw me out. I can see their point, to tell you the truth. It's probably just a matter of time before my wife does the same." Then the wrinkles in his forehead relaxed and he smiled. He lowered his voice now, speaking sotto voce, so as not to be overheard, even though there was no one else in my office. "But you know what, Doc? I like being the way I am. It's me. I've gotta be me, and all that, you know? So I blow a few grand on a cruise to nowhere. So why shouldn't she be thrilled that I give her a trip? So I ride down the highway with Dylan blasting, smoking a joint. So what? It's how I do my best thinking. I can't sit in an office and look at the nice little people in the showroom and make my plans for the day and be a good little schmuck. It's just not me. Is that so bad? Am I a worthless piece of scum just because I haven't been to the dentist in ten years? That was on their list, can you believe that? What's it to them if I go to the dentist? Who likes to go to the dentist? So I get excommunicated for that? I'm telling you, Doc, I may be obnoxious, but I don't deserve what's happening to me."

"Do you really mean that you're obnoxious?" I asked.

"Yes, I am. But I can't help it. I see something that I want to do, and before I've had the chance to think about it, I'm doing it. I've stopped making promises to Amanda, I've broken so many of them. I'm impossible, just like she says. You know what I really like to do? I like to go down to the showroom about three o'clock in the morning when I can't sleep and turn on the radios of all the cars on the showroom floor and just let 'em blast. It's a great feeling, standing in there with the lights on and all the radios blaring when outside everybody else is asleep. I can have the world to myself then, the way I like it, on my terms."

"But the family—" I started to say.

"Just about pukes," Edgar answered. "They say, 'How does that look to the rest of the world, someone playing around in the showroom in the middle of the night?' They say, 'Grow up, Edgar,' and I say, 'You're right, I'll try.' But I can't grow up. I guess that's my problem, Doc. I'm just permanently stuck in childhood."

Although Edgar's behavior was peculiar, the description of an adult with ADD as immature or childish is not uncommon. People don't know how else to make sense of this kind of behavior, so they attack it as being beneath adult standards. They hope to shame the person into changing his ways. That tactic usually doesn't work. "Edgar," I said, "why do you think you do these things?"

"I don't know, Doc! Jeez, that's why I'm here. You're supposed to tell me."

"I'll try to, but I need more information. What are some other things you do that people object to?"

"Well, there's the speeding I told you about, and the showroom. Insulting the customers, that's a biggie. I mean, what can I tell you? I don't like someone's attitude, I don't have much patience with them. I told one the other day she should work at the Department of Motor Vehicles, her personality would fit right in. I mean, she kept handing me all these forms and not speaking to me, it was annoying, you know what I mean? But they're right, I shouldn't speak like that to a customer. The customer's always right, and all that. Sometimes I just can't help myself."

"It's kind of fun, isn't it?" I said.

"It sure is. They think so, too, underneath it all. They're gonna miss having me around. Who else have they got to tell those jokers off?"

As is usually the case, Edgar's problem was not just ADD, but ADD was a big part of it. His impulsivity, restlessness, tactlessness, and high energy all contributed to the fix he was in. Despite how obnoxious he said he was, he was also quite likable, and I was sure that he was right, his family would miss having him around.

"Do you ever get sad, Edgar?" I asked.

"Try not to," he said. "Don't slow down long enough. What's the point? Red roses for a blue lady and all that? You can have it. My philosophy is live, live, live." He took off his glasses, produced a handkerchief from his back pocket, and wiped his forehead.

Later I met with Amanda and Edgar together. Amanda was a kind-faced woman a half a foot taller than Edgar who was as calm as Edgar was excitable. "I can't tell you why I love him, but I do. Isn't that a line in a song? Anyway, it's true. But he does drive me crazy. The thing about it is, he drives himself crazy, too. He's not a bad man, don't let anybody tell you that. He's like a pot that boils over, that's all. Is there any way to turn down the heat?" she asked.

"How do you manage life with him?" I asked.

"Oh, it's a trip," she said. "Never a dull moment. I'm just getting a little tired, and I know he is fed up with these messes."

After a few weeks of getting to know Edgar and getting some tests, I was confident that he had ADD. His ADD had to be discriminated from mania. In mania, the "high" is higher than in ADD. That is to say, the person with mania is under greater pressure and is more out of control than the person with ADD. The person with mania exhibits certain symptoms that the person with ADD does not show, symptoms such as pressured speech, where the words literally seem to fly out of the individual's mouth under great pressure, and flight of ideas, where the individual flies from topic to topic without a moment's pause. Mania and ADD leave a qualitatively different impression. The person with mania seems uncontrollable to the outside observer, whereas the person with ADD simply appears hurried or distracted. On the basis of Edgar's childhood history, which was suggestive of ADD, and his current situation, which showed periods of agitation but not mania, and on the basis of psychological testing, the determination was made that Edgar had ADD.

Rather than see Edgar individually, I decided to see him with Amanda. It was as important for Amanda to understand what was going on as for Edgar. His capacity for insight was minimal at first, and his ability to observe himself was not reliable. Amanda became his coach, so to speak, reminding him of what he otherwise would forget. For most situations this kind of couples therapy would not work, because it identifies one member of the couple as the patient. But for ADD it is a realistic way to proceed.

With Amanda's help, and with the help of medication, Edgar was able, over time, to develop some capacity to reflect before acting, to find relaxation and focus by other means than fast cars, loud music, and marijuana, and to think before speaking. He even made an appointment to see the dentist. He often asked me to increase the dose of the medication, or to go at him harder in therapy. "I can take it, Doc. Sock it to me." I had to explain to him that more wasn't always better, and that some of his expectations for a "total overhaul," as he called it, were a bit beyond reach just now.

After six months Edgar and Amanda felt ready to move on. The question of when to end therapy for ADD is an open one. For some people the treatment lasts just a few sessions. For most people, however, it takes longer than that. The individual—or couple—must rethink a great deal of behavior, and a good therapist can facilitate this process. Also, it can take a while to find the right dosage of the right medication. Finally, the emotional adjustment to ADD can require psychotherapy. The average duration of treatment for adult ADD is about three to six months.

I met with Amanda and Edgar together for one last visit. Edgar's family had given him his job back, conditionally, and, as Amanda told me, they had indeed missed him.

"Thanks a lot, Doc," Edgar said, still chewing a piece of gum. "I never thought I'd say that to a man in your line of work, if you know what I mean."

"Edgar!" Amanda said, slapping his knee.

"Do you know what you're thanking me for?" I asked.

"Of course, Doc," Edgar said. "Of course I know what I'm thanking you for. I'm thanking you for doing a very respectable job of shrinking my head."

"Edgar!" Amanda said again.

"That's quite all right," I said. "In fact, that's an excellent compliment. But I was wondering if what we've been saying in here makes sense to you now that we're finishing."

"I'll tell you the truth, Doc. I can't remember most of what you've told me. Amanda here, the rod and staff of my life, has written all kinds of things down and she reads them to me when we get home, and she makes lists and does all the things you've said we should do, and she sees to it that I do the things I'm supposed to do, including take the medication. But do *I* know what we've been doing here? I know I have ADD. That much I've learned. Don't ask me what it means, except whatever it is, I feel much different now. Not as edgy. Not as out of control."

"Do you miss the pot and speeding in the car?" I asked.

"The truth?" Edgar asked. "The truth is I don't, if you can believe that. Can you believe that? In fact, it scares me to think of it now. But maybe that's just because I've spent so much time lately with Amanda and you. We'll have to see what tomorrow brings."

The last I heard, Edgar and Amanda were together, Edgar was working, and life was pretty good.

■ ■ ■

There are many other issues that come up in working with couples and ADD. One of the most important, and least written about, is sexuality.

The impact of ADD upon sexuality is poorly understood. However, we have seen many people in our practice, both men and women, who complain of either an inability to pay attention during sex well enough to enjoy it, or the opposite: a hyperfocused hypersexuality.

Those who appear to be hypersexual may turn to sex as a form of intense stimulation to help them focus. Many adults with ADD are drawn to high-stimulus situations as a means of alleviating boredom or clearing their mind of distraction. Some get involved in physically dangerous activities, such as racecar-driving or vertical skiing or bungee-jumping or they get involved in risky activities like gambling or dangerous romances. They do these things as a means of focusing themselves; they focus around the high stimulation. For some adults with ADD, sex acts as a kind of stimulating medication, and they use it to find not only the pleasure of orgasm but the pleasure of being focused.

On the other hand, those who cannot pay attention often accuse themselves—or are accused by lovers—of being "frigid" or "undersexed" or involved with someone else. In fact, they may enjoy sex a great deal but simply have problems staying focused while making love, just as they have problems staying focused during any other activity.

One woman left me an anonymous note after a lecture I had given. It was the first time anyone had put plainly to me how distractibility can directly interfere with sexual activity:

Dear Dr. Hallowell,

I enjoyed your talk very much, and I wanted to ask you this question, or, more accurately make this comment during the discussion period, but frankly I was too embarrassed. So I am leaving you this note in the hope that the concerns it raises can be of help to other people.

I am a forty-two-year-old woman. I'm quite attractive, if I do say so myself, and I love my husband. He is devoted to me. I am the woman of his dreams, he says. However, until I was diagnosed with ADD a year ago, I had never had an orgasm. In fact, my husband and I never had a satisfactory sex life. He had adored me from the start—I think that's why he stayed with me. But sex between us? It was boring at best.

For the longest while I thought the problem was that I was just frigid. I was raised a Catholic, and I figured I just never got past the impact the nuns had on me. But it tore me up inside. Because I had sexual feelings. I had them all the time. I just couldn't focus them, in bed with my husband. I read lots of erotic literature, I had incredible urges toward other people, none of which I acted on—and I saw several different therapists to work on what I thought was my mental block. How could I feel so sexy, look sexy, dress sexy, be married to an incredible man, and yet think of tomorrow's shopping list as he's making love to me? Once in a while, I guess that's normal, but all the time?

The worst part was I really started to hate myself for this and to feel tremendously inadequate. I hate to say this, but I even thought of just running away—you know, the slow boat to nowhere. But I never would have left. The kids, my husband, I couldn't leave them, although, as miserable as I was at times, I think they might have been happier without me.

Then I got lucky. A friend referred me to a new therapist, and this woman knew about ADD. She made the diagnosis in two sessions and started me on treatment. What a difference! I have never read anywhere about how ADD affects sexuality, but in my case the change was incredible! Now I could focus, now I could be there. After a while I didn't even need the medication. It was a matter of realizing that it was ADD, and not some inadequacy or hidden guilt on my part. Then it was a matter of taking steps to have sex at the right time; of providing soothing music to take over the daydreaming part of my mind, and of talking to my husband openly about it. He was really great. It turns out he had been blaming himself as much as I had been blaming myself.

It is amazing how subtle, but how crucial, this discovery has been for me. I can't help but think there are a lot of women out there who are simply distractible, but who think they are sexually inadequate or just bored instead.

Now I can have orgasms, but more than that, I approach sex with enthusiasm instead of dread. I can be there, with my husband, instead of somewhere else. I have learned how to enjoy myself sexually. I would never have done this if I had not found out about ADD. The treatment has helped me in all areas of my life, but it has helped me sexually more than anything. My main problem was in staying focused, and I never knew it. I kept thinking it was something much worse, more complicated, and unfixable. And when I consider how relatively simple—yet powerful—the answer was, I wanted to share it with you in the hope you will share it with others.

Since I never had a chance to thank the anonymous author of that note, let me say now, thank you, wherever you are. Your note caused me to start paying attention to an aspect of ADD most of us have largely overlooked. So far, I have gathered a great deal of anecdotal evidence, full of inconsistency; but many people do indeed report that ADD affects their sexuality, either in the direction of nonresponsiveness or toward hypersexuality. Usually, treatment helps both groups of people.

The woman in the letter provides a good example of a person who had felt she was nonresponsive. As an example of a person whose ADD led him toward hypersexuality, consider the case of Brian, a thirty-nine-year-old unmarried man who considered himself a "sex addict." He constantly sought out flirtations or liaisons with women, and he felt that he was incapable of resisting any sort of sexual temptation. He was unable to maintain a long-term relationship because of his unremitting infidelities. Unlike some men who fit this profile, Brian was disturbed by his behavior.

He wanted to settle down into one relationship and have a family. He did not want to be a "Don Juan," as he put it, but he found that he could not resist the power of his attraction to women.

He spent years in psychotherapy trying to get at the roots of his problem. He and his therapist explored the issue from many different angles. Was he acting out some unconscious hostility toward women by seducing them and then leaving them? Was he plagued by a basic fear of intimacy that lead him to seek a new person the minute he got close to anyone? Was he trying to bolster some sense of sexual inadequacy by proving to himself over and over again that he could attract women? In therapy he took up all of these possibilities, and others as well.

When he came to see me, he and his therapist had decided that he was addicted to women. They wondered, based on an article the therapist had read, if seeing the problem through the lens of ADD might help.

Indeed it did. In reviewing Brian's history from childhood to adulthood, I found he had had problems with distractibility and impulse control all along. Many people with ADD find that certain forms of highly stimulating behavior help them focus, and they turn to these behaviors as a kind of unwitting self-treatment or self-medication of their ADD. Some people turn to gambling as a source of high stimulation and the concomitant focusing it provides. Some people turn to high-risk activities such as driving at high speeds or skydiving. In Brian's case, he was using the high stimulation of romance to help him focus.

■ ■ ■

The following guidelines or "tips" might be helpful in dealing with other issues of concern to couples in which one partner has ADD. These tips offer a starting point for discussion between the partners. The best way to use them is to read them out loud, together. Pause over each suggestion and discuss whether it might help you. As you do this, you can begin to set up your own way of dealing with ADD in your relationship. The keys to it all, as is the case with most problems in couples, are improving communication and resolving the power struggle.

1. Make sure you have an accurate diagnosis. There are many conditions that look like ADD, from too much coffee to anxiety states to dissociative disorders to hyperthyroidism. Before em-

barking on a treatment for ADD, consult with your physician to make sure what you have is really ADD and not something else. Once you are sure of the diagnosis, learn as much as you can about ADD. There is an increasing body of literature on the topic. The more you and your mate know, the better you will be able to help each other. The first step in the treatment of ADD—whether it be your partner's or someone else's—is education.

2. Keep a sense of humor! If you let it be, ADD can be really funny at times. Don't miss out on the chance to laugh when the laugh is there. At that psychological branch point we all know so well, when the split-second options are to get mad, cry, or laugh, go for the laughter. Humor is a key to a happy life with ADD.

3. Declare a truce. After you have the diagnosis and have done some reading, take a deep breath and wave the white flag. You both need some breathing space to begin to get your relationship on a new footing. You may need to ventilate a lot of stored-up bad feeling. Do that, so you won't lug it with you everywhere.

4. Set up a time for talking. You will need some time to talk to each other about ADD—what it is, how it affects your relationship, what each of you wants to do about it, what feelings you have about it. Don't do this on the run, i.e., during TV commercials, while drying dishes, in between telephone calls, etc. Set up some time. Reserve it for yourselves.

5. Spill the beans. Tell each other what is on your mind. The effects of ADD show up in different ways for different couples. Tell each other how it is showing up between you. Tell each other just how you are being driven crazy, what you like, what you want to change, what you want to preserve. Get it all out on the table. Try to say it all before you both start reacting. People with ADD have a tendency to bring premature closure to discussions, to go for the bottom line. In this case, the bottom line is the discussion itself.

6. Write down your complaints and your recommendations. It is good to have in writing what you want to change and what you want to preserve. Otherwise you'll forget.

7. Make a treatment plan. Brainstorm with each other as to how to reach your goals. You may want some professional help with this phase, but it is a good idea to try starting it on your own.

8. Follow through on the plan. Remember, one of the hallmarks of ADD is insufficient follow-through, so you'll have to work to stick with your plan.

9. Make lists. Over time, lists will become a habit.

10. Use bulletin boards. Messages in writing are less likely to be forgotten. Of course, you have to get in the habit of looking at the bulletin board!

11. Put notepads in strategic places like by your bed, in your car, in the bathroom and kitchen.

12. Consider writing down what you want the other person to do and give it to him or her in the form of a list every day. This must be done in a spirit of assistance, not of dictatorship. Keep a master appointment book for both of you. Make sure each of you checks it every day.

13. Take stock of your sex lives in light of ADD. As mentioned earlier, ADD can affect sexual interest and performance. It is good to know the problems are due to ADD, and not something else.

14. Avoid the pattern of mess maker and cleaner-upper. You don't want the non-ADD partner to "enable" the ADD partner by cleaning up all the time, in the manner that the nonalcoholic spouse may "enable" the alcoholic spouse by covering up all the time. Rather, set up strategies to break this pattern.

15. Avoid the pattern of pesterer and tuner-outer. You don't want the non-ADD partner to be forever nagging and kvetching at the ADD partner to pay attention, get his or her act together, come out from behind the newspaper, etc. People with ADD frequently need a certain amount of "down time" every day to recharge their batteries. It is better that this time be negotiated and set aside in advance rather than struggled over each time it comes up.

16. Avoid the pattern of victim and victimizer. You don't want the ADD partner to present himself or herself as a helpless victim left at the merciless hands of the all-controlling non-ADD mate. This dynamic can evolve easily if you aren't careful. The ADD person needs support and structure; the non-ADD mate tries to provide these. Unless there is open and clear communication about what is going on, the support and structure can feel like control and nagging.

17. Avoid the pattern of master and slave. Akin to number 16. However, in a funny way it can often be the non-ADD partner who feels like the slave to her or his mate's ADD. The non-ADD partner can feel that the symptoms of ADD are ruining the relationship, wrapping around it like tentacles, daily disrupting what could be, and once was, an affectionate bond.

18. Avoid the pattern of a sadomasochistic struggle as a routine way of interacting. Prior to diagnosis and intervention, many couples dealing with ADD spend most of their time attacking and counterattacking each other. One hopes to get past that and into the realm of problem-solving. What you have to beware of is the covert pleasure that can be found in the struggle. ADD is exasperating; therefore, you can enjoy punishing your mate by fighting with him or her. Try, rather, to vent your anger at the disorder, not at the person. Say "I hate ADD" instead of "I hate you," or say "ADD drives me crazy," instead of "You drive me crazy."

19. In general, watch out for the dynamics of control, dominance, and submission that lurk in the background of most relationships, let alone relationships where ADD is involved. Try to get as clear on this as possible, so that you can work toward cooperation rather than competitive struggle.

20. Break the tapes of negativity. Many people who have ADD have long ago taken on a resigned attitude of "There's no hope for me." The same can happen to both partners in the couple. As will be mentioned in many places throughout this book, negative thinking is a most corrosive force in the treatment of ADD. What I call the "tapes of negativity" can play relentlessly, unforgivingly, endlessly in the mind of the person with ADD. It is as if they click on as the sun rises and click off only when the unconsciousness of sleep shuts them down. They play, over and over, grinding noises of "You can't"; "You're bad"; "You're dumb"; "It won't work out"; "Look how far behind you are"; "You're just a born loser." The tapes can be playing in the midst of a business deal, in the reverie of a car ride home, or they can take the place of making love. It is hard to be romantic when you are full of negative thoughts. The thoughts seduce you, like a satanic mistress, into "loving" them instead. These tapes are very difficult to break, but with conscious and sustained effort, they can be erased.

21. Use praise freely. Encouragement, too. Begin to play positive tapes. Find something positive to say about your mate or about yourself every day. Build each other up consciously, deliberately. Even if it feels hokey at first, over time it will feel good and have a sustaining effect.

22. Learn about mood management. Anticipation is a great way to help anyone deal with the highs and lows that come along. This is especially true in ADD. If you know in advance that when you say "Good morning, honey!" the response you get might be "Get off my back, will you!" then it is easier to deal with that response without getting a divorce. And if the other member of the couple has learned something about his or her moods, the response to "Good morning, honey!" might be "I'm in one of my ADD funks," or something like that, instead of an attack on the other person.

23. Let the one who is the better organizer take on the job of organization. There's no point in flogging yourself with a job you can't do. If you can't do the checkbook, don't do the checkbook. If you can't do the kids' clothes shopping, then don't do the kids' clothes shopping. That's one of the advantages of being in a couple. You have another person to help out. However, the job the other person does instead of you must then be adequately appreciated, noticed, and reciprocated.

24. Make time for each other. If the only way you can do this is by scheduling it, then schedule it. This is imperative. Many people with ADD slip away like quicksilver; now you have them, now you don't. Clear communication, the expression of affection, the taking up of problems, playing together and having fun—all these ingredients of a good relationship cannot occur unless you spend time together.

25. Don't use ADD as an excuse. Each member of the couple has to take responsibility for his or her actions. On the other hand, while one mustn't use ADD as an excuse, knowledge of the syndrome can add immeasurably to the understanding one brings to the relationship.

■ 5 ■

The Big Struggle

ADD AND THE FAMILY

Consider the following scene, which is representative of many families in which one person has ADD:

"Mom, I told you I would have my homework done by Sunday night, and I will have it done by Sunday night. Now will you please just get off my back?" Tommy Eldredge kicks the trash basket next to his mother's desk as he storms out of the living room and into the kitchen.

His mother rises from her chair in pursuit. "No, I won't just get off your back. Why should I? What have you done to deserve my trust? It's spring term of your tenth-grade year, you're in the middle of high school, and you're flunking two courses. All you do is make promises and you never come through. I'm fed up with it. If you want to ruin your life—"

"Mom, calm down already. I'm not ruining my life. I've just had some bad grades, that's all."

"Some bad grades? Some? You've had nothing but bad grades. And it's not the grades I'm concerned about. It's the effort that goes into them. Or lack of effort, I should say. You just don't care. As long as you can get out of the house, you don't care what happens tomorrow. Which is why you are not leaving the house this weekend. Not even for a second. Not even for a half a second," she says, and snaps her fingers next to the back of his head.

126

Tommy turns on his mother. "You're just a bitch, you know that? You're just a fucking bitch."

At that point Tommy's mother loses her temper completely, slaps him across his face, and falls forward trying to follow the slap with a punch at his arm. When she hits the floor, she starts crying. Tommy tries to help her up, but she pushes him away as Tommy's dad walks into the kitchen. "Get out of the house," he barks at Tommy and rushes over to help his sobbing wife.

"I didn't mean to hurt her," Tommy says.

"Just get out," his dad says. "Don't come back."

"Fine," Tommy says, and leaves through the kitchen door, letting the screen slam shut behind him.

The next day, Saturday, the family has reconvened. The other kids go elsewhere while Mom and Dad sit down to talk with Tommy, who was brought home by the police after being picked up in the bus station at 3 A.M.

They all stare at each other, years of recriminations focused in this one moment. "We need to make a plan," Dad begins.

"First I want an apology," Mom interrupts.

"I'm sorry," Tommy says. "I didn't mean for you to fall down. I didn't mean to call you what I called you."

"Then why did you say it?" she asks.

"I don't know. I was mad. It just came out."

"But that's the whole problem, Tommy," his mother goes on. "You don't mean to do the things you do do, and you don't do the things you say you mean to do."

Let me stop the scene here. What Mrs. Eldredge has just said gives a pretty good short description of ADD: *You don't mean to do the things you do do, and you don't do the things you mean to do.* If she could stop herself at this point in the conversation, and say to Tommy, "Aha! I can tell by what I just said that what you have is not a case of incurable obstinacy but attention deficit disorder instead!" then the outcome might be favorable. But what usually happens is that these arguments build and ramify into conflagrations, burning down many a family in the process.

What often develops in families where one child has ADD (or one adult for that matter) is what we call the Big Struggle. The child with ADD chronically fails to meet obligations, do chores, stay up with schoolwork, keep to family schedules—get out of bed on time, arrive home on time, show up for meals on time, be ready to leave the house on time—keep his or her room tidied up, participate in family life cooperatively, and in general "get with the program" at home. This leads to chronic limit-setting by parents, with increasingly stringent penalties and increasingly tight limitations on the child. This, in turn, makes the child more defiant, less cooperative, and more alienated, which leads parents to feel more exasperated with what increasingly appears to be an attitude problem, under voluntary control, rather than the neurological problem of ADD.

As parents become more and more fed up with the child's behavior, they become less and less sympathetic to whatever excuses or explanations the child may offer, less and less willing to believe in promises to do better, and more and more apt to apply stricter and stricter consequences in a usually futile effort to control the child's behavior. Gradually, the child's role in the family solidifies around being the "problem child," and he or she becomes the designated scapegoat for all the family's conflicts and problems. An old saying about scapegoating is that the process requires a mob and a volunteer. In the case of the Big Struggle the family forms the mob, and the ADD behavior volunteers the child. Virtually anything that goes wrong in the family gets blamed on the ADD child. Over time the child is draped with a kind of blanket of derision and scorn that smothers his development of confidence and self-esteem.

The Big Struggle may last for years. It may resemble a war, with seasonal campaigns along various fronts—the homework front or the attitude front or the chores front or the cooperation-and-responsibility front, or all of these at once—attacks and counterattacks, the use of spies and special weapons, temporary negotiated settlements, momentary surrenders, occasional desertions, betrayals, treaties, and victories and defeats for both sides at various times. Unfortunately, as in most civil wars, the whole nation, or in this case the whole family, suffers.

The Big Struggle usually develops innocently enough, as one side tries to persuade the other side to do something. The first bad report card comes home, say in the fifth grade, and parents try to set up a better study program. Or Dad tries to persuade his son to get out of bed on time so he can drive him to school without being late for work himself. Or Mom gets upset at her daughter's refusal to read books. Whatever the issue, once the struggle begins, it is hard to prevent it from becoming the Big Struggle.

In the Big Struggle, parents feel they are doing their duty, that they are doing all they can to straighten their child out, that if they didn't join in the Big Struggle the child would simply goof off interminably. And the child feels he is fighting for his independence, that he is resisting becoming an automaton. Or worse, the child doesn't really know what is going on. He is simply reacting. Punch, counterpunch, you attack, I counterattack. The reason for the war is long forgotten as the battles go on and on, taking on a life of their own. After a while neither side quite remembers what is being fought for as resentments build, grudges encrust, and the family slugs it out one season into the next.

The problem is that the Big Struggle rarely achieves any constructive end. There may be short-term gains, such as getting homework done, but usually at so high a cost that it hardly seems worth it. Until a diagnosis of ADD is made and all parties can understand what is really going on, there will be little real progress.

Unfortunately, the hallmark symptoms of ADD—distractibility, impulsivity, and high activity—are so commonly associated with childhood in general that the possibility of an underlying neurological cause is often not considered. A child like Tommy is dealt with as just a rebellious adolescent, and each side ups the ante as the misunderstanding gathers force and the Big Struggle rounds into full swing.

"So what should I do?" Tommy asks. "Commit suicide?"

"You should try to get your act together," his mother answers. "You should take advantage of all the help we've tried to give you. You should show up for your tutor. You should make the effort to bring home your assignment book so we can help you check it over. You should consider telling the truth when we ask you if you have any tests on Friday. You should take that chip off your shoulder and get over thinking the whole world is against you or just doesn't understand you. You should show us a little respect. You should—"

"Wait a minute," Dad interrupts. "Tommy, you're not even listening to your mother, are you?"

Tommy has been staring at his red and purple Nikes. "I'm listening, Dad. I could recite it all back if you want. I've heard it all before."

"Then why don't you do something about it?" Dad asks through clenched teeth.

Tommy looks at his father as if he's about to tell him to piss off, then stops himself and utters the words that form the last line of defense for so many children and adolescents with ADD: "I don't know."

"What do you mean, you don't know?" his father bellows. "I can accept anything but that. That's just your way of tuning us out. You don't know. Well, why don't you know? Can't you think about it and come up with some explanation as to why you're such a screw-up? Are you just stupid? I don't think you're stupid, although I'm beginning to wonder. You just won't wise up, will you?"

Tommy's mother pushes her fingers through her hair. "I wish I could give up on you," she says. "I wish I could just let you fall and not give it a second thought."

"So do I," Tommy says glumly.

Mom and Dad look at each other and Tommy gnaws on his fingernails as the Big Struggle reaches another impasse. This family has been here many times before. Tommy is now sixteen and in the tenth grade. His school career started out well, with his teachers assessing him as a very smart and creative child, but the last several years have been downhill. Now Tommy is just barely getting by academically. His parents feel that they are taking school more seriously than Tommy is. There are so many fights in the household about Tommy that his younger brother has begun to resent him, and his older sister, a high-school senior, is trying to play peacemaker between Tommy and his parents.

The past few years read like chronicles from the war room:

March: Tommy promises to get extra help from French teacher on a regular basis. Parents believe him when he says he's doing this.

June: French teacher sends note home wondering why Tommy never came in for extra help, given that he was going to fail the course. Tommy and his father get so angry at each other that Tommy runs away from home.

October: At a parent conference the school questions Tommy's parents as to whether everything is OK at home. Tommy seems so erratic the school wonders if he is using drugs or if he is upset about something they don't know about. Tommy's parents reassure the school their marriage is fine and things at home are OK. They go home and have a big fight over what is wrong with Tommy.

January: Tommy, who has told his parents all fall that he was working on his science project on his own at school, admits, a week before it is due, that he has done nothing on the project. Dad says he can put up with anything but not lying. He says Tommy can damn well face the consequences. Mom says the consequences will be flunking science and it's not worth it. Dad says, what should I do, do it for him? Mom says, yes, and give him some punishment. In a week's time Tommy and Dad put together a prizewinning project, based on an idea about a computer program Tommy had but never got around to working up. They actually have a lot of fun doing the project. Dad forgets about the punishment, and the whole family glows for a while over winning the prize.

March: The day the family is to leave on vacation, Tommy announces he doesn't want to go. When pressed, he says he feels cramped when he's with the family. Dad explodes and gives Tommy a lecture about how much he has to be grateful for. Tommy listens passively and goes on the vacation. While away Tommy is apprehended by a hotel security man for jumping from a second-floor balcony into the pool. Tommy's explanation is that he was bored. Mom and Dad ground him for twenty-four hours and have an argument with each other.

June: Tommy promises to mow the lawn before going out to the movies with his friends on Friday. He forgets to do it. The next day he promises he'll do it after the football game. Once again he forgets. On Sunday his father tells him he cannot leave the house until the lawn is mowed. Tommy takes this as a challenge and sneaks off on his own, getting his sister to cover for him by saying he is upstairs studying. However, his father catches him as he is coming home. Enraged, he starts screaming at Tommy and then slams him against the kitchen counter. A saucepan falls from a rack, clanking on the brushed-stone floor. His father makes a fist and pulls back his arm as if to punch, but then catches himself. He bites his knuckle and kicks a cupboard door. He draws a deep breath and lets it out slowly as Tommy looks on in fear. A moment passes before his father says, "I can't tell you how disappointed I am in you, son."

Tommy winces, thinking it must be serious this time since he's never heard his father call him "son" before. "I just wanted to go over to Peter's house before I did the lawn. I knew you wouldn't let me." His father turns and walks away. "Dad, I'm sorry. I'll do the lawn now. Really, I'm sorry." His father just keeps on walking.

■ ■ ■

Finally, the Eldredges decide to seek professional help. They visit with Tommy's tutor, who suggests they get a diagnostic evaluation from a child psychiatrist. "I think more may be going on here than meets the eye," he tells Tommy's parents.

Tommy meets with a psychiatrist who interviews him alone, then his parents alone, then the three of them together. After that, Tommy is referred to a psychologist for some testing, then back to the psychiatrist for the full report.

The evaluation yields the diagnosis of ADD. As the psychiatrist explains what this means, Tommy's mother looks on intently. "Attention deficit disorder, or ADD, is a common condition," the psychiatrist begins, "and one that we have good treatments for. However, until it is diagnosed and seen for what it is, it can lead to very big misunderstandings. I think that has been happening in this family. A lot of Tommy's behavior can be explained in terms of ADD. The main symptoms of the condition are easy distractibility, impulsivity, and restlessness, all of which Tommy has."

As the psychiatrist goes on with his explanation, Tommy's mother breaks down in tears. "You mean it's not his fault? I've been after him all these years for something he can't help? I feel so guilty. This is terrible."

Often in families when ADD is diagnosed relatively late, in high school, say, rather than in elementary school, parents feel guilty and angry. They feel guilty that they didn't pick it up sooner, and angry that no one else told them about it. Keeping matters in perspective, it is quite understandable for the diagnosis to be missed, as knowledge about ADD is still spotty in schools and among many professionals. Once the diagnosis is made, many parents need help in getting past their own troubled feelings, just as the child needs help with his or her feelings. The diagnosis can require a whole rethinking of the family roles.

"So you're not the family bozo anymore," Tommy's fourteen-year-old brother pipes up at a family-therapy session designed to educate the entire family about Tommy's ADD.

"Alex, don't talk that way," Mom says.

"Well, it's true," Alex says. "He's been a bozo, but now we're supposed to say he's got a disease. It just sounds like a big excuse to me."

Alex's reaction is typical of siblings when ADD has been diagnosed. Siblings feel resentment at the amount of attention the person with ADD is getting, and they feel anger, believing that their own hard work will go unappreciated.

"You know, I work hard to get my stuff done," Alex goes on. "What if I just said, 'Ooops, can't do it this week, I have ADD.' Could I get special treatment then?"

"But you don't have ADD," Dad says.

"How do you know? I'll bet I could have it if I let myself. And I'll bet Tommy wouldn't have it if he tried not to."

"What do you mean?" Mom asks.

"Well," Alex says, "according to the doctor, with ADD you have trouble paying attention and staying focused. Who doesn't have that? I can promise you whenever I'm in Mr. Hayworth's classroom I have lots of trouble paying attention and staying focused. And I don't see how if Tommy lies about having his homework done it's anything but a lie. Does ADD make you lie? It's a license to kill, this ADD thing. He'll be able to get away with anything now."

"That's not quite true," the psychiatrist interrupts. "He'll still have to be held accountable, it's just that now we'll have a better idea of what he's up against. It's as if he's been nearsighted all these years and now we're giving him glasses."

"I don't know," Alex says, looking over at Tommy as if he had just robbed a bank, "it still all sounds like baloney to me."

Tommy leans back and gives his brother the finger. "You're such a wimp," he says.

"You see?" Alex says.

"Wait a minute," Dad interrupts. "Let's not start arguing again. We've done enough of that to last us a long while."

"So what *do* we do?" Tommy's sister asks. "This family wouldn't know what to talk about if we couldn't talk about Tommy."

"That's not true, Suzie," Mom says.

"Well, maybe it isn't, but there sure will be some empty air time to fill if we're not going to have fights about Tommy anymore."

"Who says we're not going to have fights about Tommy?" Alex asks. "I didn't say I'd go along with that."

"Nobody has said they'd go along with that," the psychiatrist interrupts. "And Suzie makes a good point. Your fights about Tommy may have been serving a purpose and may be hard to replace."

"What kind of purpose?" Dad asks.

"Well, for one thing they may be fun," the psychiatrist says.

"Fun? What do you mean, fun?" Mom gasps. "They're horrible."

"I'm not sure," the psychiatrist says, "but I think as horrible as they may be, they may also be a form of family entertainment."

"I think that's true," Suzie says, looking at Alex. "I can think of at least one person who likes them a lot."

"So what if I do," Alex responds. "He's got it coming to him."

"There may be other reasons to keep the fights going as well," the psychiatrist goes on. "As long as Tommy takes the heat, it takes it off other people."

"You make it sound as if Tommy is just an innocent victim," Dad says.

"I don't mean to," the psychiatrist says. "I'm just suggesting you all might want to keep things the way they are rather than see things change."

Families, by and large, like most groups, resist change. If one member of a family wants to move away, this is often regarded as a betrayal, for example. If one member of a family is fat and tries to lose weight, often other members of the family will sabotage the effort. If one member of a family wants to get out of a role he or she has been playing for years, this is usually difficult to do because the rest of the family tries not to let it happen. If your role is clown, you remain the clown. If your role is responsible oldest child, you probably keep that role, within your family, for your entire life. If you are the black sheep, you'll find it very difficult to change colors in the eyes of your family no matter how many good deeds you do.

So it is with ADD. When the diagnosis is made and the family is faced with the challenge to change, this challenge is often met with great resistance. In the scene above, Tommy's brother Alex voices the resistance, but he is speaking not only for himself, but for the family system as well. If you think of a family as an interconnected group, a system rather than a set of discrete individuals, it is easier to see how movement by one member sets off movement by another, as in a reverberating circuit. And in the family system one member can speak an opinion that everyone in the family holds to some extent but doesn't have to voice as long as that one member stays in his role. In the example above, by expressing his skepticism and resentment at the diagnosis of ADD, Alex allows the other members of the family to be more understanding toward Tommy. Let's see what happens when Alex wavers.

"You mean I might not want Tommy to get this diagnosis because it will make me take more heat?" Alex asks.

"Something like that," the psychiatrist says.

Alex grunts. "I think you may have a point there."

"Alex, are you feeling OK?" Mom asks with a forced smile.

"Yes, Mom, I am. Can't I have my own opinion without you questioning it?"

"I think Alex is trying to beat us to the punch," Dad says. "He wants to agree before we force him into it."

"Alex is trying to be noble," Suzie says sarcastically.

"Alex is full of it," Tommy says, folding his arms. "Don't trust him for a second."

By even tiptoeing out of his role, by even considering changing his assigned lines, Alex receives rapid-fire attack from every member of his family. He has a job to do, a role to play. If he doesn't do it, even if he just wavers, the family gets uneasy and attacks.

This kind of invisible process, common in families yet hard to pin down, can get in the way of the changes the family needs to make once ADD has been diagnosed.

"Wait a minute," the psychiatrist intervenes. "Give Alex a chance. Maybe he is opening the door to the possibility of change." With some help from the psychiatrist Alex is allowed to leave his role as antagonist and skeptic for a while and look at the possibility that Tommy does have a bona fide medical condition that warrants a rethinking of family roles and family procedures. Although in this case Alex is the point person, it is a family decision. Once this happens, once the family gives its permission for change to occur, or at least to be explored, then the Big Struggle can begin to deescalate, and a negotiated peace can be worked out.

Once the fist of the Big Struggle has unclenched, then the family can begin the commonsense process of negotiation. The two keys to reaching this point are first, making the diagnosis of ADD, and second, persuading the family unconscious to grant permission for there to be change within the family system. How do you talk to the family unconscious? How do you get it to grant permission to change? The methods a therapist typically uses include interpretation, which the psychiatrist did in the example above when he suggested there might be reasons the family did not want to stop fighting with Tommy, or confrontation, as when the psychiatrist said to the family, "Wait a minute. Give Alex a chance." In this instance, the psychiatrist was confronting the family before the members could stop Alex from stepping out of his role. Other techniques the therapist may use include direction, support, and suggestion. These may or may not take place within family therapy. Usually, some kind of family meeting or family-therapy session helps to get change going. A family need not feel it *must* go into family therapy to negotiate change, but it would help if the family was aware of some of the pitfalls in family negotiation. Whatever the course of action, you should be aware that there is such a thing as a family unconscious, and that it may try to sabotage the most constructive and well-meaning efforts toward change.

As the family is trying to change, the watchword should be "negotiation." Although it may be quite difficult at first, the family should try to bear the tension of reaching consensus, of listening to and putting up with each other long enough for everybody to feel heard and for everybody to have taken part in reaching the final solution. It is easier to hold people to a negotiated settlement than a dictated one.

For example, at a later session with just Tommy and his parents, Tommy's mom began, "We really have to come up with a plan about homework."

Tommy slumped down in his chair. The psychiatrist noticed this—it was hard to miss—and simply said, "Let's try to have this discussion in a new way."

Tommy and his parents looked at the psychiatrist for a moment, then at each other. There was a pause, as anxiety mounted. "OK," Tommy's dad said. "I'll take the lead on this. I think I can see how my way has not been the smartest way. What can I tell you? It was how I was brought up. My father was just as dumb and stubborn as I am. If I didn't do what he told me to do, he took off his belt and hit me with it until I did what he told me to do."

"Did that method work?" the psychiatrist asked.

"Oh, sure," Dad said. "In the short run. I did what he told me to do. But I learned to hate the son of a bitch. I've forgiven him now, I guess, because he was just doing what he knew, probably just what had been done to him. But it cost us a relationship. I still can't talk to him. I just can't imagine talking to him about anything that matters. So we have really stilted conversations that both of us can't wait to end. Then we go off and wish we had a better relationship with each other."

Tommy was looking at his father, obviously interested. "You never told me about that, Dad," Tommy said.

"No, I guess I didn't," his father said. "But I don't want to make the same mistake with you. And I won't, damn it. Don't get me wrong, kiddo, I have never hit you with a belt and I do not intend to let you manipulate me into doing whatever you want, but coming here has made me think about some things, and I really don't want to end up not talking to you. I don't know why, but I like the look of your ugly puss and the sound of your squeaky voice."

"Hey, Dad, I just love your forty-inch waist," Tommy said.

Tommy's mother sat watching and listening. At one point, when neither her son nor her husband could see her, she nodded approvingly at the psychiatrist.

"Thirty-eight," Dad said.

"OK, I'll give you two inches. So you also want homework?" Tommy said.

"Yes. I would say *you* should want homework, but I know you don't. So what do you want?"

"Free time, money, girls, music, and fast cars," Tommy said with a big grin.

With these positions as starting points, Tommy and his dad, with Mom's silent encouragement, started to negotiate a plan they could each live with. The key to doing it was to establish a tone of support and cooperation first, and not come at the negotiation struggling.

Unfortunately, what often happens in families is that the ADD so threatens the parents' sense of control that one parent or the other—or both—overreacts to the threat by trying to control every last detail. This person insists on dictating how everything should be done, as well as when, where, and why. As appealing as enlightened monarchies may be in the abstract, in families torn by ADD they rarely work well. This is for several reasons. First, monarchs are usually not as enlightened as they think they are. Second, members of the family understandably resent constantly being told what to do. And third, such a controlling hand serves to raise, rather than reduce, tension and conflict within the family. For example, in the session above, had Tommy's dad led off by saying something vaguely combative or confrontative like, "Now see here, Tommy, you have got to know that we are in charge, and you have got to live by our rules," it is unlikely the session would have gone well. The sides would have polarized. Tension would have risen, and, even if Tommy did partially agree with what his father was saying, he never could have acknowledged that out of fear of losing face.

Negotiation, of course, is at times impossible. And with younger children it is often not desirable. Younger children with ADD especially need structure and limits. They want them, and they will test parents until they get them. With a younger child it makes more sense to say, "We're going to McDonald's," than to say, "Which of the five fast-food restaurants in this area would you like to go to tonight?" A younger child gets caught up in the stimulation of making such a vast decision. He or she gets preoccupied with all the options and excited by all the possibilities, and could take an hour or two to decide where to have dinner. It is best in these moments to use one's common sense and intervene decisively. "We are going to McDonald's," may be met with protests, but it is also met with an inner, unspoken sense of relief.

The art of negotiation, a key to the family management of ADD, should be introduced at an early age, but not relied upon with younger kids. Sometimes they are just unable to bear the tension it requires. At other times they will turn negotiation into argument and find it to be a lot of fun. Argument is stimulating, and people with ADD love stimulation. A child with ADD who is bored may instigate a family fight, just because he enjoys the stimulation of it. When this happens it is fair to exercise parental control and say, "We'll do it my way because I said so," and engage in no further discussion until the situation has calmed down.

As children grow older, negotiation becomes more important in all families. Negotiation is key to managing any family's or any group's behavior. But getting on the track to negotiation in a family with ADD is very difficult. Don't get discouraged if you keep falling back into a struggle as you try to negotiate. First, bear in mind that it is in the nature of the person with ADD at any age to prefer a struggle to a negotiation because a struggle is often more stimulating. It can be more exciting to have a family fight than to act reasonably and cooperatively and peacefully. It may be more fun to throw mashed potatoes at your sister than to pass the bowl politely. Most people with ADD love excitement and stimulation. So the Big Struggle is usually more inviting—more engrossing—than some boring negotiation.

Second, the process of negotiation is inherently difficult for someone with ADD because it entails bearing frustration. This is difficult for all people. But it is particularly difficult for the person with ADD who would rather deal with frustration by blowing it off, or by reaching closure too quickly—even if that means sabotaging his own interests—than by the excruciatingly painful ordeal of bearing with it. Like sitting still in class, it is almost impossible for the child or adult with ADD to sit still with frustration. (A practical suggestion here is to encourage the person with ADD to pace about the room while the negotiation is proceeding.)

With those cautions, are there some general principles that will aid in negotiation in families? One of the best books written on the art of negotiation comes from the Harvard Negotiation Project. It is *Getting to Yes: Negotiating Agreement Without Giving In*, by Roger Fisher and William Ury. Originally intended for application to business and diplomacy, this book is better than almost any psychology or family-therapy text for learning how to negotiate effectively in families.

The authors recommend a method of negotiation they call *principled negotiation* or *negotiation on the merits*. The method rests on four basic points:

1. "People: Separate the people from the problem."* The idea here is to get people's ego and pride disentangled from whatever the problem is so that the problem can be attacked without fear of attacking any person in the process. If the person is attached to the problem, the person may never change his mind, no matter how reasonable the solution, because he doesn't want to lose face.

2. "Interests: Focus on interests, not positions." This is what separates negotiation from debating. A debating team defends —or attacks—a certain position, no matter what. It is its sole interest to do that. Like an infantry, its position is its interest. Negotiation should never become debating (or trench warfare). In negotiation people have many interests, and it is the interests, not some debating position, that need to be satisfied. Indeed, one's position may sometimes go against one's interests and one does not want to be so identified with one's position that one cannot change it. This is particularly true with adolescents, who

* Quotation marks set off direct quotations from *Getting to Yes: Negotiating Agreement Without Giving In*, rev. ed., by Roger Fisher, William Ury, and Bruce Patton (Penguin Books, 1991), pp. 10–11.

can back themselves into a corner during an argument so that they end up, out of pride, defending a position they really don't want at all.

3. "Options: Generate a variety of possibilities before deciding what to do." This is particularly important in ADD families, because it is the tendency of the person with the ADD to bring premature closure to the discussion just to avoid bearing the tension of the discussion itself. Don't feel everything has to be wrapped up in one meeting. Get the problem out and then let everybody take a few days to think about it, to come up with various options and solutions. It is much easier to think freely when you are not under pressure. Be very careful not to bully anyone into some agreement too soon.

4. "Criteria: Insist the result be based on some objective standard." This allows the members of the negotiation to appeal to some standard other than their own will or opinion. Examples of objective standards that might be useful in family negotiations would be: What do other families in this area do about this problem? What does the school recommend? What would the open market pay for this service or item? What is the relevant medical information regarding the safety of this activity? What sort of practice schedule does the coach recommend? What does the law say? Is there an agreed-upon set of values or a religious concept that could help the negotiation?

Often in family negotiations parents switch back and forth between "hard" and "soft" negotiation. One day, or one moment, they will be setting strict limits and proposing severe punishments. The next day, or the next moment, they feel unhappy about their "hard" position and switch to a "soft" one, which also becomes ineffective. One day Tommy is being thrown out of the house, and the next day his mother may bake cookies for him in an effort to prop him up. In principled negotiation, as described by Fisher and Ury, the idea is neither to be soft nor hard but to negotiate on the merits, on the principles and issues, always looking for ways of finding mutual gain, and where interests conflict, reconciling them on the basis of some fair standard rather than strength of will or power.

For example, in Tommy's case it was important to get past the power struggle between Tommy and his parents and into the problem of managing school performance. As long as the power struggle predominated, as long as the people were attached to the problem, to use Fisher and Ury's terminology, the Big Struggle would go on. Once Tommy and his dad were able to meet amicably on some common ground, true negotiation could begin.

After Tommy's family had worked out their plan, something happened that often happens in families with ADD. One member of the family tried to rekindle the struggle. Tommy had agreed to go over his homework every other day with a tutor. One night at dinner Tommy's brother, Alex, decided to tease Tommy about having to see a tutor. "Tutors are for retards," Alex said.

"Why don't you go—" Tommy started.

"Wait a minute," Mom interrupted. "Alex, why are you baiting your brother? Can't you see he's trying? Would you like me to make fun of you the next time Sharon McCall comes by?"

Alex blushed. Tommy laughed. For the time being, dinner proceeded without mayhem.

Quashing the Big Struggle takes work—work on a daily basis. Like weeds, it will come back if allowed to.

Here is a summary of some more of the principles of the management of ADD in families.

■

TWENTY-FIVE TIPS
ON THE MANAGEMENT OF ADD
WITHIN FAMILIES

1. Get an accurate diagnosis. This is the starting point of all treatment for ADD.

2. Educate the family. All members of the family need to learn the facts about ADD as the first step in the treatment. Many problems will take care of themselves once all family members understand what is going on. The education process should take

place with the entire family, if possible. Each member of the family will have questions. Make sure all these questions get answered.

3. Try to change the family "reputation" of the person with ADD. Reputations within families, like reputations within towns or organizations, keep a person in one set or mold. Recasting within the family the reputation of the person with ADD can set up brighter expectations. If you are expected to screw up, you probably will; if you are expected to succeed, you just might. It may be hard to believe at first, but having ADD can be more a gift than a curse. Try to see and develop the positive aspects of the person with ADD, and try to change his family reputation to accentuate these positive aspects. Remember, this person usually brings a special something to the family—special energies, special creativity, special humor. He (or she) usually livens up any gathering he attends, and even when he is disruptive, it's usually exciting to have him around. He punctures bombast and does not tolerate fools. He is irreverent and not afraid to speak his mind. He has a lot to give, and the family, more than any group of people, can help him reach his potential.

4. Make it clear that ADD is nobody's fault. It is not Mom's or Dad's fault. It is not brother's or sister's fault. It is not Grandmother's fault, and it is not the fault of the person who has ADD. It is nobody's fault. It is extremely important that this be understood and believed by all members of the family. Lingering feelings that ADD is just an excuse for irresponsible behavior or that ADD is caused by laziness will sabotage treatment.

5. Also make it clear that ADD is a family issue. Unlike some medical problems, ADD touches upon everybody in the family in a daily, significant way. It affects early-morning behavior, it affects dinner-table behavior, it affects vacations, and it affects quiet time. Let each member of the family become a part of the solution, just as each member of the family has been a part of the problem.

6. Pay attention to the "balance of attention" within the family. Try to correct any imbalance. Often, when one child has ADD, his siblings get less attention. The attention may be negative, but the child with ADD often gets more than his share of parents' time and attention day in and day out. This imbalance of attention can create resentment among siblings, as well as deprive them of what they need. Bear in mind that being the sibling of a child with ADD carries its own special burdens. Siblings need a chance to voice their concerns, worries, resentments, and fears about what is going on. Siblings need to be allowed to get angry as well as to help out. Be careful not to let the attention in the family become so imbalanced that the person with ADD is dominating the whole family scene, defining every event, coloring every moment, determining what can and cannot be done, controlling the show.

7. Try to avoid the Big Struggle. A common entanglement in families where ADD is present but not diagnosed, or diagnosed but unsuccessfully treated, the Big Struggle pits the child with ADD against his parents, or the adult with ADD against his spouse, in a daily struggle of wills. The negativity that suffuses the Big Struggle eats away at the whole family. Just as denial and enabling can define the alcoholic family, so can the Big Struggle define (and consume) the ADD family.

8. Once the diagnosis is made, and once the family understands what ADD is, have everybody sit down together and negotiate a deal. Using the principles outlined earlier, try to negotiate your way toward a "game plan" that everyone in the family can buy into. To avoid the family gridlock of the Big Struggle, or to avoid an ongoing war, it is wise to get into the habit of negotiation. This can take a lot of work, but over time negotiated settlements can usually be reached. The terms of any settlement should be made explicit; at best they should be put into writing so they can be referred to as needed. They should include concrete agreements by all parties as to what is promised, with contingency plans for meeting and not meeting the goals. Let the war end with a negotiated peace.

9. If negotiation bogs down at home, consider seeing a family therapist, a professional who has experience in helping families listen to each other and reach consensus. Since families can be explosive, it can be very helpful to have a professional around to keep the explosions under control. Also consider buying a book to help in negotiation, such as Fisher and Ury's *Getting to Yes*.

10. Within the context of family therapy, role-playing can be helpful to let members of the family show each other how they see them. Since people with ADD are very poor self-observers, watching others play them can vividly demonstrate behavior they may be unaware of rather than unwilling to change. Video can help in this regard as well.

11. If you sense the Big Struggle is beginning, try to disengage from it. Try to back away. Once it has begun, it is very hard to get out of. The best way to stop it, on a day-to-day basis, is not to join it in the first place. Beware of the struggle's becoming an irresistible force.

12. Give everyone in the family a chance to be heard. ADD affects everyone in the family, some silently. Try to let those who are in silence speak.

13. Try to break the negative process and turn it into a positive one. Applaud and encourage success when it happens. Try to get everyone pointed toward positive goals, rather than gloomily assuming the inevitability of negative outcomes. One of the most difficult tasks a family faces in dealing with ADD is getting onto a positive track. However, once this is done, the results can be fantastic. Use a good family therapist, a good coach, whatever —just focus on building positive approaches to each other and to the problem.

14. Make it clear who has responsibility for what within the family. Everybody needs to know what is expected of him or her. Everybody needs to know what the rules are and what the consequences are.

15. As a parent, avoid the pernicious pattern of loving the child one day and hating him the next. One day he exasperates you and you punish him and reject him. The next day he delights you and you praise him and love him. It is true of all children, but particularly true of those with ADD, that they can be little demons one day and jewels of enchantment the next. Try to keep on an even keel in response to these wide fluctuations. If you fluctuate as much as the child, the family system becomes very turbulent and unpredictable.

16. Make time for you and your spouse to confer with each other. Try to present a united front. The less you can be manipulated the better. Consistency helps in the treatment of ADD.

17. Don't keep ADD a secret from the extended family. It is nothing to be ashamed of, and the more the members of the extended family know about what is going on, the more help they can be. In addition, it would not be unlikely for one of them to have it and not know about it as well.

18. Try to target problem areas. Typical problem areas include study time, morning time, bedtime, dinnertime, times of transition (leaving the house and the like), and vacations. Once the problem area has been explicitly identified, everyone can approach it more constructively. Negotiate with each other as to how to make it better. Ask each other for specific suggestions.

19. Have family brainstorming sessions. When a crisis is not occurring, talk to each other about how a problem area might be dealt with. Be willing to try anything once to see if it works. Approach problems as a team with a positive, can-do attitude.

20. Make use of feedback from outside sources—teachers, pediatrician, therapist, other parents and children. Sometimes a person won't listen to or believe something someone in the family says, but will listen to it if it comes from the outside.

21. Try to accept ADD in the family just as you would any other condition and normalize it in the eyes of all family members as much as possible. Accommodate to it as you might a family member's special talents or interests like musical ability or athletic skills whose development would affect family routines. Accommodate to it, but try not to let it dominate your family. In times of crisis this may not seem possible, but remember that the worst of times do not last forever.

22. ADD can drain a family. ADD can turn a family upside down and make everybody angry at everybody else. Treatment can take a long while to be effective. Sometimes the key to success in treatment is just to persist and to *keep a sense of humor*. Although it is hard not to get discouraged if things just seem to get worse and worse, remember that the treatment of ADD often seems ineffective for prolonged periods. Get a second consultation, get additional help, but don't give up.

23. Never worry alone. Try to cultivate as many supports as possible. From pediatrician to family doctor to therapist, from support group to professional organization to national convention, from friends to relatives to teachers and schools, make use of whatever supports you can find. It is amazing how group support can turn a mammoth obstacle into a solvable problem, and how it can help you keep your perspective. You'll find yourself saying, "You mean we're not the only family with this problem?" Even if this does not solve the problem, it will make it feel more manageable, less strange and threatening. Get support. Never worry alone.

24. Pay attention to boundaries and overcontrol within the family. People with ADD often step over boundaries without meaning to. It is important that each member of the family know and feel that he or she is an individual, and not always subject to the collective will of the family. In addition, the presence of ADD in the family can so threaten parents' sense of control that one or another parent becomes a little tyrant, fanatically insisting on control over all things all the time. Such a hypercontrolling attitude raises the tension level within the family and makes everybody want to rebel. It also makes it difficult for family members to develop the sense of independence they need to have to function effectively outside the family.

25. Keep up hope. Hope is a cornerstone in the treatment of ADD. Have someone in mind whom you can call who will hear the bad news but also be able to pick up your spirits. Always bear in mind the positive aspects of ADD—energy, creativity, intuition, good-heartedness—and also bear in mind that many, many people with ADD do very well in life. When ADD seems to be sinking you and your family, remember, things will get better.

ADD can tear families apart, no matter what the ages of the people involved. George was a fifty-seven-year-old man who came from a conservative, respectable New England family. He had bumped around from job to job all his life, supporting his wife and children but never living up to his potential or the higher expectations his aristocratic family had for him. When he discovered, at age fifty-seven, that he had ADD, that indeed there was a reason for his underachievement, he became elated and couldn't wait to share the news with his older sister, the family matriarch since his mother had died. She responded coldly, saying, "I'm happy for you, George, if you've found something that makes you happy."

"I didn't expect much," George said. "Maybe just a 'holy cow.' But nothing? I don't understand it."

George wrote the following letter just after talking to his sister, but he did not mail it. He presented it to me during one of his sessions, with this note as a preface: "An unsent letter to my older sister, a seemingly ideal daughter, married to a business executive, having become the seemingly ideal mother, wife, and pillar of her community, a classic product of an ideal family. Since I shared the recent discovery of my ADD with her in mid-March, I have not heard from her. This is curious, since she pretty much spends her life doing all good things to all who come in contact with her. As an exercise, I have written this letter. Perhaps it will help me even if it never does get sent."

Dear Patricia,

As you are undoubtedly aware, it has been some time since we have spoken. As I recall, it was mid-March when I called and explained to you my revelation regarding the ADD. We spoke again ever so briefly Easter weekend when you passed me rather quickly (and rather unceremoniously, I might add) to David. I actually tried to call you a couple of times without any luck, and, as time passed, it became apparent that you were not making any noticeable effort to reach me. As more time has passed, it seemed appropriate to come at this from another direction. I am not sure what is actually happening and, therefore, am unsure of proper protocol, but I have decided to communicate my thoughts to you as clearly and sincerely as I can.

As you may or may not know, ADD has only recently become even reasonably understood with children and continues to cause a good deal of uncertainty with regard to adults. What you may or may not also know, is that . . . wait a minute, that's not where I want to head. Actually, sharing information about ADD is not really the primary thrust here. What really interests me is trying to explain a bit more about what is going on in my life and perhaps have the opportunity to hear the same about you.

To review, my call to you in March was to share with you what is unquestionably the single most significant realization of my life. This ADD thing has not only silently blocked me from successfully doing those things that have been expected of me, but it has done so in such a way that I (along with most others similarly blessed) came to believe that my inability to perform was a matter of choice and therefore a massive character flaw. I have genuinely felt that to be true for as long as I can remember. In addition, it has been apparent to me as well as to all with whom I have had contact that I have had the ability, intelligence, good looks, sense of propriety, and whatever else seemed important in the quest for success . . . another false start.

What I really want to know is, what the hell is going through your head? Your brother for whom you have professed genuine love and affection tells you that he has a neurological disorder of extremely significant proportion, ADD, and that its by-products have literally warped my every action, relationship, and thought. Why have you not offered me encouragement, sympathy, expressions of interest, or anything of the sort? If for some reason you feel none of those things, why have you not indignantly confronted me as a sham, an embarrassment, a blemish on our all-American family picture? Why in the bloody hell have you not done anything at all? Am I that insignificant a pimple of irritation to your fat-ass, do-gooder life that you don't even deem me worthy of a snappy, superior (perhaps even condescending) retort?

None of these options makes any sense at all, Patty. I am your brother, George. I have a neurological impairment called attention deficit disorder. It is no one's fault that I have it and no one has intentionally contributed to the effects it has had on me. While I am not angry or bitter about it, it has caused me no end of trouble in doing even the most simple of things that I have expected of myself and others have expected of me. I have not had control over those functions of my mind that allow me to sustain interest in almost anything of significance in my life. I have appeared to myself and to others to be lazy and unmotivated, wasteful of an abundance of natural talent. This has become so chronically discouraging that I have not been able to generate a whit of real enthusiasm for anything (other than getting out of my debt) for a long, long time. This is *not* a figment of my imagination or some café syndrome to be used as an excuse for a failed life. As it affects me, it also affects thousands of others like me. There is no doubt about my diagnosis. It has been confirmed conclusively by three independent specialists in adult ADD. I have read account after account of how people have lived with ADD unknown to them and, for most, I could have written the anecdotes myself. The diagnostic definitions fit as though they were written to describe me. Lucky me, though, I am not in jail like lots of ADD aficionados, or an alcoholic, or any one of a number of other distasteful, yet not uncommon, ends.

I am now in the process of trying various combinations of medicine that will allow me to control the focus of my mind. At the same time, I am trying to unravel years of creative behavior patterns that have provided variations of success, failure, frustration, confusion, and even some laughs. While I am not convinced that I am blessed to have this insidious thriller, I do recognize that I am at least better off knowing about it than bluffing my way through the duration of a life that hasn't actually been that much fun.

Would you please let me know what is going through your mind? I am not expecting any particular attitude from you. What I do want is to know your honest feelings whatever they may be. It would be nice if our past relationship of blood, family, and sharing of life experience could continue on some positive level, but if that is somehow not something that can work for you, I can deal with it. Why don't you just let me know.

Sincerely,

Your brother,

George

After some consideration George decided not to send the letter. "I think it's time for me to give up trying to get some sort of approval from her that she will never be able to give. I don't know why at my age I should even want it. But I do."

Over time George began to get that approval from others, and mostly from himself. His lifelong struggle could at last be understood, at least by himself and by his wife and children. His ordeal would have been eased, however, if his sister could have understood his situation.

Families in general have tremendous power both to heal and to inflict pain. If the family is willing to cast a new eye upon a chronically wounded member, if the family is willing to help heal him, it can be more effective than all the medications, therapies, and incantations ever devised. However, if the family is unwilling to look differently upon its George, if the family instead sneers and snorts, "Just another one of your lame excuses! Why don't you just shape up?" then the family can undermine whatever good treatment he may receive. Few of us ever outgrow the power of our families both to deflate us and to fill us up. Few of us ever get past the wish for love and approval from mother or father, sibling or kin. That wish can be used in our favor, to support us as the wish is granted, or it can be used in our destruction as the wish is perpetually denied.

For the family to use its considerable power to heal, it must be willing to accept the challenge of change. All groups, most especially families, feel threatened by a change in the status quo, no matter how bad the status quo may be. As the person with ADD seeks to change, he is also asking his family to change with him. This is never easy. It is not the troubled family that has a hard time with change; it is all families. But with education and information as guides, with encouragement and support as reinforcers, most families can successfully adapt. As there is less suffering in the family system, life at home can even be fun.

▪ 6 ▪

Parts of the Elephant

SUBTYPES OF ADD

We do not yet have one concise definition for ADD. Instead, we have to rely on descriptions of symptoms to define ADD. Often the descriptions focus on one part of the syndrome or another, highlighting this aspect or that, in a way that is reminiscent of the story of the blind men describing an elephant. One blind man feels the trunk and describes something long and tubular emitting warm air. Another feels the tail and describes something narrow and pliable. Another feels a leg and describes something like a tree trunk. Still another feels the belly and describes something massive yet spongy. None of the blind men is able to step back and see the elephant as a whole.

So it can be with ADD. When we focus in on one part of the syndrome, we are at risk of overlooking another, quite different part. For example, if we focus in on inattentiveness, we can overlook the fact that most people with ADD can hyperfocus at times. Or if we focus in on hyperactivity, we can overlook the many people with ADD who are quiet and daydreamy. It is difficult to step back and see that all of these aspects are part of a greater whole. By examining the various parts, or subtypes, of ADD, however, one can gain a better understanding of this complex syndrome. The formal diagnostic nomenclature recognizes only two subtypes of ADD: ADD with

151

hyperactivity and ADD without hyperactivity. ADD in children and ADD in adults constitutes another broad classification.

We would like to introduce some other subtypes, not all formally recognized, but, based upon our clinical experience, useful in identifying the most common and distinct ways in which ADD is manifested. Because many of the secondary symptoms associated with ADD develop over time, these subtypes apply mainly to ADD as it is seen in adults. We list them, roughly speaking, in descending order of frequency.

The subtypes include:

1. ADD without hyperactivity

2. ADD with anxiety

3. ADD with depression

4. ADD with other learning disorders

5. ADD with agitation or mania

6. ADD with substance abuse

7. ADD in the creative person

8. ADD with high-risk behavior, or "high-stim" ADD

9. ADD with dissociative states

10. ADD with borderline personality features

11. ADD with conduct disorder or oppositional disorder (in children) or antisocial personality features (in adults)

12. ADD with obsessive-compulsive disorder

13. Pseudo-ADD

ADD without Hyperactivity

One of the most common misconceptions about attention deficit disorder is that it only occurs with hyperactivity. Many people believe that if the child is not "bouncing off the walls," then he or she does not have ADD.

If the child is not a behavior problem, or a discipline problem, or at least a fidgety nudge, then the child does not have ADD. Or, if the adult is not a restless whirling dervish, then he or she cannot have ADD. The diagnosis seems to rest, in many people's minds, upon the symptom of motoric hyperactivity.

While untrue, this is understandable. ADD was first described in the population of hyperactive children. Our comprehension of the disorder is rooted in studies of hyperactive kids. It is only fairly recently that we have come to understand that ADD can occur without hyperactivity, or, for that matter, that it can occur in adults. Just as reputations die hard, so does dated knowledge fade slowly.

But the evidence now shows that there are hosts of children and adults who have all the other symptoms of ADD but who are not hyperactive, or even overactive. If anything, they are motorically slow, even languid.

These are the daydreamers. These are the kids—often girls—who sit in the back of the class and twirl their hair through their fingers while staring out the window and thinking long, long thoughts. These are the adults who drift off during conversations or in the midst of reading a page. These are the people, often highly imaginative, who are building stairways to heaven in the midst of conversations, or writing plays in their minds while not finishing their day's work, or nodding agreeably and politely while not hearing what is being said at all. They steal away silently, without the noisemaking of their hyperactive brethren, but they steal away just the same.

Perhaps due to the manner in which the ADD gene is expressed, or due to the absence of the Y chromosome, girls seem to have ADD without hyperactivity more often than boys do. It can occur in both sexes, but it is more common in girls or women.

Usually in these people the core symptom is distractibility. It is a quiet phenomenon, their shifting of attention. It happens as silently, but as definitely, as a cut in a film sequence. Imagine, one moment you are in one place, and in the next moment you are somewhere else. You don't really notice it. Rather you go along with it, as you go along with a cut in a movie. The narrative carries you, as you view your own internal story, your own internal screening of the day's events.

In some ways it is a charming symptom. The mind meanders like a brook, winding through the contours of the land, bending here, falling there, quietly making its way, in its own time, to some larger river of thought.

But in other ways it is anything but charming. It can be downright disabling not to be able to rely on your own mind to remember things, to prompt you to get to places on time, to keep you involved in a conversation when you want to be, or focused on a page you really do want to read, or concentrated on a project you need to complete. The meandering brook, in its desultory way, seems to be forever carrying you away from where you want to be.

"I can be working on a project at my desk," reports one patient, "when, without really knowing it, I begin to think about some other idea my work suggests. Then I follow that thought, or I may even leave my desk to go get something, and by the time I've gone to get the thing, I've forgotten what it was I was going to get. I'm almost sleepwalking. Hours can pass in this unfocused state. Lots of interesting thoughts pass by, I can be engaged in lots of creative enterprises, but relatively little gets done. I can combat it consciously for a few minutes, but the moment I get into anything, the moment I stop monitoring what I'm doing and get into the flow of the work, then I'm at the mercy of my whims. If I could just stay focused for even one hour, I could probably get my whole day's work done."

After this woman was treated for ADD, her life changed. "It was amazing," she says. "I didn't really feel any different, but I started getting all my work done. Projects I'd had on the back burner for years began to get finished, and at the end of a day I couldn't believe how much I'd actually accomplished. But it was more than just my productivity that changed. My whole way of looking at myself changed, too. I stopped thinking of myself as some kind of spaceshot and started realizing I was just as smart as anybody else. I started realizing I was not defective. In fact, I was pretty good. It was quite a change, I can tell you. My only regret is that I didn't find out about my condition sooner in my life."

Many factors other than ADD can contribute to an inability to focus consistently. The most common of these include the hectic pace of everyday life, traumatic events in the present or the past, depression, substance abuse or overuse of prescribed medication, anxiety disorders, grief reactions, major life changes, and various medical conditions, such as certain seizure disorders, that require a visit with a physician to evaluate. However, the cause may also be untreated ADD.

Particularly when hyperactivity is not present, the diagnosis of ADD is easy to miss. The individual simply appears to be one of the many people who "can't get their act together." You want to take them and shake them and say, "Shape up! Get with it! Don't you realize you're frittering your life away?!" But if someone in the person's life could stop to consider that the problem might be rooted in something more complex than laziness or general fecklessness, then a new light could shine on the situation, and, perhaps, a better life could begin.

ADD with Anxiety

For some people, the experience of ADD is one of chronic anxiety. What bothers them most is not the inattentiveness or impulsivity of ADD, but the attendant anxiety they so frequently feel.

This anxiety can be separated into two parts, one logical and obvious, the other irrational and hidden. The "logical" anxiety is the anxiety that one would expect to feel if one were chronically forgetting obligations, daydreaming, speaking or acting impulsively, being late, not meeting deadlines—all the typical symptoms of ADD. Living in such a state naturally leaves one feeling anxious: What have I forgotten? What will go wrong next? How can I keep track of all the balls I have in the air?

The hidden anxiety is hard to believe, but we see it frequently in clinical practice. This is the anxiety or worry that the individual actively seeks out. The person with "anxious ADD" often starts the day, or any moment of repose, by rapidly scanning his or her mental horizon in *search* of something to worry about. Once a subject of worry has been located, the individual locks in on it like a heat-sensing rocket and doesn't let go. No matter how trivial the subject or how painful the worry, the individual keeps the worry alive, returning to it magnetically, obsessively. Some of these people do in fact have obsessive-compulsive disorder, but the majority do not. They are actually using worry as a means of organizing their thinking. Better to have the pain of worry, they seem to feel, than to have the disquietude of chaos.

Listen to one patient's description: "The minute I have my mind cleared of one problem, I go out and look for another. They are usually really stupid things like an unpaid bill or something someone said to me two days before or whether or not I'm too fat. But I brood over them until they ruin my whole mood."

This tendency to organize around worry defines the subtype of ADD with anxiety. It is common. Why is it so persistent? In part because the individual doesn't know why he's doing it. Like most habits of mind, it persists until insight can begin to try to change it.

Another explanation for this ruminative, often extremely painful style of thinking has to do with what we call the startle response in ADD. It is a sequence of events that goes as follows:

1. Something "startles" the brain. It may be a transition, like waking up, or going from one appointment to the next, or it may be the completion of a task, or the receiving of some piece of news. It may be, and usually is, trivial, but the "startle" requires some reorganization on the part of the brain.

2. A minipanic ensues. The mind doesn't know where to look or what to do. It has been focused on one thing and is now being asked to change sets. This is very disorganizing. So the mind reaches out for something red-hot, something to focus on. Since worry is so "hot," and therefore so organizing, the mind finds something to worry about.

3. Anxious rumination replaces panic. While anxious rumination is painful, it is at least organized. One can say over and over in one's mind, thousands of times a day, "Will I get my taxes paid on time?" or "Does that look she gave me mean she is angry with me?" or "Did I pass the exam?" The panic induced by the "startle" is replaced by the focused ache of anxious rumination.

The whole point of the sequence is to avoid chaos. No one likes chaos, but most people can endure milliseconds, or even seconds, of it as they go from one task to another, one state to another, one stimulus to another. The ADD mind often cannot. Instead, it fixates on worry and gets organized—or stuck—around it.

ADD with Depression

Sometimes the first symptom that brings a person with ADD to a psychiatrist is some form of mood disorder, particularly depression. While ADD is usually defined in terms of other symptoms—distractibility, impulsivity, and restlessness—and consequently is not considered when someone says he or she is depressed, the fact is that ADD and depression frequently coexist.

This is not hard to understand when one considers the typical life experience of someone with ADD. Since childhood, the person with ADD has felt a sense of chronic frustration and failure. Underachieving all along, accused of being stupid or lazy or stubborn, finding the demands of everyday life extraordinarily difficult to keep up with, tuning out instead of tuning in, missing the mark time and again, living with an overflow of energy but an undersupply of self-esteem, the individual with ADD can feel that it is just not worth it to try anymore, that life is too hard, too much of a struggle, that perhaps it would be better if life were to end than go on.

It is heartening how valiantly people with undiagnosed ADD try in the face of their despair. They don't give up. They keep pushing. Even when they've been knocked down many times before, they stand up to get knocked down again. It is hard to keep them down for good. They tend not to feel sorry for themselves. Rather, they tend to get mad, to get up, to have at it again. In this sense one might say they are stubborn: they just don't give up. But they may remain depressed.

While life experience can lead to some of the depression one often sees among people with ADD, there may be a biological factor at work as well. It may be that ADD partakes of a common pathophysiology with biological depression (i.e., depression not caused by life events but by biology). That is to say ADD and biological depression may be physiologically, and genetically, related. Whatever goes wrong in depression, whatever the "patho" part of the physiology is, that part may also go wrong in ADD.

James Hudson and Harrison Pope at the Harvard Medical School, in their innovative research, have speculated that eight separate disorders, among them depression and ADD, may share a common physiologic abnormality. They call the group affective spectrum disorder. (It also includes bulimia, obsessive-compulsive disorder, cataplexy, migraine, panic disorder, and irritable-bowel syndrome.) The grouping is supported by response to similar medications, as well as by clinical evidence. If, as is the case, a medication that successfully treats major depression also successfully treats ADD, might we not suppose that there is a link between the two disorders? Although it is not necessarily so—indeed, there are unrelated disorders in medicine that the same medication treats—it is worth wondering about. Hudson and Pope did just that. Their research shows strong evidence for a physiologic linkage among the eight disorders they include within the "affective spectrum."

On the basis of both biology and life experience, then, it is not surprising to find depression associated with ADD.

Often, however, the mood problem in ADD is subtle. It is not severe enough to be called depression, but it is more severe than the ordinary dips in mood of everyday life. Listen to this description from a patient:

> I don't think I've ever really been happy. For as long as I can remember, there's always been a sadness tugging at me. Sometimes I forget about it. I guess that's when you could say I was happy. But the minute I start to think, then the bad feeling comes back. It isn't despair. I've never attempted suicide or anything like that. It's just that I've never felt good, about myself or about life or about the future. It's all been an uphill battle. I guess I always thought that's just what life was—one long series of disappointments interrupted by moments of hope.

This patient's description brings to mind a remark made by Samuel Johnson, a man for whom there is ample evidence of having ADD and depression. Johnson observed that "life is a process not from pleasure to pleasure, but from hope to hope." Elsewhere he wrote, "Life is a state everywhere in which there is much to be endured and little to be enjoyed." He also said that "we live in a world that is bursting with sin and sorrow."

Such persistent sadness, or lack of pleasure, often accompanies ADD. Sometimes, when the ADD is treated, the sadness lifts. As if a mote had been removed from the eye, the person can see pleasure where there had only been confusion or a blur. In people with this subtype of ADD the distractibility that is part of the syndrome interferes with the process of apprehending pleasure, of perceiving order, and of sensing that life can be all right.

It had never occurred to the patient quoted above that matters could work out in her life because she never recognized it when they did. She was always distracted by some relatively benign worry. But she was so distractible, so subject to the disruptions the worries caused her, that she could never see the forest for the trees. Her sense of chronic disappointment was as much a function of her inability to perceive order or stability in her world as it was of actual failures.

We are not suggesting here that all depression is due to ADD. Far from it. However, there are some people who are chronically sad who do in fact have ADD and don't know it.

The primary disorder—an inability to attend—can lead to the secondary problem of depression. Or the two—ADD and depression—may coexist, both arising independently from the same physiological abnormality.

ADD with Other Learning Disorders

The pain of a learning disorder resides not only in the strain one feels in trying to function but in the disconnections one can suffer, a disconnection from language and from thought, from expression and creativity, from books and from words, as well as from people and from feelings.

Equally, it can be said, I believe, that one of the pleasures of the various disorders is the fanciful variations they bring up. While the child with dyslexia or ADD may stammer, stumble, and reverse, while he may disconnect from the word or the page or the person, he may also soar. He may connect in new and unexpected ways. He may, in his stumbling, stumble onto something new and wonderful. It is therefore vital that we keep the windows of these children's minds clean, that we keep them free of the smudge and grease of shame, criticism, defeatism, and devaluation.

Let me tell a story. There was once a little boy who was pronounced writing-phobic. This pronouncement was made by a psychologist. "Karl is writing-phobic," the report read. "I reach this conclusion based upon psychometric testing as well as projective testing which reveals a partial inability to retrieve certain words under stress as well as an incomplete release of the preverbal memory structures as initiated by image recall and impromptu stimulation. This leads to a relative inhibition of the capacity to form written expressives, that is to say a tendency to avoid external prompts or stressors related to the act of writing. These neurological factors are complicated, on a psychodynamic level, by the fact that Karl has a precocious awareness of his parents' own internal conflicts. For a boy of eight, he displays an unusual understanding of his mother's unfulfilled literary ambitions as well as his father's shame-slash-pride over certain verbal successes vis-à-vis his own career, namely that he is a successful writer for what are commonly referred to as television sitcoms. Thus, the neurological and the psychodynamic combine to create in Karl an intense ambivalence as to whether or not he wants to write, whether or not he should write, whether or not he can write, and what, exactly it means *to* write. Until these issues are resolved he will remain writing-phobic. It is my advice not to tamper with this delicate balance, but rather to respect Karl's defensive structure and wait for the issues to resolve. Failing this, resource room time might prove invaluable."

My friend, Priscilla Vail, a learning specialist, read this report and laughed out loud. "What does this mean?" she asked herself. Not quite believing the report, Priscilla decided to take a different tack from the one the psychologist had recommended. She told Karl that as much as he might want to write, he would have to constrain all his written output within the bounds of one three-by-five note card per day. She then began to work with him on all sorts of fun projects that involved writing—games, puzzles, mazes, wish lists, fan letters. In no time Karl was asking for a bigger note card. "I don't know about that," Priscilla said, stroking her chin. "That's an awful lot of space you'd have to fill."

"Oh, please, Mrs. Vail!" Karl pleaded.

"Well, if you think you can handle it—"

"Handle it?" Karl interrupted. "I can handle much more than that!" he said proudly.

Soon Karl's written output exceeded that of most professional writers. The "writing phobia" and the resource room were forgotten as Karl eagerly got busy with words without knowing that he wasn't supposed to be able to.

I think people come to words much as lovers get together. They stumble onto each other, at the oddest of times, in the strangest of places. They will meet in an empty laundromat on a rainy Sunday afternoon, or they will catch each other's eyes across a ballroom dance floor in the middle of a wedding waltz. They will meet without appointment and strike up a relationship without an agenda. There may be a long courtship or a whirlwind romance. There may be protracted avoidance, even what looks like a phobia, as in Karl's case, or there may be an instant avidity, what amounts to love at first sight. Some carry on a kind of epistolary relationship with words, expressing their feelings through the formal prose of elegant notes, while others jump at words and bark them out at the world in the immediate poetry of certain street-corner vendors. Some slap their words up on posters on telephone poles, while others keep them in reserve, like a pistol concealed in a pocketbook. Some read haltingly, like the nervous lover, hat in hand, while others seem born to orate. We all woo language differently, and language grants us her favors in different ways. Sometimes the relationship takes off, although it is rare there is a ride without bumps. While utterly beautiful, endlessly varied, and thoroughly transfixing, language can also be frustrating, confusing, exasperating, and unforgiving.

Priscilla Vail, one of the great couples counselors we have for troubled-language relationships, knew intuitively and from great experience how to bring Karl together with words. She knew how to coax him from the periphery and onto the dance floor. She knew if she played the right music and showed him a few simple steps, the allure of the dance would overcome Karl's shy way with words.

Priscilla knew what all who work with words know: that one's language is not an inert tool that you take down from the shelf like a hammer. Rather, it is a living companion, whose company you keep for most of your waking life. For many people language is a best friend they take for granted.

For some others, though, language never comes easily. The company of words is always an effort to keep. These people—and I count myself among them as one who is dyslexic and has ADD—never know quite what to expect from words. Our relationship with words is rooted in unpredictability. One moment we are Abraham Lincoln composing a Gettysburg Address, and the next moment we are as clumsy with words as a boy on his first date.

When I was in high school, back in the sixties, the classification of learning disorders was really pretty simple. There was basically one learning disorder: stupidity. And there was basically one treatment: work harder. Oh, people talked a good game about "special help" and tutoring, and we all knew that some people were good at math and others were good at

English and a lucky few were good at both, and some people had heard of dyslexia, but we had no more sophisticated understanding of what was going on than that.

Now the science of learning has grown in scope and depth. Of course, as our knowledge has increased, matters have grown more complicated. The jargon in the field is cumbersome and test reports are often difficult to comprehend. The terms tossed around include "auditory processing problem," "visual-spatial dysfunction," "receptive language disorder," "nonverbal learning disability," "word-retrieval problem," "language-based learning disorder," etc., etc. All very pungent concepts, but almost impossible to keep straight unless you deal with them every day. Experts in the field appropriate their own set of terms and then compete with each other to see whose lexicon will win out. Committees meet and decree terms and then they meet again and change the terms just as you've learned the first set. The committee that convened not very long ago to write the definition of ADD for the *Diagnostic and Statistical Manual of Mental Disorders* third edition, revised (or, for short, DSM-III-R), will soon come out with a new definition for DSM-IV.

One can hardly hope that science will slow down so that we can keep up with its nomenclature. However, it is important not to be intimidated by science. Too often, practitioners in the field of learning problems and ADD confuse rather than clarify through their use of arcane terms or references. One should be able to gain access to the important information in this field without the use of a translator's dictionary.

Priscilla Vail's term for many of the children we have described in this book is "conundrum kids." These kids don't fit any one mold exactly, and we can't explain all of what is going on. These kids puzzle us as they flounder one day and shine the next, read to beat the band one day and stare out the window the next, solve complex math problems in their spare time but find themselves unable to do any of the math on the test. Anyone who would like to know these children well—and how to help them—should read Priscilla Vail, especially *Smart Kids with School Problems* and *The World of the Gifted Child*.

While the conundrum kids (or, for that matter, the conundrum adults) puzzle us, one part of the puzzle they present is often ADD. In dealing with ADD it is important to know that it is often accompanied by other difficulties in learning. Depending upon what difficulty you are referring to and how you define it, the incidence of other learning disorders coexisting with ADD ranges from 10 percent to 80 percent. Much of the variability here has to do with definition. An excellent book that sorts out the various terms and gives lucid explanation to them all is *Diagnosing Learning Disorders* by Bruce Pennington. Another example of a clear writer in an unclear field, Pennington brings together research and interpretation in a framework that is useful to both the lay and professional reader.

In Pennington's neuropsychological framework, ADD is one of several so-called learning disorders. A learning disorder refers to a problem in the individual's neuropsychological system that adversely affects school performance. One can, of course, underachieve in school without having a learning disorder if the poor performance is due entirely to emotional or social factors. Mental retardation constitutes one large grouping of learning disorders, while Pennington's book takes in the others. The disorders he discusses include, in decreasing order of frequency, dyslexia and other developmental language disorders, ADD, right-hemisphere learning disorders (which includes specific problems with math, handwriting, and art, as well as associated problems with social cognition), autism spectrum disorder, and acquired memory disorders (most commonly due to a closed head injury or a seizure disorder). Learning disabilities—specific problems with math, reading, or language—are a subset of learning disorders in Pennington's classification.

ADD, then, is one kind of learning disorder. It may be accompanied by other learning disorders, such as dyslexia or an acquired memory disorder. It may also be accompanied by a specific learning disability, such as a math disability.

This distinction between disorder and disability may be confusing at first. The disabilities are a subset of the disorders. The disabilities impair specific abilities: math disability, language disability, spelling disability. The disorders, on the other hand, are not so specific; they affect cognition in general.

Since ADD affects all areas of cognition, it will exacerbate any learning disability. ADD is not a specific learning disability in itself; it does not disable any one cognitive function, but is broader than that. A specific math disability may often be found with ADD, as may other specific learning disabilities, particularly difficulty in learning foreign languages.

Math difficulties warrant careful evaluation. There are different kinds of math problems, ranging from culturally induced problems as may be found among girls who are brought up to believe they should be bad at math and over time become math-phobic, to neurologically based learning difficulties. There are different kinds of difficulties among the neurologically based, some having to do with problems with spatial relations, others having to do with conceptualization, others having to do with memory and data-processing. Once you understand precisely what kind of difficulty you are dealing with, you are then equipped to make the delicate decision of how far to push. There is remedial help available for math disabilities and language disabilities. The help ranges from tutoring to the use of special devices such as Cuisenaire rods (manipulable colored sticks of different lengths that help little children learn calculation) to special schools where intensive support and technical expertise may be found. The special assistance can help a great deal, but it is not curative. The disability does not go away; one simply learns to cope with it as best one can.

When do you decide that the individual has worked long and hard enough at math or at a foreign language before letting it drop? This kind of decision is best made in concert with the school, the family, the individual, and a learning specialist. You do not want to give up too soon, thus limiting what the person can learn. On the other hand, you do not want to slog away endlessly with no apparent gain, losing time and self-esteem in the process. The matter should be evaluated repeatedly, and programs should allow flexibility so that the individual can learn as much as possible without damage to self-confidence.

The most common learning disorder, and the one about which we know the most, is dyslexia. Its prevalence in this country, depending on how it is defined, is from 10 to 30 percent. Briefly stated, dyslexia is a problem with reading or writing one's native language that cannot be explained by some other cause such as limited schooling, poor vision or hearing, brain damage or retardation. Since not all dyslexia is the same, we should probably refer to it in the plural, the dyslexias. Some dyslexics have particular trouble spelling. Others are what used to be called "mirror readers," reversing letters in words, reading "was" for "saw" and so forth. Others do not reverse letters per se, but anticipate letters or sounds incorrectly, and so misread words, for example mistaking "battlefield" for "bachelor" or "filament" for "firmament" or even "metaphor" for "medical." According to the work of Albert Galaburda at Harvard, the brains of dyslexics appear to be different from normal brains in that they have aberrant nodules on the cerebral cortex. These nodules may interfere with how the brain perceives and processes the phonemes or sound bits that make up words. The underlying phonological processing problem in turn leads to the problems in reading, spelling, and writing characteristic of the dyslexias. The primary symptoms of ADD—erratic attention span, impulsivity, and restlessness—can make reading difficult, and therefore can mimic dyslexia. However, the two are separate disorders. The distinction is of practical significance because the treatments for the two conditions are different.

The two disorders can coexist or they can occur separately. In terms of overlap, ADD occurs more frequently among dyslexics than in the population at large. However, there is not an increased incidence of dyslexia among the ADD population. Put differently, you are more likely than the average person to have ADD if you have dyslexia; but you are no more likely than the average person to have dyslexia if you have ADD.

Auditory processing problems also occur frequently with ADD. As the term suggests, an auditory processing problem interferes with the brain's ability to comprehend fully what it "hears." The child or adult with this problem has no hearing deficiency; sound enters the brain without problems. However, once the sound gets into the brain, the cerebral cortex has trouble processing it or fully making sense of it.

For example, a child in class may "hear" the teacher say "George Washington was the first president of the United States" but comprehend it as "George Washington is the president of the United States." If, when asked about George Washington, he repeats his "revised" version, he will appear foolish or stupid.

Or a child may have trouble socially because he or she does not process properly what is being said. The same problems can affect an adult, both at work and socially.

We do not yet appreciate how profoundly auditory processing problems interfere with learning and interacting with others. Particularly in individuals who also have ADD, auditory processing problems can greatly interfere with everyday life.

■ ■ ■

A learning disorder, whatever the definition or cause, usually hurts. As an example, consider this, from the novelist John Irving's recollections of his days as a student at Phillips Exeter Academy:

I simply accepted the conventional wisdom of the day—I was a struggling student; therefore, I was stupid.

I was such a poor student, I needed five years to pass the three-year foreign language requirement; and in my fifth year at Exeter—in my second "senior" year—I was taking Math III for the second time (I had already taken Math II twice). I was such a weak student, I passed Latin I with a D—and flunked Latin II; then I switched to Spanish, which I barely survived. . . .

I wasn't diagnosed as learning-disabled or dyslexic at Exeter; I was just plain stupid. I failed a spelling test and was put in a remedial spelling class; because I couldn't learn how to spell—I *still* can't spell—I was advised to see the school *psychiatrist*! This advice made no sense to me then—it makes no sense to me now—but if you were a poor student at Exeter, you would develop such a lasting sense of inferiority that you'd probably be in need of a psychiatrist one day. . . .

I wish I'd known, when I was a student at Exeter, that there was a word for what made being a student so hard for me; I wish I could have said to my friends that I was dyslexic, or learning-disabled. Instead, I kept quiet, or—to my closest friends—I made bad jokes about how stupid I was.

It is struggle enough to have a learning disorder, but to have that struggle compounded by a string of invidious labels—stupid, lazy, and the like—puts one's whole self-esteem in jeopardy. The experience of moral condemnation is so frequent among the learning disordered as to be commonplace. Indeed, it is only recently that anything like an informed, compassionate view has developed. Still, one hears snide jokes all the time in reference to this population: they are "intellectually challenged," or they are just looking for an excuse to get better grades in school or file a discrimination grievance at work.

It is worth mentioning here the moral bias in our society that often prevents the diagnosis of ADD—and other learning disorders—from being made. A streak of Puritanism runs deep within American society. Permissive and pioneering as we may be on the one hand, we are strict and conservative on the other. As much as we may be a country of mavericks and entrepreneurs, we are also a country of finger waggers and name callers. As much as we may be a country of compassion for the underdog, we are also a country that believes in self-reliance.

This is apparent in the field of learning disorders. In our educational system, despite reform, the operative principle is still sink or swim. School is a fair marketplace, we seem to believe. The smart will excel. If you don't excel, well, then you are not smart. Pretty words to the contrary, most students, parents, and teachers still seem to agree on the concept of smart/stupid. They seem to think that the idea that intelligence may be a more complicated matter than smart versus stupid is just a fancy way of dancing around the truth: you either have it or you don't.

Such thinking can turn school into one long, dismal ordeal.

We now have the knowledge to identify children with learning disorders early on and thus spare them the emotional trauma of daily being misunderstood, daily being labeled dumb, daily not getting it, and daily wondering why.

Think for a moment of the importance of the innocent curiosity a child brings to school. Think of the little tendrils of knowledge and of self-esteem embedded in that curiosity. If nourished, those tendrils will grow, over the many years the child will spend in school, college, and beyond, into a solid store of knowledge, a feeling of confidence around learning new ideas, and a buoyant sense of self. Think of the look on the face of a three-year-old as she tries to blow bubbles, or the face of a four-year-old trying to make a house of cards, or a five-year-old balancing on his first bicycle. Think of the look of concentration on that face and think of how important it is to the child to get it right. Remember in your own life, when you were a child, the feeling of excitement and danger as you tried something new. Remember how the one thing you feared more than anything else was not failure but being made fun of, being humiliated. Think of the faces of children everywhere as they open their minds to learn.

Keep those faces in mind, the little girls and boys in the early grades, all trusting the adults to show them the way, all eager and excited about life and what will come next, and then just follow those faces over time. Follow the face of a little girl who doesn't read very well and is told to try harder; who tends to daydream and is told she better pay attention; who talks out in class when she sees something fascinating, like a butterfly on the windowpane, and is told to leave the class and report to the principal; who forgets her homework and is told she will just never learn, will she;

who writes a story rich in imagination and insight and is told her hand-writing and spelling are atrocious; who asks for help and is told she should try harder herself before getting others to do her work for her; who begins to feel unhappy in school and is told that big girls try harder. This is the brutal process of the breaking of the spirit of a child. I can think of no more precious natural resource than the spirits of our children. Life nec-essarily breaks us all down somewhat, but to do it unnecessarily to our children in the name of educating them—this is a tragedy. To take the joy of learning—which one can see in any child experimenting with something new—to take that joy and turn it into fear—that is something we should never do.

And yet it happens every day with children with learning problems. We can prevent it by applying the knowledge we have in defining the learning style of each individual child.

In my work with adults with ADD I hear many stories of school days gone wrong. People tell these stories much in the same manner as victims of trauma. There is a numb period when I hear all the facts. Not much emotion, just a long narrative of what it was like to be in school. Gradually, as I empathize with what it must have been like for them, the emotion begins to emerge: the hurt, the anger, the disappointment, the fear.

"You just don't know how much I hated going to school," Franny, a woman in her thirties, said to me. "It was all a blur. My main idea was just to get through the day without getting hurt. I always said 'I don't know' rather than risk giving a wrong answer. I actually loved to read and to make up stories, but all the teachers saw was the slow reader, the late papers, the messy handwriting, the bad spelling. One teacher actually said to me, 'Your handwriting looks like a moron's.' She wasn't even a mean teacher. She just thought she was motivating me to try harder. But a ten-year-old doesn't hear things that way. I began to think I was a kind of moron: one that liked to read and make up stories, but could never do anything with them because she couldn't write or spell. I really thought I was defective. My whole self-image became one of being different. I became afraid of making friends. Each year I'd have one or two sort-of friends. The other most marginal kids in the class. We became friends by default. One year we actually called ourselves the rejects, you know, pronounced *ree*-jex."

It turned out that Franny had both dyslexia as well as ADD. Her treatment was complicated by the damage school had done to her self-esteem. However, she ended up doing well, starting her own business as a remedial tutor specializing in women with learning disorders.

If there is any question of an associated learning disorder or learning disability in the presence of ADD, neuropsychological testing can help elucidate exactly what the obstacle to learning is. The more specific the definition of the problem, the better targeted the therapy can be. Testing can address such questions as: Is there a specific math disability or is there only ADD? At what level is this individual reading? What are the relative cognitive strengths and weaknesses in the individual's profile?

The tests are part of what is called a neuropsychological battery. These are mostly paper-and-pencil tests. Some are like the reading-comprehension tests we all took in grade school. Others are like games. The subject is asked to put together parts of a maze or is asked to trace a geometric figure from memory. Others ask the subject to make up a story based on a picture or a series of statements, while others ask him to solve math problems. All in all, if the tests are done by a sensitive examiner, they are not unenjoyable, and sometimes they are quite fun. Usually, they are most revealing. Included in the battery are tests of attention, tests of memory, tests of observational acuity, tests of auditory comprehension, tests of spatial relations, tests of word retrieval, tests of vocabulary, tests of computational ability, tests of general knowledge, and tests of impulsivity. Sometimes tests of vision and hearing are included in the battery, and sometimes there is a neurological examination as well.

People with both dyslexia and ADD are often the most creative and intuitive of the ADD population. With proper diagnosis and treatment they can do very well.

ADD with Agitation or Mania

Sometimes ADD can look like manic-depressive illness due to the high energy level involved in both syndromes. Manic-depressive illness is characterized by periodic momentous mood swings, from very high to very low. The very high moods, called periods of mania, can resemble ADD in that they include highly active behavior, easy distractibility, impulsivity, and an apparent disregard for personal safety.

One can distinguish mania from the high energy of ADD by the level of intensity. An average person could simulate the energized state of ADD, but could not voluntarily reproduce the energy level of mania. Mania is the most extreme form of non-drug-induced drivenness that we know. The manic person can go without sleep for days, traveling the globe or spending his life's savings on wild schemes or making grandiose claims of self-importance or talking nonstop from morning until night.

The manic individual is truly out of control. He cannot slow down. He does not just talk fast, he talks as if the words were being propelled from his mouth, a disconcerting symptom referred to as "pressured speech." Listening to someone who is in the grip of mania gives one the feeling of wanting to duck; the words seem to be thrown at you. A manic's mind leaps from topic to topic, like a frog jumping lily pads, alighting for a moment here only to spring away to another place. This symptom is aptly called "flight of ideas." It makes logical conversation of any length just about impossible. Let me give an example, taken from my days working on a psychiatric inpatient unit:

> "Good morning, Mr. Jones."
>
> "Why good morning, Doctor, and good morning to all the lovely little squiggles you have on your tie, and to squiggles everywhere, who, by the way, are outward representations of chaos, a soon-to-be-quantified branch of physics and mathematics, which, if you haven't boned up on your integrals, will leave you without much hope of doing more than passing over the topic, as the cow passes over the moon in the ditty which you may have heard when you were a child. You were once a child, Doctor? It is safe to assume that we all were children once, that is a safe assumption, the first three letters of which are a-s-s so don't be an ass and assume anything, as my old teacher used to say. Sound advice, especially for a planetary stargazer, wouldn't you say? There is more in the stars than there is in every brain put together, like link sausages, a delicious breakfast at that!"

While the individual with ADD can branch from topic to topic, he does not do so with the suddenness or pressuredness that the manic does, as in the example above. And while the person with ADD may be restless and full of energy, he is not driven by nearly the same horsepower as the manic.

The two syndromes can actually coexist. The person with ADD may become manic for a period of time, and may cycle into depression as well.

On the other hand, the person who has ADD with a high degree of agitation may be incorrectly diagnosed as having manic-depressive illness. This has practical significance in that the drug most commonly used to treat mania, lithium, usually does not help ADD. Indeed, it may make ADD worse. Therefore, it is important to consider ADD as a possible diagnosis in the agitated individual thought to be manic but who is nonresponsive to lithium. That person may have ADD and may get better when treated with one of the medications used for ADD.

Let me give an example. A forty-three-year-old man—we'll call him James—came for an evaluation for adult ADD. He had carried the diagnosis of manic-depressive illness—or in the formal nosology, bipolar disorder—for twelve years. As medication, he was taking 1,800 mg of lithium per day, a very large dose. He told me the dose had been gradually increased since he started taking lithium twelve years ago. He seemed to remain in a constant state of distraction. He didn't think the lithium had helped him much, but he was afraid to stop it.

His history was indeed remarkable, particularly his job history. During the year before the diagnosis of bipolar disorder was made, he had held no less than 124 jobs, actual jobs with W-2 forms to prove it. The pattern of getting fired and getting hired in such rapid succession was what had led to his being diagnosed manic. The reasons for his job endings were suggestive of mania. He would get fired because he would go into a loquacious tirade about the evils of the world in the midst of the working day. He would get fired because he would insult his boss, believing his solutions to problems were smarter. Or he would quit because of grandiose ideas of better jobs. Or he would leave to pursue some wild scheme, such as the time he got hoodwinked by a hustler in the mail-order business who promised him riches. Or he would get fired because he was too "hyper" to get along with coworkers.

A very bright man, with a tested IQ of 144, he was currently working as a night watchman from midnight to 8 A.M. and taking college classes in the evening. He'd held this job longer than he'd held any job, seventeen months, probably because there was no one around to tell him what to do or for him to insult or get carried away with. His classes were not going well, however; he was barely passing, because of an inability to pay attention.

It seemed to me that James's history was compatible with ADD as well as with manic-depressive illness. Since the lithium did not appear to be controlling his symptoms, and because other second-tier medications for mania, such as Tegretol, had been tried without success, we decided to give Ritalin a trial. While tapering his lithium gradually, so we could watch for any emergent symptoms of mania, James started taking the Ritalin.

The results were dramatic. James felt much more alert, focused, and, as he put it, "alive," on the new medication. His grades at night school soared, averaging around 95. His wife couldn't believe the difference. "He's a totally new man. I always knew he was smart, it's just that now he can use it."

Over six weeks he stopped taking lithium completely. No mania emerged. He continued to do well.

ADD with Substance Abuse

Of the many masks that ADD wears, substance abuse is one of the most difficult to see behind because the substance abuse itself causes such problems. When someone is alcoholic, is abusing cocaine, or is dependent upon marijuana, we often become so preoccupied with the problems the drug use creates that we fail to consider what purpose the drug must be serving for the user. ADD is one of the underlying causes of substance abuse that is particularly important to look for, because it can be treated.

There are a host of reasons people drink, or use cocaine, or smoke dope. To find a moment's pleasure, to flee pain, to fit in, to relax, are common reasons for using drugs. When the use becomes abuse, then it can become an illness in itself. It is widely accepted now that alcoholism is a disease, with its own genetics, natural history, treatment, and prognosis. Whether it is "the pain of being a man," to use Samuel Johnson's phrase, that leads people to drink, or drink that creates the alcoholic's pain is still an open debate. However, it may be that alcoholism is its own cause, without any other factor underlying it.

But perhaps more subtle than the disease concept of alcoholism, and of substance abuse in general, is the self-medication hypothesis advanced by Edward Khantzian, a psychoanalyst as well as a specialist in the field of substance abuse. He proposes the idea that people use drugs to treat some underlying bad feeling. They use the drug, whether it be alcohol, cocaine, tobacco, marijuana, or whatever, as a kind of self-prescribed medication for what ails them emotionally. The drug then creates physical and emotional problems of its own, so that repeated use of the drug becomes an attempt to treat the drug's own side effects, as in having a drink to cure a hangover. But the abuse begins in an attempt to cure some bad feeling. One may use alcohol, for example, to treat depression, or use marijuana to alleviate feelings of low self-esteem.

This concept is especially useful in understanding the relationship between ADD and substance abuse. Many people who have undiagnosed ADD feel bad and don't know why. Some feel depressed, as we have mentioned above. Some feel agitated or anxious. Many more feel distracted and unfocused, living in a sort of disjointed limbo, waiting to come in for a landing. This feeling of unease or what psychiatrists call "dysphoria," doesn't have a context or even a name. It's just life, in the minds of the people who feel it. You can live with something all your life but not be aware of it in its own right; it is simply a part of you. So it is with many of our feelings. Until we name them, they are entwined in our sense of self. Naming the feelings gives us some leverage over them. Being able to say "I am sad" can make the sadness less disabling. Once we recognize a feeling, we can attempt to control or change it. On the other hand, people who cannot say "I am sad" or "I am angry" are often directed or overpowered by these emotions in ways they are quite oblivious to.

So, too, for the dysphoria associated with ADD. It is a peculiar kind of feeling, the distractibility-within-self many ADD people feel. The feeling, unrecognized and untreated, often leads to substance abuse through attempts at self-medication.

Take cocaine as an example. Cocaine is in the class of drugs we call stimulants. Ritalin, one of the standard prescription medications for the treatment of ADD, is also a stimulant. Most people feel a rush of unfocused energy when they take cocaine. However, people with ADD feel focused when they use cocaine, just as they do when they take Ritalin. Rather than getting high, they suddenly feel clearheaded and able to pay attention. When those who don't know they have ADD stumble upon cocaine, the drug seems like a cure in that it temporarily alleviates their ADD symptoms, and so they become chronic users. Interestingly enough, in the literature about cocaine, approximately 15 percent of addicts report feeling focused by the cocaine, rather than feeling high. This 15 percent probably have adult ADD and are self-medicating, albeit unwittingly, with cocaine.

While cocaine, among the drugs of potential abuse, offers the most specific treatment for the dysphoria associated with ADD, both alcohol and marijuana can be used as well. Alcohol tends to quiet the internal noise many adults with ADD complain of. It also reduces, in the short term, the anxiety commonly associated with ADD. Unfortunately, in the long run, alcohol is a depressant, and the daily withdrawal or hangover associated with chronic abuse increases anxiety. Similarly, marijuana tends to quiet the noise inside, to help the individual, in the words of one of my patients, "chill out." Unfortunately, this is also only a short-term effect, and the repeated use of marijuana as an antianxiety agent is associated with a decrease in motivation.

For those addicts who do in fact have ADD, it is essential that the ADD be treated as well as the addiction. By treating the ADD one reduces the likelihood that the individual will go back to abusing the original drug.

As an example, let me discuss the case of a twenty-three-year-old man I will call Peter. Peter came to me after being released from jail, where he'd spent six months for dealing marijuana. Prior to his arrest, he had developed such a severe marijuana-abuse problem that his whole life centered around the drug. While in jail he read an article about ADD and sent it to his mother. In piecing together his childhood history, both from school and home, she decided it was quite likely he had ADD. However, after Peter was released from prison, he found himself in a bind familiar to many people who have been prosecuted for drug abuse. These people come up against a great deal of prejudice and fear, if not contempt, from the medical community. Most doctors do not welcome convicted felons into their practices. While this is understandable, it is also unfortunate. The very treatment these people are denied is the key to keeping them off drugs and out of jail. It only takes a few rejections from legitimate caregivers to send these people back to their self-medicating, drug-abusing ways.

Peter was able to convince me of his sincerity in seeking help, and I took him on as a patient. I reviewed the school records his mother gave me, and I listened to both Peter's and his mother's account of his childhood. It was classic for ADD. In fact, one pediatrician had made the diagnosis of hyperactivity, but there had been insufficient follow-up. Peter's academic performance declined through high school. Even though he was very bright—an IQ of 126, which due to ADD probably measured lower than it actually was—he could not do satisfactory work in high school, and he dropped out.

One problem led to another, and this handsome, smart, middle-class boy ended up in jail. After his release from jail he began to turn his life around on his own. Angry, cynical, and bitter on the one hand, he was also full of determination: to stay off drugs, to get an education, to make up for lost time.

The treatment for his ADD provided a key he'd been looking for. "Now I don't even want to smoke dope anymore," he said. "It's like the medication takes away the urge." He got a job and began attending night school as well. He set high goals for himself and got the highest grades in his class. His job reports were outstanding. His girlfriend, who had stood by him even through his days in jail, said she felt confident now that things would work out. But the most dramatic report on the effectiveness of the treatment came from Peter's mother, who wrote me a letter that I excerpt here:

> Dear Dr. Hallowell,
>
> The last time your eyes passed over this handwriting, I was a mother filled with desperate hope. Peter was home this weekend for the first time since he has been on medication. It is really almost impossible to put the words down on paper that fill my heart.
>
> The Peter that came home this weekend was the Peter who I always knew he was and wished he would let himself be. This was the first time in his life he actually *sat* down in a chair and carried on a conversation with his father and me.
>
> My heart would always pound in my chest when he and his father would ever try to do anything together, or even simply talk. It would be like a time bomb ticking and you knew it would go off. I watched them talk, laugh, load a van together (they could never even do that without disagreement). His father's reaction was, what a pleasure to have Peter home.
>
> My reaction cannot be done justice in writing. He and I talked the whole time he was here—until 3 A.M. Sunday morning. There is this strange feeling I seem to have always had through all of the years, the nightmare times included. Maybe it is just a mother wanting that certain image, but I really have been, I feel, not your June Cleaver type. Under the rough edges, the long hair, Grateful Dead, the period from "hell," I see and always have seen something very special in Peter,

and now it is coming to the surface. Maybe it is something as simple as seeing him with Lorraine [his girlfriend], their laughter, their caring for each other, hearing plans for the future, of him heading for a field where I know his talent would be utilized.

To see your son you love heading on a collision course, involved with the wrong people, drugs, negative self-esteem, clashes with the system, prison, the heartbreak—any parent finds it hard to continue to keep putting one foot in front of the other, to keep their life going, but they have to.

Then, how does it happen? This young man, my son, finds an article in a woman's magazine of all unlikely places, talks to his mother about it, and sends the article which leads to the knowledge that changes a life. . . .

The young man that came home this weekend, the peace and love that was felt by *both* of those parents who couldn't give up, who refused to write this child off, who were given the strength to persevere. . . .

It's been a year now since I met Peter. He has remained drug-free. He is doing well.

ADD in the Creative Person

While creativity is commonly found in people who have ADD, we discuss it here as a separate subtype in order to highlight some of the issues involved in ADD and creativity.

A full definition of creativity and its psychological and neurological roots is well beyond the scope of this book. For our purposes we define creativity as a tendency to see life's elements in new ways, a tendency to combine bits of personal experience into new forms, a tendency to give shape to new ideas.

Several elements of the ADD mind favor creativity. First of all, people with ADD have a greater tolerance of chaos than most. Living in distraction as they do, bombarded by stimuli from every direction and unable to screen out what is extraneous, people with ADD live with chaos all the time. They are used to it, they expect it. For all the problems this might pose, it can assist the creative process. In order to rearrange life, in order to create, one must get comfortable with disarrangement for a while. One must be able to live with the unfamiliar without, to use Keats's phrase, any "irritable searching after fact and reason." In bearing with the tension of the unknown or the unfamiliar, one can enable something new to come into existence. If one forecloses a thought too quickly, because it seems too weird or strange or disorganized, then the pattern or beauty that may be hidden within the fantasy will get lost.

When someone with ADD receives a stimulus of some sort—an image, a sentence, an idea, a person's face, a question—he does not immediately put it in its "proper" place. He doesn't even know where that place is. So, for example, the water bill gets filed with concerns over a fishing trip, and the next thing you know an idea is being generated that has to do with entrepreneurial fishing expeditions. The very uncertainty with which people with ADD react to most stimuli allows for these messages to metamorphose before they solidify in the mind. This tendency to get confused or to confuse things—so often regarded as a chief bedevilment of the ADD brain—can enhance creativity most advantageously.

Second, one of the cardinal symptoms of ADD is impulsivity. What is creativity but impulsivity gone right? One does not plan to have a creative thought. Creative thoughts happen unscheduled. That is to say they are impulsive, the result of an impulse, not a planned course of action. One can set up conditions that maximize the chances of a creative moment occurring, chance favoring the prepared mind, but the actual idea, or phrase, or image comes, as it were, out of nowhere. Nowhere is where many ADD people live all the time. Neither here nor there nor anywhere in particular, but rather here and there, not in any one place, but all over the place, nowhere precisely. And it is out of nowhere, on the wings of impulse, that creativity flies in.

A third element that favors creativity among people with ADD is an often-overlooked capacity they have. This is the ability to intensely focus or hyperfocus at times. As mentioned earlier, the term "attention deficit" is a misnomer. It is a matter of attention inconsistency. While it is true that the ADD mind wanders when not engaged, it is also the case that the ADD mind fastens on to its subject fiercely when it is engaged. A child with ADD may sit for hours meticulously putting together a model airplane. An adult may work with amazing concentration when faced with a deadline. Or an adult with ADD may become obsessed with a project and complete it in a tenth of the time one would have predicted. This ability to hyperfocus heats up the furnace in the brain, so to speak, and melts down rigid elements so they may easily flow and commingle, allowing for new products to be formed once they hit the cool light of day. The intensity of the furnace when it heats up may help explain why it needs to cool down, to be distracted, when it is not heated up.

A fourth element contributing to creativity is what Russell Barkley has called the "hyperreactivity" of the ADD mind. Cousin to the traditional symptom of hyperactivity, hyperreactivity is more common among people with ADD than hyperactivity is. People with ADD are always reacting. Even when they look calm and sedate, they are usually churning inside, taking this piece of data and moving it there, pushing this thought through their emotional network, putting that idea on the fire to burn, exploding or subsiding, but always in motion. Such hyperreactivity enhances creativity because it increases the number of collisions in the brain. Each collision has the potential to emit new light, new matter, as when subatomic particles collide.

The trick for the person with ADD is to harness these processes productively. Some people spend a lifetime trying. They burst with creative energy but like a live wire without a socket to plug into, they dispel their energy unchanneled. The child may dissipate his or her creativity just in making wise remarks in class, or the adult may have a long list of marvelous ideas but have no plan for enacting them. In the chapter on treatment we will discuss ways of marshaling this energy constructively.

ADD with High-Risk Behavior, or "High-Stim" ADD

"What is my ideal fantasy?" said one adult with ADD. "To live my day in a room with three TVs going, me holding the blipper, my PC running, the fax operating, a CD playing, portable phone held to one ear, the newspaper spread out before me, with three deals about to close."

Such a search for highly stimulating situations is often a central part of the syndrome of ADD in adults and in children.

Some children with ADD always seek action. The roots of high-stimulation-seeking adult behavior can be seen in those children who are hyperactive (but not in the dreamy, nonhyperactive kids). The hyperactive child with ADD craves novelty and needs excitement. He tends to like life to be lively and fast-paced. If there is no conflict present, nothing to spice the scene up, he might create some. For example, the child might pick a fight with a sibling, not because he is angry but because he is bored. Or he might disrupt a quiet evening at home, not because he is upset but because he feels understimulated. Or he might make a clown of himself in class not because he is particularly witty or in need of attention but because he finds the class dull. The excitement and danger of causing an uproar in the classroom can far surpass any reward for being a "good" student. It is important that the parent or teacher understand this. Taking the behavior too seriously, letting the child get a big rise out of you, can backfire. The excitement of a strong reaction may be just what the child wants.

So it can be with the adult with ADD who seeks intense stimulation, often through high-risk behavior. While most people with ADD are easily bored and seek diversion quickly, the adult with high-stim ADD particularly abhors boredom. He—and it is usually a he—may seek high stimulation through relatively safe avenues—creating tight deadlines to work under; regularly engaging in heavy exercise; keeping many projects going simultaneously; carrying games or crossword puzzles around in case a moment of tedium arises; taking on very challenging work; living on the brink of chaos by not tending to checkbooks, appointment books, and the like; provoking testy conversations for the fun of it—or through more risky means, such as gambling, having dangerous romantic liaisons, making very risky business deals, putting himself in physical danger through such activities as vertical skiing (an extraordinarily dangerous and exhilarating kind of skiing that entails going straight down an almost sheer face of ice), bungee-jumping, car-racing, or other high-risk activities of his own creation. A calm place or relaxing scene can stress such an ADD adult to the point of exhaustion. However, that same person paradoxically may find calm and relaxation in hubbubs of activity or in risky, even very dangerous situations.

Brian Jones, a thirty-seven-year-old insurance executive, is a good example. He shows up at the office at 6:30 A.M. after running six miles and spending twenty minutes on his Stairmaster. He is not a fitness freak; it's just that without his morning workout he feels as if he would explode within the confines of the workday. As it is, his company uses him as a kind of human time bomb, strategically placing him in meetings that need an explosive element or with clients who won't get off the dime. Behind his back the junior employees call him "Boom-Boom" because of his legendary eruptions. He's always on the brink of getting fired or of being promoted.

On weekends Brian goes on the prowl in search of action. He has tried vertical skiing, which he loves. He has raced Formula One cars. He skydives regularly. Sometimes he'll just drive around town playing chicken with traffic lights, speeding through stop signs, taking safaris down one-way streets, anything to combat what he calls "the endless redundancy of everyday life." He loves to gamble, and he's been pretty lucky. However, of late, he's taken to making blind five-hundred-dollar bets at the racetrack: he puts down his wager without even looking at the racing form, picking a horse with nothing but whimsy to guide him. He came for a consultation after losing four of these bets consecutively.

"It's not the losing per se that bothers me," he said. "What bothers me is how much I like the action. I mean, Doc, I don't just like it. I love it. I want to go back and make a hundred-thousand-dollar bet blind. Now that much could get me into big financial trouble fast. But I want to do it. I imagine it's like someone who's having an affair with someone they know they shouldn't, but they just can't hold back, it's got such a grip on them. I've finally found something that gets my attention. It gets my juices flowing like nothing else, but in a strange way it also calms me and relaxes me. All the other distractions of my life, the little mosquitoes that are buzzing around my brain trying to bite me, they all go away when I'm at the track. I mean, after I put that bet down, I'm there. I'm alive. I can see and hear. After that, everything else seems dull. I have to really hammer myself in the morning to get myself to work now."

Brian had adult ADD. He responded well to treatment, which included medication and psychotherapy. The medication helped him focus, thus reducing his appetite for high stimulation, which he had been using as a focusing device. The psychotherapy helped him identify and stay with his feelings a bit, rather than having to blast past them. One of the reasons people like Brian seek high stimulation is that they cannot bear the tension of an ordinary feeling for very long. If they feel sad or lonely or afraid or above all bored, they swing into fast action for relief. Once medication helped him focus, Brian used psychotherapy to learn to stay with an emotion. He began to find that his emotions could be stimulating in their own right, and in a safe and useful way.

He has given up gambling and is working on ways of modulating his appetite for high stimulation so that he can enjoy the pleasures of ordinary life. He has not become a boring person, which was his fear, but his means of sustaining interest in life have changed.

Problem gambling is a common disorder in this country, afflicting some 3-to-5 million people. We do not yet have any reliable figures as to what percent of problem gamblers have ADD, but a rough estimate would be 15 to 20 percent. A corollary to problem gambling, which is also associated with high-stim ADD, is chronic overspending. Just as lotteries have brought ease and convenience to gambling, so have credit cards made overspending insidiously easy. The overspender is often relieving some bland ennui with the excitement of a blitz through the shopping mall. For both the gambler and the overspender, treatment can avert financial disaster.

Any of the following might be a tip-off for high-stimulation adult ADD:

Chronic, high-risk behaviors of any sort

Type A personality

Thrill-seeking personality

Addictive behaviors

Explosive temper

Exercise addiction

Irascible impatience

Habitual gambling

Violent behavior

Accident-proneness

Repetitious whirlwind romances

Chronic overspending

Other disorders of impulse control like
  kleptomania and pyromania

The essence of this subtype of adult ADD is the hunger for intense stimulation. Once you understand the tendency and have a name for it, you can feel it when you are with persons who have it. They radiate energy and create zones of action wherever they go. It is as if they carry within them a radioactive element, emitting energy at all times. They are always trying to strike up the band, go for the gusto, seize the moment and make it last. They will make deals in the midst of siestas, turn the vacation house's back room into a newsroom or a business center, make banquets out of leftovers, leave conversations in mid-sentence to go pursue an idea, or bring a brass band to an after-funeral party. These people can be a lot of fun to be with, and they can be very trying as well. As with Brian Jones, they can be productive and successful, but they can also be on the edge of ruin. They can be the ones who "dare to go where no man has gone before." However, they can also be in danger when they go there. They may be in need of help.

While we do not understand exactly why the danger or thrill is so appealing to a certain kind of adult with ADD, we do see the pattern often. It may be that the thrill or danger helps focus the individual in a way similar to that of stimulant medication, inducing changes at the neurotransmitter level. Stimulant medications, the standard medications for ADD, enhance the release of epinephrine (adrenaline) in the brain. High-risk behavior does the same thing. Hence such behavior may constitute a form of self-medication.

In addition, a high-risk situation may supply the extra motivation that we know can help with focusing. When one is highly motivated, once again there is a change at the neurotransmitter level that enhances focusing. Situations of danger can do this particularly. As Samuel Johnson said, "Depend upon it sir, when a man knows he is to be hanged in a fortnight, it concentrates his mind wonderfully."

Whatever may be going on, it is important that we consider ADD in adults who tend toward thrill-seeking, dangerous risk-taking, or a chronic inability to relax or have fun in the absence of intense stimulation. Even those people we simply chalk up to having the well-known Type A personality may have covert ADD. While psychological conflict can certainly contribute to such behavior, psychodynamic therapy alone may miss the biological component. Without taking into account the biology, the therapy may be ineffective.

ADD with Dissociative States

Probably the most difficult symptom of ADD to evaluate accurately is what we call "distractibility." While we all know, pretty much, what "distractible" means, it can be very difficult to ascertain exactly what is causing a person to be distractible. A partial list of causes of distractibility would include:

ADD

Depression

Anxiety states

Drug use or withdrawal

Stress

Seizure disorder (petit mal)

Caffeinism

Sleep deprivation, fatigue

Dissociative disorders

This list is only partial, but it highlights the importance of accurately understanding the cause of a symptom before making a diagnosis. It is the last cause listed above, dissociative disorders, that this section takes up.

Dissociation refers to the dis-association of a feeling with the cause of that feeling. A dissociative state is a blank, emotionally neutral state of mind wherein one is cut off from one's external situation and internal feelings. Victims of trauma often dissociate to escape the pain associated with the memory of the trauma or even during the trauma itself they dissociate as their only means of defending themselves against the unendurable. The trauma may be childhood abuse of some kind, experiences in combat, or any event that was of such enormous emotional and/or physical pain as to be psychically unbearable.

The dissociated state that trauma may produce can closely resemble the distracted state caused by ADD. In recent years, due to the excellent work of investigators like Judith Herman and Bessel Van der Kolk, we have learned a great deal about emotional trauma. As more and more accounts appear of childhood abuse, we are finding more and more people who have suffered trauma but have been unable to speak of it. One of the research questions that has yet to be answered is how much of an overlap exists between the population of people who have suffered trauma and developed dissociative states, and those people with ADD.

In differentiating the dissociative state from distractibility, the first factor to consider is the individual's history. Does he or she have a history of trauma? Of course, many victims of trauma cannot recall the trauma they suffered. Frequently, an individual, in the midst of psychotherapy, will gradually remember some awful events that had been forgotten for years. The safe and protective context of psychotherapy allows the person to feel secure enough to recapture the memory and try to work through the pain.

On the other hand, does the individual have a history that reflects ADD, even if it has not yet been diagnosed? People with a history of ADD do not forget the events, the evidence, of their ADD; they often just do not know what it means.

Even if one discovers a history of ADD and no history of trauma, this is no guarantee that a history of trauma will not emerge as the therapy moves along. One should always bear in mind that what looks like distractibility may be confused with a dissociative state.

ADD with Borderline Personality Features

When the diagnosis of borderline personality disorder was first described in the 1950s, it referred to the "borderline" between psychosis and neurosis.

Our knowledge of the condition has increased considerably since the fifties, although the original diagnostic label remains. Now we understand the syndrome as follows: Individuals with a borderline personality disorder have a poorly defined inner sense of self. They hunger after relationships on the one hand, with a pressing urge almost to merge with the other person, but on the other hand they abruptly terminate relationships and flee intimacy as soon as it is established. They are given to periods of deep psychic pain, full of rage, fear, and depression. They often feel suicidal, and characteristically make many gestures of suicide during young adulthood, typically by wrist-cutting or overdosing. Usually, their suicide attempts do not end in death but rather serve a kind of self-soothing function. It may seem incongruous to talk of a suicide attempt as self-soothing, but many people with borderline personalities speak of a tremendous difficulty in regulating their feelings. Sometimes a kind of monster of emotion grows inside that feels as if it will overwhelm the individual utterly. The act of cutting into one's wrist, physically painful as it might be, cuts into the monster inside, and as the blood is let, the bad feelings dissipate in a soothing trickle.

One of the primary feelings of the borderline syndrome is rage, which can come clawing out unexpectedly and apparently unprovoked. Borderline individuals are exquisitely sensitive to rejection. They tend to draw others into their personal drama magnetically, and they tend to split these people, usually their caregivers, into the good and the bad. They have difficulty seeing other people as combinations of both good and bad, and they resolve this difficulty by idealizing some and totally devaluing others. They often treat their inner pain with drugs and/or alcohol. This constellation of extreme symptoms makes their lives chaotic, painful, unpredictable, and often tragic.

What does this have to do with ADD? If one reviews the symptoms named above, several points of intersection with ADD can be seen. The poorly defined inner self of the borderline can closely resemble the distracted, fragmented self of the person with ADD. The abrupt breaking off of relationships is not uncommon in ADD when the individual inadvertently simply tunes out. The person with ADD seeks high stimulation in order to focus, while the borderline person seeks high stimulation to deal with painful feelings. Both syndromes are marked by a high degree of impulsivity. The person with ADD carries a great deal of anger, due to frequent frustration over not getting things right, while the person with a borderline syndrome carries much anger due to frequent frustration over not getting his or her emotional needs met. In both syndromes substance abuse is not uncommon as a form of self-medication. These similarities are summarized in the table below.

■

SIMILARITIES BETWEEN ADD
AND BORDERLINE PERSONALITY

ADD	BORDERLINE
Distracted inner self	Poorly defined inner self
Tunes out in relationships	Breaks off relationships
Organizes around high stimulation	Eases pain with high stimulation
Impulsivity common	Impulsivity common
Anger over performance frustration	Anger over unmet emotional needs
Substance abuse not uncommon	Substance abuse not uncommon
Mood instability	Mood instability
Underachievement common	Underachievement common

We have seen a number of cases in our practice, and have had reports from others, of patients diagnosed as borderline who in fact have ADD. The practical significance of this is that the treatment for ADD is quite different from the treatment for borderline personality disorder.

As an example, consider the case of Bonnie. As a child, Bonnie was physically aggressive at home and impulsive and unproductive at school. By the third grade she was referred to as "a terror" by her parents and teachers alike and was locked into a power struggle with her mother that would last for years. She felt extremely resentful of her mother's attempts to "force me into the conventional mold," and so she rebelled as often as possible. In her teenage years she often used drugs and spent the night away from home. Visits to various family and individual therapists throughout adolescence did not help. Bonnie was attractive, and had a constant entourage of boys throughout high school. She encouraged sexual rumors about herself in order to worry her mother, who responded by trying, unsuccessfully, to set limits on her. Although Bonnie had poor grades, she scored high on the college admission tests, and so went off to a good university.

Bonnie settled down in college, falling in love with literature. Although she had great trouble completing papers on time, she did graduate. Soon thereafter she became pregnant and married a man she liked but did not love.

Her child became the organizing principle in Bonnie's life, much as literature had been in college. However, once the child left for school, Bonnie became obsessed with suicidal fantasies. When the child was away, Bonnie felt empty. She could not reassure herself that even though her child was not at home, the child was still connected to her. Her old insecurities swirled up and began to choke her. To combat these feelings she started drinking heavily, until finally her husband had her committed to a detoxification center where she was diagnosed as a borderline personality.

After two years of therapy she felt no better. She was chronically depressed and, as she put it, "distracted from having any goals." Then, by chance, she happened to read about ADD. After consulting with her therapist, who quite open-mindedly recommended she follow up with an evaluation for ADD, Bonnie came to our clinic.

After reviewing her history and some psychological testing, I could certainly see why the diagnosis of borderline personality had been made. However, by highlighting other aspects of her history, I could also see ample grounds for a diagnosis of ADD. Bonnie and her therapist agreed to a trial of medication for ADD.

The results were dramatic. What Bonnie had perceived as depression was in retrospect "a state of aimless distractibility." As the medication helped her focus, she began to develop goals. She enrolled in school, and is now a successful participant in a Ph.D. program in English. Her work with her therapist suddenly became productive, rather than frustratingly off target. She was able to start working through many of the problems from her childhood, rather than avoiding or forgetting them. In addition to the help in focusing the medication provided, the diagnosis of ADD lifted some of the guilt and self-recrimination Bonnie had carried while considering herself borderline.

Unknowingly, in her past, she had been treating her ADD by finding axes around which to organize herself. First there was the axis of the struggle with her mother. While this damaged her psychologically in many ways, it did serve the constructive purpose of organizing her thoughts and feelings. Then there was the axis of the study of literature in college, followed by the axis of taking care of her baby at home. However, when the child left for school, that relationship no longer filled her day; the organizing axis was gone, and the forces of distractibility took over and she began to self-medicate with alcohol.

We do not know how common this picture of ADD with borderline features really is. As the diagnosis of ADD gains wider attention, it would not be surprising to see it more frequently. The combination of sudden anger, the search for high stimulation, impulsivity, suicidal thoughts or gestures, self-recrimination, underachievement, and disorganization, which sounds like a borderline personality, could well be hidden ADD.

ADD with Conduct Disorder or Oppositional Disorder (in Children) or Antisocial Personality Features (in Adults)

In both children and adults, especially among males, certain kinds of aggressive or defiant behavior can mask ADD or occur concurrently.

"Conduct disorder" and "oppositional defiant disorder" are two different diagnoses that apply to particular patterns of aggressive behavior in children. Although the terms may conjure up all one's worst fantasies of some kind of psychiatric enforcement agency, handing down frumpish norms of good versus "disordered" behavior, there are children who have great trouble peacefully coexisting with others in any environment. These children get into frequent fights; they can't obey rules; they resist limits; they disrupt the work and play of others; they may even break the law. While there is a genetic factor in these disorders we are just learning about, there is also a significant environmental factor. Often these children come from severely troubled families, families where the parents may be absent or uninvolved, where there may be drug use, physical or sexual abuse, extreme neglect, little food, poor housing, little education, few supports of any kind. The "disordered" conduct of these children is often a critical warning sign of the need for intervention and assistance at home.

The restless, hyperreactive behavior of a child with ADD can resemble that of a child with conduct or oppositional disorder. One must look closely to distinguish between the two. They may indeed coexist. More frequently, however, children with ADD are incorrectly diagnosed as having a conduct disorder and vice versa. In the children with just ADD, one will not find the angry edge, or the premeditation one sees in conduct or oppositional disorders. When an ADD child trips and falls, he may get flustered. When an oppositional-disorder child trips and falls, he immediately looks to blame someone else and plot his revenge at recess. The disruptive outbursts of the child with ADD tend to be impulsive and spontaneous, whereas these outbursts in the conduct-disordered child tend to be planned or in response to some perceived insult or injury. The child with conduct disorder alone, on the other hand, does not show the distractibility or restlessness of the child with ADD. It can be difficult to get an accurate diagnosis for these children because everybody—parents, teachers, school officials—becomes so upset over the "bad" behavior that they don't attempt to understand what's causing it before trying to stamp it out.

A typical example is the child in school who is "bouncing off the walls." I'm not sure why that is the phrase used, because usually it is not walls but other people the child is bouncing off of, but I know I hear it all the time, and when I do, it is usually in reference to a little boy, age six to twelve, who, wherever he goes, leaves people shaking their heads and muttering to themselves. This is the boy who overturns the table at the birthday party, or upsets the jar of paint in art class, or pushes over a little girl during recess, or bumps into the teacher as she's bending to pick up a piece of chalk. Or worse. This is the child who uses four-letter words when he's told to do something, who has a tantrum in the classroom, breaking windows and chairs, who falls on the floor kicking and screaming when asked to go to gym class, who stabs a pencil into his friend's arm while waiting in line.

In responding to these children, it is important to figure out the cause of their aggression rather than simply punishing them for the behavior. Among the many possible causes are conduct or oppositional disorder or ADD, or a combination.

There is a similar group of adults, usually men, whose behavior causes such problems that to many people treatment seems pointless, a liberal-minded luxury. Some of them are in jails, or in mental hospitals with a diagnosis of antisocial personality. Like the borderline population and those with disorders of impulse control, many who are diagnosed as antisocial personalities actually have ADD.

People with an antisocial personality disorder, those who are sometimes called sociopathic or psychopathic, are the transgressors in our world.

They break the law, they test the limits, they deceive, they lie, cheat, and steal. They also can be, often, very likable and charming.

In the case of adults with antisocial personalities who have a clear childhood history of ADD rather than oppositional disorder, it may be the case that the antisocial diagnosis is incorrect, or that while the antisocial behavior may meet the technical requirements for that diagnosis, yet the individual still responds favorably to treatments specific for ADD.

Particularly in males with a history of violent behavior—the kinds of people that fill jails and mental hospitals—one finds many who have a classic history of ADD. Their violence is not due to a defect in their conscience or to psychosis or to some morbid familial conflict, but to the frustration intolerance and impulsivity of ADD. When they are properly diagnosed and receive the appropriate treatment, often their course changes for the better.

ADD with Obsessive-Compulsive Disorder

Interestingly enough, much of the best research we have on both ADD and obsessive-compulsive disorder (OCD) come from the same person, Dr. Judith Rapoport at the National Institute of Mental Health in Washington, D.C. Her book on OCD, *The Boy Who Couldn't Stop Washing*, is an excellent example of psychological thinking made clear.

As Rapoport points out in her book and elsewhere, OCD can occur with other syndromes, ADD being one of them. The symptoms of OCD include driven, ritualistic thinking; compulsive, repetitive behavior; intrusive, unpleasant thoughts; superstitions that control one's behavior; and an inability of the "will" to counteract these symptoms, try as it might. Like ADD, it is a biologically based disorder.

When OCD occurs with ADD, the ADD may go undetected at first because the symptoms of OCD are more troublesome. Or if the disruptive symptoms of ADD predominate, then one may miss the underlying OCD. Since the treatments for the two syndromes are different, it is important to diagnose them both when they occur together.

Pseudo-ADD

In concluding this chapter on the subtypes of ADD, we mention one subtype that is not ADD at all. It is not really a subtype, but it is mentioned here because it is directly linked to true ADD. This is the phenomenon of culturally induced ADD, what we call pseudo-ADD.

American society tends to create ADD-like symptoms in us all. We live in an ADD-ogenic culture.

What are some of the hallmarks of American culture that are also typical of ADD? The fast pace. The sound bite. The bottom line. Short takes, quick cuts. The TV remote-control clicker. High stimulation. Restlessness. Violence. Anxiety. Ingenuity. Creativity. Speed. Present-centered, no future, no past. Disorganization. Mavericks. A mistrust of authority. Video. Going for the gusto. Making it on the run. The fast track. Whatever works. Hollywood. The stock exchange. Fads. High stim.

It is important to keep this in mind or you may start thinking that everybody you know has ADD. The disorder is culturally syntonic—that is to say, it fits right in.

It is true that the prevalence of ADD—the frequency with which it occurs in the population over a given period of time—is higher in America than it is overseas. We do not know why this is so. The British think that we overdiagnose ADD in America. Until recently, Michael Rutter, one of the leading British child psychiatrists and an expert on epidemiology, doubted that ADD, as we think of it, actually existed as a valid syndrome. He thought we were lumping other syndromes under the heading of ADD. He has since changed his mind, acknowledging that ADD does indeed exist, but he finds it in the British population at lower rates than we diagnose it here.

One possible explanation for this is that our gene pool is heavily loaded for ADD. The people who founded our country, and continued to populate it over time, were just the types of people who might have had ADD. They did not like to sit still. They had to be willing to take an enormous risk in boarding a ship and crossing the ocean, leaving their homes behind; they were action-oriented, independent, wanting to get away from the old ways and strike out on their own, ready to lose everything in search of a better life. The higher prevalence of ADD in our current society may be due to its higher prevalence among those who settled America.

Certain qualities are often associated with the American temperament. Our violent, rough-and-tumble society, our bottom-line pragmatism, our impatience, our intolerance of class distinctions, our love of intense stimulation—these qualities, which are sometimes explained by our youth as a country, may in part arise from the heavy load of ADD in our gene pool.

Since we suspect that ADD is genetically transmitted, this theory makes some sense. Although it is impossible to ascertain the prevalence of ADD in colonial Boston or Philadelphia, as you read through the lives of the adventurous souls who lived there, you can see that more than a few of them liked risk and high stimulation, balked at custom and formality, lived by innovation and invention, and rose to action rather quickly. It is dangerous to diagnose the dead, but Benjamin Franklin, for example, seems like a man with a case of ADD. Creative, impulsive, inventive, attending to many projects at a time, drawn to high stimulation through wit, politics, diplomacy, literature, science, and romance, Franklin gives us ample ground to speculate that he may have had ADD and was the happier for it.

If it is true that part of the high energy and risk-taking of our ancestors was due to ADD, then that would explain, to some extent, why our rates of ADD are higher than other people's. But even taking that into account, might we be overdiagnosing it, or might our definition of it be so broad as to be overinclusive? Frequently, people remark when they hear a description of ADD for the first time, "But doesn't everybody have that?" or, "Isn't that just a variation on normal behavior?" or "How can you call it a disorder when it's so common?"

It may seem that our cultural norms are growing closer and closer to the diagnostic criteria for ADD. Many of us, particularly those in urban areas live in an ADD-ogenic world, one that demands speed and splintering of attention to "keep up." The claims on our attention and the flow of information we are expected to process are enormous. The explosion of communications technology and our standard way of responding to its most ubiquitous form—television—provide good examples of ADD behavior. Remote-control switch in hand, we switch from station to station, taking in dozens of programs at once, catching a line here, an image there, getting the gist of the show in a millisecond, getting bored with it in a full second, blipping on to the next show, the next bit of stimulation, the next quick pick.

Because we live in a very ADD-oid culture, almost everybody can identify with the symptoms of ADD. Most people know what it feels like to be bombarded with stimuli, to be distracted by overlapping signals all the time, to have too many obligations and not enough time to meet them, to be in a chronic hurry, to be late, to tune out quickly, to get frustrated easily, to find it difficult to slow down and relax when given the chance, to miss high stimulation when it is withdrawn, to be hooked to the phone and the fax and the computer screen and the video, to live life in a whirlwind.

That is *not* to say, however, that most people have ADD. What they have is what we call pseudo-ADD. As we will discuss in the chapter on diagnosis, true ADD is a medical diagnosis requiring evaluation by an expert. What differentiates pseudo-ADD from true ADD, what differentiates the people who can only identify with it from those who actually have it, is a matter of duration and intensity of the symptoms.

This is true of many psychiatric diagnoses. For example, most of us know what it feels like to be paranoid. We have all felt, at one time or another, that someone is out to get us who really isn't. We have, most of us, felt suspicious and nervous, wondering: Are they watching me? Is the IRS out to get me? Is my boss setting me up? Was that joke at the meeting a veiled reference to me? That we experience moments of paranoia does not make us paranoid personalities, however. In the true paranoid personality, the paranoia besets the individual chronically and intensely. It is the intensity and duration of symptoms that differentiates the insecure person from the truly paranoid.

Similarly, we have all been depressed at one time or another. That does not mean we have suffered major depression. Most of us have gambled at some time—bought a lottery ticket or put a nickel in a slot machine—and felt a thrill when we won. That does not make us pathological gamblers. Most people have felt a fear of heights at times, or had trouble with closed spaces, or felt frightened of snakes, but not to the extent of developing a phobia. Only if the symptoms are more intense than is normal, if they last a long while, and if they interfere with one's everyday life, only then can one entertain an actual diagnosis.

So it is with ADD. The person with true ADD experiences the symptoms most of the time and experiences them more intensely than the average person. Most important, the symptoms tend to interfere with everyday life more than for the average person.

It is important to keep true ADD separate from pseudo-ADD for the diagnosis to retain any serious meaning. If everybody who gets distracted or feels hurried or gets easily bored is diagnosed with ADD, then the diagnosis will signify nothing more than a passing fad. While pseudo-ADD may be interesting as a kind of metaphor for American culture, the true syndrome is no metaphor. It is a real, and sometimes crippling, biologically based condition that requires careful diagnosis and equally careful treatment.

How Do I Know if I Have It?

THE STEPS TOWARD DIAGNOSIS

It is arbitrary, really, where the line of diagnosis is drawn, where "normal" leaves off and ADD begins. And yet, as Edmund Burke remarked in differentiating night from day, "though there be not a clear line between them, yet no one would deny that there is a difference."

There is a logical set of steps that lead to a diagnosis of ADD. The key to it is the history, one's own recollection of one's life, confirmed and amplified (particularly in diagnosing ADD in a child) by the observations of those close to one: parents, spouse, teacher, sibling, friend. There is no definitive test for ADD, no blood test or electroencephalogram reading, or CAT scan or PET scan or X ray, no pathognomonic neurological finding or psychological testing score.

It is important to underline this point: the diagnosis of ADD is based first and foremost on the individual's history or life story. The most important step in determining whether one has ADD is sitting down and talking to somebody who is knowledgeable in the field. The most important "test" in making the diagnosis of ADD is the taking of the individual's history. This is old-fashioned medicine, not high-tech. This is a doctor talking to a patient, asking questions, listening to answers, drawing conclusions based upon getting to know the patient well. These days we often

195

don't respect or trust anything medical that doesn't depend upon fancy technology. Yet the diagnosis of ADD depends absolutely upon the simplest of all medical procedures: the taking of a history. This is the most powerful (and, ironically, the least expensive) tool we have in making a diagnosis. Your doctor should be sure to trust it and use it before ordering complex, expensive, and sometimes unnecessary tests.

The logical steps toward diagnosis proceed as follows:

1. You Seek Help

Something happens to lead you to look for help. In children this is usually academic underachievement or disruptive behavior. In adults the inability to "get one's act together," chronic disorganization or procrastination, underachievement professionally, trouble staying close in a relationship, chronic anxiety or depression, substance abuse, gambling, or chronic distractibility are the leading reasons one seeks help. Most adults who have ADD do not suspect they have it. They just feel that something is amiss in some unnameable way. Many are being treated for some condition other than ADD, the ADD lying masked and undetected.

2. Review Your History

The first step in the diagnostic process is for you to find a physician knowledgeable in the field of ADD and to sit down with him or her and go over your life story. If after reviewing your history your physician decides (1) that you have the symptoms of ADD, (2) you have had them since childhood, (3) you have the symptoms to a much greater degree than your peers of the same mental age, and (4) there is no other diagnosis that can explain your symptoms, then a presumptive diagnosis of ADD can be made.

You should keep in mind a few points concerning your history. First of all, it is best if at least two people relate the history. People with ADD are notoriously poor self-observers. The history will be much more reliable if another person is present to corroborate, enlarge upon, or give a different point of view on what you say. In the case of children, the history should be taken from the child, from parents, and from schoolteachers' written or telephoned reports. With adults, the history should be taken from the individual in question as well as his or her spouse, or a friend or relative. If available, documents from past school and college experience can contribute to the history as well.

In reviewing your history, your physician will want to know about the following ten areas. It will make your first visit more efficient and productive if you go over these in your mind beforehand:

a. Family history. In your parents, grandparents, or extended family, is there any history of ADD or hyperactivity (not likely, since the diagnosis was not made frequently a generation ago, but if it was, it is highly significant)? Any history of related disorders such as depression, manic-depressive illness, alcoholism or other substance abuse, antisocial behavior, or dyslexia or other learning disabilities? If you are adopted, that itself is a significant finding, as ADD is much higher among the adopted than among the general population.

b. Pregnancy and birth history. Were there risk factors such as maternal drug use during pregnancy (including cigarettes and heavy alcohol use), inadequate health care during pregnancy, any trauma or oxygen deprivation during birth, any illness during the period just after birth?

c. Medical and physical factors. Your doctor will take a standard medical history, asking about past illnesses, surgeries, injuries, and so forth. There will also be questions about what medications you currently take, as well as about your use of alcohol, tobacco, cocaine, marijuana, and other drugs. A sexual history should also be included. People with ADD often have a variety of sexual problems, most commonly hyposexuality or hypersexuality.

Your physician will ask about certain specific physical factors that are often associated with ADD, including left-handedness or ambidextrousness, frequent ear infections in childhood, upper respiratory infections or other illnesses as a child, allergies, sleep disturbances, especially great difficulty in falling asleep, or frequently waking up during the night or trouble getting up in the morning, awkwardness or clumsiness or poor hand-eye coordination, bed-wetting as a child, accident-proneness as a child, or high frequency of somatic complaints as a child.

d. Review what is called your "developmental history." At what age did you walk, talk, learn to read, etc? There are often erratic developmental patterns in people with ADD. They will have been advanced in some areas and delayed in others.

e. School history. How did you feel about school? What was it like for you? This is a key question in your history. Many people with ADD point to school as the first place they realized anything was different about them. Were you slow to learn to read, to write? Did you have trouble with organization, promptness, impulsivity? Were teacher comments full of statements such as "If only Johnny could sit still and pay attention . . ." or, "Johnny could do so much better if only he would buckle down . . ." or "Johnny is more interested in socializing than studying . . ."? Was underachievement a pattern? Was performance inconsistent, erratic?

f. Home history. Where younger children are concerned, the physician will ask about behavior at key times of day, such as when getting dressed in the morning, leaving for school, eating dinner with the family, making the transition from one activity to another, getting to sleep at night and getting up in the morning. In diagnosing adolescents and adults the questions will likely be about such topics as the appearance of their desks, any mess piles about house or study, and the general level of disorganization or impending chaos. There might also be questions about the number of high-stimulation gadgets owned (i.e., computers, stereos, CDs, fax machines, answering machines, video recorders, exercise machines, video games, televisions, intercoms, satellite dishes, and portable or car phones), and about length of time spent interacting with family as opposed to going from project to project or sleeping.

g. College and other educational experience. Do you recall themes of underachievement or special struggles? Any formally diagnosed learning disabilities?

h. Job history. Have you seen a pattern of underachievement, trouble with bosses, frequent job changes, or trouble with deadlines and procrastination? Do you have a tendency to be a maverick at work? Are you particularly innovative or creative? Are you a hard worker? Is saying or doing the wrong thing at the wrong time a recurring problem?

i. Interpersonal history. Have you experienced trouble staying connected, either in a conversation or in a long-term relationship? Do you particularly like people? Have you had a tendency to be misunderstood interpersonally, your inattentiveness often being mistaken for indifference?

j. Before your first visit with a professional, compare your history (or your child's) with the defining lists of symptoms in Tables I and II and the Utah Criteria.

The formal diagnostic criteria for ADD in children, as set forth in the standard psychiatric manual, DSM-III-R (*Diagnostic and Statistical Manual*, third edition, revised), are summarized in Table I.

The above criteria cover children. These criteria have been statistically assessed—that is to say, they have been tested against other criteria and with various groups of children to ascertain which factors are most discriminating in diagnosing ADD. These criteria are included in the diagnostic manual of psychiatry.

As yet, we do not have formal, statistically validated criteria for the diagnosis of ADD in adults. It is only fairly recently that the syndrome has even been recognized in the adult population. However, based upon our clinical experience with hundreds of adults with ADD, we set forth the criteria in Table II for making the diagnosis of ADD in adults (this is an abbreviated version of the symptoms discussed in chapter 3).

In addition to the criteria above, also rate yourself using Paul Wender's Utah Criteria. (These are referred to as the Utah Criteria because Wender is professor of psychiatry at the University of Utah School of Medicine.)

Whatever diagnostic criteria one refers to, it cannot be stressed too firmly how important it is not to diagnose oneself. While the information and examples presented here may lead you to suspect that you or your child or a relative has ADD, an evaluation by a physician to confirm the diagnosis and to rule out other conditions is essential.

3. Consider All Possibilities

In making the diagnosis, your physician must also rule out other conditions that can look like ADD as well as look for conditions that may occur with ADD. Often the diagnosis of ADD is missed because the ADD is masked by some coexisting condition such as substance abuse, depression, or anxiety. At other times the diagnosis is made incorrectly when some medical condition such as hyperthyroidism is causing the symptoms.

Table IV lists some of the conditions that may resemble ADD and need to be ruled out in making the diagnosis, and some of the conditions that may accompany or mask ADD. While you may not know the exact nature of all the diagnoses in the list, it can be used as a point of reference to ask your doctor about.

Most of these require an evaluation by a physician. Certain blood tests

■ TABLE I ■

DIAGNOSTIC CRITERIA FOR ATTENTION-DEFICIT HYPERACTIVITY DISORDER IN CHILDREN
(according to *DSM-III-R*)

NOTE: Consider a criterion met only if the behavior is considerably more frequent than that of most people of the same mental age.

A. A disturbance of at least six months during which at least eight of the following are present:

1. Often fidgets with hands or feet or squirms in seat (in adolescents [or adults] may be limited to subjective feelings of restlessness).
2. Has difficulty remaining in seat when required to do so.
3. Is easily distracted by extraneous stimuli.
4. Has difficulty awaiting turn in games or group situations.
5. Often blurts out answers to questions before they have been completed.
6. Has difficulty following through on instructions from others.
7. Has difficulty sustaining attention in tasks or play activities.
8. Often shifts from one uncompleted activity to another.
9. Has difficulty playing quietly.
10. Often talks excessively.
11. Often interrupts or intrudes on others.
12. Often does not seem to listen to what is being said to him or her.
13. Often loses things necessary for tasks or activities at school or at home.
14. Often engages in physically dangerous activities without considering possible consequences.

NOTE: The above items are listed in descending order of discriminating power based on data from a national field trial of the DSM-III-R criteria for disruptive behavior disorders.

B. Onset before the age of seven.

C. Does not meet the criteria for a pervasive developmental disorder.

■ TABLE II ■

SUGGESTED DIAGNOSTIC CRITERIA
FOR
ATTENTION DEFICIT DISORDER IN ADULTS

NOTE: Consider a criterion met only if the behavior is considerably more frequent than that of most people of the same mental age.

A. A chronic disturbance in which at least twelve of the following are present:

1. A sense of underachievement, of not meeting one's goals (regardless of how much one has actually accomplished).
2. Difficulty getting organized.
3. Chronic procrastination or trouble getting started.
4. Many projects going simultaneously; trouble with follow-through.
5. A tendency to say what comes to mind without necessarily considering the timing or appropriateness of the remark.
6. A frequent search for high stimulation.
7. An intolerance of boredom.
8. Easy distractibility, trouble focusing attention, tendency to tune out or drift away in the middle of a page or a conversation, often coupled with an ability to hyperfocus at times.
9. Often creative, intuitive, highly intelligent.
10. Trouble in going through established channels, following "proper" procedure.
11. Impatient; low tolerance of frustration.
12. Impulsive, either verbally or in action, as in impulsive spending of money, changing plans, enacting new schemes or career plans, and the like; hot-tempered.
13. A tendency to worry needlessly, endlessly; a tendency to scan the horizon looking for something to worry about, alternating with inattention to or disregard for actual dangers.
14. A sense of insecurity.

15. Mood swings, mood lability, especially when disengaged from a person or a project.
16. Physical or cognitive restlessness.
17. A tendency toward addictive behavior.
18. Chronic problems with self-esteem.
19. Inaccurate self-observation.
20. Family history of ADD or manic-depressive illness or depression or substance abuse or other disorders of impulse control or mood.

B. Childhood history of ADD. (It may not have been formally diagnosed, but in reviewing the history, one sees that the signs and symptoms were there.)

C. Situation not explained by other medical or psychiatric condition.

■ TABLE III ■
UTAH CRITERIA FOR
ADULT ADD

I. A childhood history of ADD with both attentional deficits and motor hyperactivity, together with at least one of the following characteristics: behavior problems in school, impulsivity, overexcitability, and temper outbursts.

II. An adult history of persistent attentional problems and motor hyperactivity together with two of the following five symptoms: affective lability, hot temper, stress intolerance, disorganization, and impulsivity.

may need to be ordered, such as thyroid-function tests, or other kinds of medical diagnostic tests may be indicated, such as an electroencephalogram. These are not always indicated, however. Your physician will determine if they are.

Although a full discussion of what physicians call the differential diagnosis—the complete list of possibilities that must be considered before confirming one diagnosis—would require more medical knowledge than this book presumes, a few remarks should be made.

■ TABLE IV ■
CONDITIONS THAT MAY ACCOMPANY, RESEMBLE, OR MASK ADD

Anxiety disorder
Bipolar disorder or mania
Caffeinism (excessive coffee or cola drinking)
Conduct disorder (in children)
Depression
Disorders of impulse control (stealing, fire-setting, and the like)
Fatigue, chronic
History of fetal alcohol syndrome
Hyperthyroidism or hypothyroidism
Lead poisoning
Learning disabilities
Medications (e.g., phenobarbital and Dilantin)
Obsessive compulsive disorder
Oppositional disorder (in children)
Pathological gambling
Personality disorders, such as narcissistic, antisocial, borderline,
    and passive-aggressive personality disorders
Pheochromocytoma
Posttraumatic stress disorder
Seizure disorder
Situational disturbances such as divorce or job loss or other
    disruption in one's life
Substance abuse (e.g., cocaine, alcohol, marijuana)
Tourette's syndrome

As was pointed up in chapter 6 on the subtypes of ADD, attention deficit disorder often hides behind other diagnoses, such as depression; alcohol, marijuana, and cocaine abuse; pathological gambling; and the others mentioned before. These diagnoses may mask an underlying case of ADD or they may be hard to distinguish from it. The childhood history is particularly helpful in untangling this knot. Was there evidence of ADD in childhood? If there was, then the presenting symptom of, say, substance abuse, may overlie a case of ADD.

More difficult to distinguish are those conditions that develop out of ADD, organically, like a limb. These are the personality styles that people with ADD may evolve. They can look like what psychiatry calls personality disorders. For example, consider the passive-aggressive personality. This is the person who cannot express aggression directly. Instead, he expresses it passively, through nonaction or nonresponse. Instead of telling his boss he disagrees with him, he skips his appointment with him. Instead of telling his wife he is angry with her, he buries his head behind the newspaper. Instead of competing for the job he wants, he "forgets" to send in the application on time. Traditionally, we understand the passive-aggressive style in psychodynamic terms and try to help the patient work out, through psychotherapy, whatever fears he may have of directly expressing aggressive feelings. However, forgetting, being late, finding it difficult to tune in to conversations—these are what ADD is all about. What gets labeled "passive-aggressive" may be caused by a case of ADD.

Similarly, ADD may be the cause of behavior that seems narcissistic. The narcissist, in simple terms, has trouble paying attention to other people. He appears to be wrapped up in himself, preoccupied with his own place in the world, and incapable of genuine empathy or love. If this inability to attend to others can be traced to the individual's early life experiences of deprivation, narcissism is a probable diagnosis, and the proper treatment would then be psychotherapy or psychoanalysis. However, if the inability to attend is due to ADD, psychotherapy or psychoanalysis will not help. If the person receives treatment for ADD, the "narcissistic" symptoms will fade, and the person will be able to engage with others meaningfully.

It is critical that these distinctions be made as early as possible in an individual's life. A great deal of time can be lost treating the wrong condition, or not treating the right one.

4. *Proceed with Psychological Testing*

Once your physician has made the diagnosis through consideration of your history (or your child's), and he has ruled out other conditions, he then must decide whether to proceed with psychological testing.

Psychological testing can be very helpful in elucidating any associated learning disabilities or in uncovering other problems that may not have surfaced in the history, such as a hidden depression or problems with self-image or a hidden thought disorder or psychosis. For example, projective testing examines what the subject projects, without knowing it, onto the test stimulus. The classic example of a projective test is the inkblot test (the Rorschach test is the most famous). The person being tested is asked to look at a series of standardized inkblots. What the subject "sees into" the inkblot is of his own creation, and can help reveal what might be on his unconscious mind. Sometimes people see scenes of extraordinary violence or destruction in an inkblot; these people may be dealing with pent-up rage or repressed memories of traumatic abuse. Some people make up stories of great sadness based upon the inkblot; these people may be dealing with hidden depression. Other people see nothing but chaos and unrecognizable shapes in the blots; these people may have an information-processing problem or even an undetected psychosis.

Psychological testing can also offer evidence that helps confirm the diagnosis of ADD. Certain subscales on the Weschler tests of intelligence, called the WISC in children and the WAIS in adults, are typically low in people with ADD.

There are other tests of attention as well in what is called a neuro-psychological battery for ADD. It is up to the tester what test to employ. There is no standard battery, but rather a range of tests from which the tester may select. Testing of this kind is as much an art as a science. The psychologist chooses which test to use depending upon what question is presented. When ADD is the problem, or the question, some psychologists use a test in which the subject is asked to copy an abstract drawing from memory after looking at it for ten seconds. Others use a test called the continuous-performance task in which the subject must attend to patterns of flashing lights. Whenever a prespecified pattern appears, the subject is supposed to press a button; if that pattern does not appear, he is not supposed to press the button. Taking this test is a lot like playing "Simon Says." Sometimes you press the button when you shouldn't, and sometimes you should press the button but you don't. It all depends upon how alert you can be. The test tries to assess both attention span and impulsivity: pressing the button when you should is a measure of paying attention, and pressing the button when you shouldn't is a measure of impulsivity. The test is far from infallible, however. Extraneous factors such as the subject's motivation and mood, the conditions of the room where the test is conducted, and the ease of operation of the machine can greatly influence results.

Other examiners use the TOVA or Test of Variability of Attention in which the subject responds to different shapes flashed on a screen under similar conditions as the continuous-performance task. Whatever the test, they all try to quantify attention, distractibility and impulsivity. No test pattern, however, can definitively rule in or rule out the diagnosis of ADD. It can only support or detract from the clinical evidence for the diagnosis.

A strong word of caution should be added here with respect to psychological testing. Often people rely too heavily on psychological testing to make the diagnosis of ADD. This is a grave error, however, because psychological testing is often falsely negative. That is to say, many people who do in fact have ADD appear not to have it when given psychological tests.

This is because the testing procedure may temporarily treat the ADD, obliterating the symptoms during the time of the testing. Three of the best treatments for ADD are one-to-one tutoring, high motivation, and novelty. People with ADD typically can focus in a one-to-one setting while they become distractible in a group setting such as a classroom, the workplace, or a party. Also in settings where the individual is highly motivated, the symptoms of ADD often disappear. And novel settings—unusual or new places—can stimulate the person with ADD to such a degree that their attention becomes focused. The procedure of psychological testing involves all three of these "treatments" for ADD. It is done one-on-one, with the psychologist guiding the individual orally through the tests, making it difficult for him to tune out. The subject is typically highly motivated, trying to "do well" on the test. And the testing situation is highly stimulating due to its novelty. These three factors combine to make the testing situation an almost ideal treatment for ADD, but a far-from-ideal setting in which to detect ADD. One must be highly skeptical of psychological testing that finds no evidence of ADD if the clinical, real-life data supports the diagnosis.

Often the history is so complicated that no one thinks of ADD as being part of the diagnosis. A patient whom I shall call Andrea came to see me and recounted a three-year history of misunderstanding and misery in the mental-health system. Brought to an emergency room one morning in June because of light-headedness, Andrea began a long process of being evaluated. All kinds of tests were done, including X rays and MRIs and various blood tests and metabolic studies and tests of immune function, even a pregnancy test. When no physical cause of her episode of light-headedness could be found, Andrea was referred to a psychiatric unit.

Because of a series of misunderstandings, Andrea was found to be violent and suicidal. What actually happened was one of those comic-horror stories from the movies where one wrong conclusion leads to another. She met with a psychiatrist and stated she was not crazy. The psychiatrist, who was a rather by-the-book sort of fellow, nodded and wrote down what she said. This angered Andrea. "Why are you writing down what I say?" she asked. "Why don't you talk to me instead?"

"Have you been ignored a great deal in your life?" the psychiatrist responded.

By the end of her psychiatric evaluation Andrea was so frustrated that she picked up an ashtray from the psychiatrist's desk and threatened to throw it through the window if she were not released immediately.

"Please do not do that," the psychiatrist said calmly.

"How can you be so calm?" Andrea asked. "Can't you see how upset I am?"

"I can see that you are upset," the psychiatrist replied.

"But you're just sitting there like a bump on a log," Andrea went on. "No emotion. No response. Would it help if I said I was suicidal? Then would you react?"

The psychiatrist did indeed react. Andrea was involuntarily committed to the psychiatric unit on the grounds of being potentially violent and suicidal.

By the time all the confusion had been resolved, Andrea had developed quite a dislike for the mental-health field. On the other hand, she needed help. While the light-headedness had not recurred, her hospitalization had brought forth a number of complaints Andrea's husband had been sitting on. He was concerned that she was nervous, forgetful, and unreliable. He was concerned that she was moody and hot-tempered. He was concerned that she was inconsistent with the children, and he was especially concerned that she was drinking too much.

Andrea and her husband went into couples therapy. Their relationship, if anything, got worse. Andrea's symptoms did not improve, and her husband was growing tired of the whole situation.

After a six-month trial separation, Andrea voluntarily checked into an alcohol treatment unit. She had felt terribly guilty about the separation and had indeed started drinking uncontrollably. A counselor at the alcohol unit reviewed Andrea's history and raised the possibility of ADD. The question had never been raised before. This was no one's fault; it was at a time when almost nobody knew about ADD. But the counselor at the alcohol unit did. His son was being treated for ADD, and he had read a great deal on the subject.

"When that man described to me the symptoms of ADD," Andrea said to me, "I felt as if I was being given a reprieve. Suddenly, there was an explanation other than my being a neurotic. I read everything I could find. It all fit. I got my school records, and sure enough, they were full of comments about how I couldn't sit still and how I was such a daydreamer."

"What happened next?" I asked.

"My husband had to learn about ADD. It made sense to him, too. Even if the medication hadn't worked as well as it did, it was great just to come out of the psychiatric nightmare. Finally, I had the right diagnosis."

If you think you may have ADD, first consult someone who has experience with the condition. Child psychiatrists, neurologists, psychologists, and pediatricians are the professionals most likely to have developed expertise in recognizing ADD. Be sure to ask whomever you consult if they have experience in diagnosing and treating ADD, and whether that experience is with children, adults, or both. The most important factor is not what degree the person has but that he or she have considerable experience in evaluating ADD. At some point in the process an M.D. should be involved to make sure no medical condition is overlooked. If psychological testing is deemed indicated, this should be done by someone with a Ph.D. in clinical psychology. Make sure this person is trained in what is called neuropsychological testing and has experience in testing for ADD and learning disabilities.

Since ADD in adults is a relatively new "discovery," it may be difficult to find a clinician in your area with experience in treating this disorder. Later in this chapter, and at the end of this book, you will find listings of ADD resources. In addition, a good starting point in locating a specialist is a medical school in your area. Also the state medical society, psychiatric society, or psychological association can be of assistance.

■ ■ ■

The following set of questions reflects those an experienced diagnostician will ask. While this quiz cannot confirm the diagnosis, the questions can increase the reader's feel for what ADD is, and offer a rough assessment as to whether professional help should be sought to make the actual diagnosis of ADD.

The more questions that are answered "yes," the more likely it is that ADD may be present. Since everybody will answer "yes" to some number of questions, and since we have not established norms for this questionnaire, it should only be used as an informal gauge.

1. Are you left-handed or ambidextrous?

2. Do you have a family history of drug or alcohol abuse, depression, or manic-depressive illness?

3. Are you moody?

4. Were you considered an underachiever in school? Now?

5. Do you have trouble getting started on things?

6. Do you drum your fingers a lot, tap your feet, fidget, or pace?

7. When you read, do you find that you often have to reread a paragraph or an entire page because you are daydreaming?

8. Do you tune out or space out a lot?

9. Do you have a hard time relaxing?

10. Are you excessively impatient?

11. Do you find that you undertake many projects simultaneously so that your life often resembles a juggler who's got six more balls in the air than he can handle?

12. Are you impulsive?

13. Are you easily distracted?

14. Even if you are easily distracted, do you find that there are times when your power of concentration is laser-beam intense?

15. Do you procrastinate chronically?

16. Do you often get excited by projects and then not follow through?

17. More than most people, do you feel that it is hard for you to make yourself understood?

18. Is your memory so porous that if you go from one room to the next to get something, by the time you get to the next room you've sometimes forgotten what you were looking for?

19. Do you smoke cigarettes?

20. Do you drink too much?

21. If you have ever tried cocaine, did you find that it helped you focus and calmed you down, rather than making you high?

22. Do you change the radio station in your car frequently?

23. Do you wear out your TV remote-control switch by changing stations frequently?

24. Do you feel driven, as if an engine inside you won't slow down?

25. As a kid, were you called words like, "a daydreamer," "lazy," "a spaceshot," "impulsive," "disruptive," "lazy," or just plain "bad"?

26. In intimate relationships is your inability to linger over conversations an impediment?

27. Are you always on the go, even when you don't really want to be?

28. More than most people, do you hate waiting in line?

29. Are you constitutionally incapable of reading the directions first?

30. Do you have a hair-trigger temper?

31. Are you constantly having to sit on yourself to keep from blurting out the wrong thing?

32. Do you like to gamble?

33. Do you feel like exploding inside when someone has trouble getting to the point?

34. Were you hyperactive as a child?

35. Are you drawn to situations of high intensity?

36. Do you often try to do the hard things rather than what comes easily to you?

37. Are you particularly intuitive?

38. Do you often find yourself involved in a situation without having planned it at all?

39. Would you rather have your teeth drilled by a dentist than make or follow a list?

40. Do you chronically resolve to organize your life better only to find that you're always on the brink of chaos?

41. Do you often find that you have an itch you cannot scratch, an appetite for something "more" and you're not sure what it is?

42. Would you describe yourself as hypersexual?

43. One man who turned out to have adult ADD presented with this unusual triad of symptoms: cocaine abuse, frequent reading of pornography, and an addiction to crossword puzzles. Can you understand him, even if you do not have those symptoms?

44. Would you consider yourself an addictive personality?

45. Are you more flirtatious than you really mean to be?

46. Did you grow up in a chaotic, boundariless family?

47. Do you find it hard to be alone?

48. Do you often counter depressive moods by some sort of potentially harmful compulsive behavior such as overworking, overspending, overdrinking, or overeating?

49. Do you have dyslexia?

50. Do you have a family history of ADD or hyperactivity?

51. Do you have a really hard time tolerating frustration?

52. Are you restless without "action" in your life?

53. Do you have a hard time reading a book all the way through?

54. Do you regularly break rules or minor laws rather than put up with the frustration of obeying them?

55. Are you beset by irrational worries?

56. Do you frequently make letter or number reversals?

57. Have you been the driver and at fault in more than four car accidents?

58. Do you handle money erratically?

59. Are you a gung-ho, go-for-it sort of person?

60. Do you find that structure and routine are both rare in your life and soothing when you find them?

61. Have you been divorced more than once?

62. Do you struggle to maintain self-esteem?

63. Do you have poor hand-eye coordination?

64. As a kid, were you a bit of a klutz at sports?

65. Have you changed jobs a lot?

66. Are you a maverick?

67. Are memos virtually impossible for you to read or write?

68. Do you find it almost impossible to keep an updated address book, phone book, or Rolodex?

69. Are you the life of the party one day and hang-dog the next?

70. Given an unexpected chunk of free time, do you often find that you don't use it well or get depressed during it?

71. Are you more creative or imaginative than most people?

72. Is paying attention or staying tuned in a chronic problem for you?

73. Do you work best in short spurts?

74. Do you let the bank balance your checkbook?

75. Are you usually eager to try something new?

76. Do you find you often get depressed after a success?

77. Do you hunger after myths and other organizing stories?

78. Do you feel you fail to live up to your potential?

79. Are you particularly restless?

80. Were you a daydreamer in class?

81. Were you ever the class clown?

82. Have you ever been described as "needy" or even "insatiable"?

83. Do you have trouble accurately assessing the impact you have on others?

84. Do you tend to approach problems intuitively?

85. When you get lost, do you tend to "feel" your way along rather than refer to a map?

86. Do you often get distracted during sex, even though you like it?

87. Were you adopted?

88. Do you have many allergies?

89. Did you have frequent ear infections as a child?

90. Are you much more effective when you are your own boss?

91. Are you smarter than you've been able to demonstrate?

92. Are you particularly insecure?

93. Do you have trouble keeping secrets?

94. Do you often forget what you're going to say just as you're about to say it?

95. Do you love to travel?

96. Are you claustrophobic?

97. Have you ever wondered if you're crazy?

98. Do you get the gist of things very quickly?

99. Do you laugh a lot?

100. Did you have trouble paying attention long enough to read this entire questionnaire?

▪ 8 ▪

What Can You Do About It?

THE TREATMENT OF ADD

General Principles of Treatment

Most people who discover they have ADD, whether children or adults, have suffered a great deal of pain. The emotional experience of ADD is filled with embarrassment, humiliation, and self-castigation. By the time the diagnosis is made, many people with ADD have lost confidence in themselves. Many have been misunderstood repeatedly. Many have consulted with numerous specialists, only to find no real help. As a result, many have lost hope.

Individuals with ADD may have forgotten what is good about themselves. They may have lost any sense of the possibility of things working out. They are often locked into a kind of tenacious holding pattern, needing all their considerable resiliency and ingenuity just to keep their heads above water.

And yet their capacity to hope and to dream is immense. More than most people, individuals with ADD have visionary imaginations. They think big thoughts and dream big dreams. They can take the smallest opportunity and imagine turning it into a major break. They can take a chance encounter and turn it into a grand evening out.

But like most dreamers, they go limp when the dream collapses. Usually, by the time an individual seeks help, this collapse has happened often enough to leave them wary of hoping again.

215

Hope begins with the diagnosis. More than with most disorders, often just the making of the diagnosis of ADD exerts a powerful therapeutic effect. The walls of years of misunderstanding come crashing down under the force of a lucid explanation of the cause of the individual's problems.

While with other medical conditions the diagnosis directs the treatment, with ADD, to a large extent, the diagnosis *is* the treatment. The diagnosis brings great relief in and of itself. For example, if you were nearsighted and had never heard of nearsightedness, and for years you had thought your blurry vision and subsequent learning problems were due to lack of effort or moral turpitude, imagine your relief in discovering that there was this condition called nearsightedness, and it had nothing to do with effort or morality, but rather was a neurological condition. So it is with ADD. The diagnosis is liberating.

Everything else in the treatment evolves logically from an understanding of the diagnosis.

EDUCATION

Once the diagnosis has been made, the next step is to learn as much as possible about the condition. The more you know, the better you will be able to construct your treatment to meet your own needs, and the better able you will be to understand your life story in terms of ADD. Effective treatment often requires a radical rethinking of your view of yourself. Understanding the many forms ADD takes will help you not only to recognize how it affects you, but also to explain the syndrome to those around you —family, friends, colleagues, teachers.

The ability to educate those around you is crucial. ADD has a deep social impact: it affects your home, work, or school environments, as well as your internal life. You need to be able to explain what is going on inside you to those who share the world you move in. For example, if you are able to explain what ADD is to your boss in terms that he or she can understand and sympathize with, you may be able to greatly improve the conditions under which you work. Similarly, if you can explain ADD to your spouse or partner in human terms, you may be able to put the relationship on a whole new footing. In general, the ability to advocate for yourself intelligently is crucial in the successful management of a life with

ADD, and it depends upon knowing as much as possible about the syndrome.

As you learn about ADD, you change yourself. You give yourself a power you never had before, and the power resides in the knowledge. Your knowledge becomes a part of you and silently, subtly works to move you to a new place.

The treatment of ADD is not passive, not something one reclines to receive. Rather, the treatment is an active process involving work and study.

In adults the process of education is straightforward: through reading, attending lectures, talking to experts and to others who have ADD, you gradually learn as much as you can about it. In children, however, the process raises questions in most parents' and teachers' minds. How much do we tell a child? At what age is he or she old enough to know what ADD is? Should other children in the class know if one child has it? What if the child thinks the diagnosis really means he or she is stupid? How much should a child know about medication?

These are difficult questions. There is no "right" answer. However, based on extensive experience with many children, families, and schools, I have found the following principle to be the best guide: tell the truth.

Telling the truth to the child, and to the school, helps destigmatize ADD. It helps normalize the syndrome. By not requiring one to skip over certain points or invent childlike euphemisms, it also allows one to convey the information in the simplest and most accurate way. Instead of resorting to some disguised version of the truth—which the child can usually see through anyway, and which conveys a message of secrecy and danger— telling the truth implies there's nothing to hide, nothing to fear, nothing to be ashamed of.

When I explain ADD to a child, I usually do so in the presence of one or both parents. I do not use a script, but a typical introduction to ADD might go like this (bear in mind that throughout I pause frequently for questions and I make sure the child does ask a question or two; it is a complete waste of time to deliver a monologue to children with ADD— they stop listening after two sentences):

> "As you know, Jimmy, you and your mom and dad have been coming here to talk about how things are going at home and at school. I have found out something about you that I think will help you. We

have talked about what school is like for you, and you have told me that you have a lot of trouble paying attention and listening and that you like to look out the window and that it is hard for you to sit still and wait in line and raise your hand and all those kinds of things. Boy, do I know how you feel. Do you know why that is? It is because both you and I have something called attention deficit disorder.

"Attention deficit disorder, or ADD, is sort of like being nearsighted and needing glasses, except the nearsightedness isn't in our eyes. It's in how we think. We need glasses for how we think, to help us focus our attention so we won't daydream so much or change the subject so much or forget things so much or have so much trouble getting organized in the morning or after class.

"Having ADD does not mean we are stupid. Lots of really smart people have had ADD, like Thomas Edison and Mozart and Einstein and the actor Dustin Hoffman—do you know who he is? What we people with ADD do need is special help—like glasses—so we can do the best we can. Only the special help we need isn't glasses exactly, but other things that help us focus and get organized. Sometimes lists, reminders, and schedules help us. Sometimes a tutor or a coach can help. And sometimes medication can help.

"Lots of other kids have ADD. If anyone asks you about it, it is up to you what you want to tell them, but remember, there is nothing wrong with having ADD, any more than there is anything wrong with wearing glasses."

I try to be as simple and honest as possible. I believe what I say: there is nothing wrong with having ADD, and there is nothing to be ashamed of. Most children take some time to get used to the idea of having ADD. Most children are ashamed or embarrassed at first. However, I have found that the sooner the topic can be brought out into the open and all questions addressed clearly, the sooner the condition can be accepted by the child as just another part of his or her everyday life.

I give the same advice to classroom teachers. Tell the truth. If a child is receiving special treatment for ADD, the other kids should be told about this and told why. The other children will notice something is going on anyway; they might as well know what it is. Otherwise the treatment will be shrouded in secrecy, and secrecy always implies there is something to hide. I suggest that the teacher first of all get the permission of the parents and the child, and then explain to the class what ADD is, and what special treatment the child will be receiving, such as sitting close to the teacher, taking untimed tests, having permission to leave the classroom when he or she feels overstimulated or to get medication if that is part of the regimen, receiving individualized homework assignments, and so forth. Since an individualized classroom treatment plan should be set up for the child with ADD anyway, and since the other children will notice it, it is best if they have an accurate explanation for it, rather than allowing the rumor mill to generate an inaccurate one. Furthermore, it is almost certain that other children in the class will have either ADD or some other form of learning disorder. The sooner these conditions can be normalized and understood for what they are, the better for everyone.

These suggestions to parents and teachers for explaining ADD to children are summarized as follows:

■

TEN TIPS
FOR PARENTS AND TEACHERS
ON EXPLAINING ADD TO CHILDREN

1. **Tell the truth.** This is the central, guiding principle. First, educate yourself about ADD, then put what you have learned into your own words, words the child can understand. Don't just hand the child a book or send the child off to some professional for an explanation. Explain it to yourself, after you have learned about it, then explain it to the child. Be straightforward and honest and clear.

2. **Use an accurate vocabulary.** Don't make up words that have no meaning, or use inaccurate words. The child will carry the explanation you give him wherever he or she goes.

3. **The metaphor of nearsightedness** is a useful one to use in explaining ADD to children. It is accurate and emotionally neutral.

4. Answer questions. Ask for questions. Remember, children often have questions you cannot answer. Don't be afraid to say you don't know. Then go find the answer. Books by professionals who deal with ADD are good sources of information; see, for example, Paul Wender's *Hyperactive Children, Adolescents, and Adults*, and Russell Barkley's *Attention Deficit Hyperactivity Disorder*, and CHADD (Children with Attention Deficit Disorders), a national organization devoted to educating parents, teachers, and professionals about ADD (CHADD, 499 NW 70th Avenue, Suite 308, Plantation, FL 33317; telephone: 305-587-3700).

5. Be sure to tell the child what ADD is *not*: stupidity, retardation, defectiveness, badness, etc.

6. Give examples of positive role models, either from history, such as Thomas Edison, or from personal experience, like a family member (Mom or Dad?).

7. If possible, let others know the child has ADD. Let the others in the classroom know (after discussing this with the child and parents), and let others in the extended family know. Again, the message should be that there is nothing to hide, nothing to be ashamed of.

8. Caution the child not to use ADD as an excuse. Most kids, once they catch on to what ADD is, go through a phase of trying to use it as an excuse. ADD is an explanation, not an excuse. They still have to take responsibility for what they do.

9. Educate others. Educate the other parents and children in the classroom. Educate members of the extended family. The single strongest weapon we have to ensure that children get proper treatment is knowledge. Spread the knowledge as far as you can; there is still a great deal of ignorance and misinformation out there about ADD.

10. Coach the child on how he might answer questions other people might have, especially peers. The guiding principle is the same: tell the truth. You might try role-playing a scene where a peer is teasing the child in order to anticipate and deal with such a problem in advance.

STRUCTURE

The new understanding of oneself that the diagnosis and education provide leads naturally to a rearranging or restructuring of one's life, both internally and externally. By taking ADD into account and trying to get rid of long-held negative perceptions of oneself, one rethinks or reshapes one's self-image; this is the internal restructuring. And one rearranges the nuts and bolts of one's daily life, setting up means of improved organization and control; this is the external restructuring.

Structure is central in the treatment of ADD. The word "structure" is a homely one, perhaps conjuring up dull images of blueprints or two-by-fours. However, structure can dazzle with its results. Structure makes possible the expression of talent. Without structure, no matter how much talent there may be, there is only chaos. Think of what a tight structure Mozart worked within. The very tightness of the structure helped create the intensity of the expression of Mozart's genius. Whether it be the iambic pentameter of Shakespeare or the rhymed couplets of Pope or the rhythm of the long-distance runner or the timing of the short-order cook, all creative expression requires structure. Many adults with ADD have not fulfilled their considerable creative potential because they have been unable to shape and direct their creative energies.

Think of a thermometer and the mercury it contains. If you have ever broken a thermometer, you know what happens to the mercury. The ADD mind is like spilled mercury, running and beading. Structure is the vessel needed to contain the mercury of the ADD mind, to keep it from being here and there and everywhere all at once. Structure allows the ADD mind to be put to best use, rather than dissipating itself like so many tiny beads of mercury on the floor.

Structure refers to essential tools like lists, reminders, notepads, appointment books, filing systems, Rolodexes, bulletin boards, schedules, receipts, IN and OUT boxes, answering machines, computer systems, alarm clocks, and alarm watches. Structure refers to the set of external controls that one sets up to compensate for unreliable internal controls. Most people with ADD cannot depend upon their internal controls to keep things organized and to keep themselves on task over time. For them a reliable system of external controls is essential. Setting up a system does *not* have to be boring; in fact, one can be quite creative in devising a workable structure. And once in place, the system will be calming and confidence-building.

We particularly recommend a scheme of reorganizing one's life that we call pattern planning. This system of time management operates on the same principle as automatic withdrawals from your bank account: by making the withdrawals (of money or time) from your account automatic, you don't have to plan them every time; they just happen. You plug certain regular appointments or obligations into the pattern of your week so you attend to them automatically. This frees up your limited planning time to focus on other activities. Simple in its conception, pattern planning can reduce the stresses of planning one's life considerably.

It is easy to set up. You start by making a list of all the regular tasks, obligations, and appointments you have every week—your fixed-time expenditures, so to speak. You then make a grid of your week on a calendar or appointment book and plug each fixed obligation into a regular time slot. For example, you may decide you will pick up your dry cleaning every Thursday afternoon at 4:30; you will work out Wednesday and Friday at 7 A.M.; you will go to the bank Monday and Thursday at noon; and you will attend your professional seminar alternate Tuesdays at 6 P.M.

Before you know it, these regular appointments take root in your subconscious. Thursday afternoon becomes dry cleaners' time, and after a while you drive to the cleaners almost without thinking about it. Wednesdays and Fridays become work-out time, and not only does the time become automatically reserved for you, but also you do not have to worry about when you will find the time to work out. You have decided in advance, not impulsively, what you want to make enough of a priority to pre-plan, and where to put each such activity or obligation. You know that you will do these things, and you know when you will do them. This means you do not need to wonder every day *when* you will get to the dry cleaners, or *if* you will get to the bank, or *how* you will find time to work out, or *whether* you can ever make it to that professional seminar again.

Through the use of pattern planning you can streamline your life considerably. It is remarkable how much mental energy the planning of these humdrum, everyday tasks can take, and how easy pattern planning can make them.

People with ADD can spend a lifetime dodging the necessity of organizing themselves. They avoid getting organized the way some people avoid going to the dentist: repeatedly postponing it as the problem gets worse and worse. One man hadn't paid his taxes in eight years, not because he was protesting or didn't have the money but because he couldn't face up to the organizational task of doing so. A woman was on the brink of divorce because her inability to throw anything away had led to her house being overrun with junk. Another man cost himself literally tens of thousands of dollars a year in tax deductions because he felt constitutionally incapable of saving receipts. The task of getting organized, one that bedevils us all, particularly vexes the ADD mind.

"Vexes" is an understatement in children with ADD. The failure to get organized can be the ruination not only of the child with ADD but of the whole family. Disorganization is a time-honored component of any normal, ordinary childhood, or one hopes it is. The "too-neat" child has problems of his or her own. But the child with ADD can go to the other extreme.

For example, I once treated an eleven-year-old boy named Charlie. A Tom Sawyer clone, Charlie was unintentionally making his family crazy due to his completely disorganized ways. Together, as a family, we zeroed in on key problem areas. One in particular enraged Molly, his fifteen-year-old sister: Charlie left the bathroom a mess every morning just before Molly used it. He would leave his underwear on the floor, a dirty towel in the bathtub, bits of toothpaste stuck to the sink, dirty handprints on the mirror, the toilet seat up (often covered with evidence of Charlie's poor aim), the water dripping, and the fan turned off so that steam still filled the room. Molly had asked Charlie a hundred times about these things, and he always told her he'd try to do better, but nothing changed. She wanted to kill him, or at least maim him severely.

After some negotiation we came up with the following plan. Charlie and his sister wrote up a list of ten items that Charlie needed to check off before leaving the bathroom each morning. They posted the list on the inside of the bathroom door where Charlie could not miss seeing it. Each morning Charlie checked off the list before he left the bathroom. He also added an eleventh item to the list which he happily checked off last. It read, *"I'm outta here!!!"* This simple plan, this bit of structure, worked very well. Charlie and Molly made up, with Charlie unmaimed.

Some tips might be useful in helping children with ADD get organized.

■

TEN TIPS
ON STRUCTURING
AND ORGANIZING
THE LIFE OF THE CHILD
WITH ADD

1. Write down the problem. Sit down with the child—or the whole family—and write down exactly where the problem areas are—the dining-room table, the bedroom, the bathroom, wherever. It is good to define, and thereby limit, the problem instead of leaving it in the realm of the infinite.

2. Come up with specific remedies for each problem area.

3. Make use of concrete reminders like lists, schedules, alarm clocks, and the like.

4. Incentive plans are fine. Don't think of them as bribes, but rather as incentives. Children with ADD are born entrepreneurs.

5. Give frequent feedback. Kids with ADD often don't see what they are doing as they are doing it. Don't wait until the house is completely torn apart before suggesting that it be put back together.

6. Give responsibility wherever possible. For example, if the child is old enough to get up on his own in the morning, give him the responsibility for doing that. If he misses his ride to school, let him pay for a cab out of allowance or other earnings.

7. Make copious use of praise and positive feedback. More than most people, people with ADD blossom under the warmth of praise.

8. Consider using a coach or tutor when it comes to schoolwork. You do not want to give up your role as parent to an ad hoc role of supervisor-tutor-badgerer-teacher.

9. Provide the child with whatever devices he or she demonstrates can help. Ask the child what will help. Experiment with different plans and devices. One child organized his homework by setting his alarm clock to go off at twenty-minute intervals; he would plan out his homework in twenty-minute chunks. Another child found that a word processor made the task of writing immensely easier. Another found that studying with earphones on allowed for better concentration. Use as your guiding principle: whatever works (but isn't illegal or dangerous).

10. Always remember: negotiate, don't struggle.

PSYCHOTHERAPY AND COACHING

The person with ADD can best get started in treatment for ADD by establishing a relationship with a therapist who knows about both ADD and psychotherapy.

Your therapist must keep several issues in mind. While attending to your neurological problems, the therapist should help you grapple with your emotional problems as well. He or she should remain attuned to the omnipresent therapy issues of hidden meanings, covert signals, concealed motives, repressed memories, and unspoken desires. Your therapist should leave aside all preconceived ideas derived from diagnosis and should seek first of all to know you as you really are. You should feel understood. This may sound simple, but there is probably no act between two humans that requires greater skill.

We must underline this point with a thick red pencil: the treatment of ADD should never overlook that the patient is a person first, and a person with ADD second. While the symptoms of ADD may dominate the picture, they should never be allowed to supercede the patient's humanity. The patient needs the chance, as we all do, to be heard and understood as an individual, with a specific history, an idiosyncratic set of habits and tastes, a personal chest of drawers of memories and mementos, not as just another person who has ADD.

While your therapist may know a lot about ADD, he or she knows nothing of your particular life. Indeed, what keeps the therapy fresh and exciting is not what your therapist knows, but what he or she does not know. Your therapist must stand ready and eager to learn from you.

The feeling within you of being understood can heal more wounds than any medication or kind words or bits of advice. And the only way for you to find this feeling of being understood is for your therapist to take the time to listen, and it does take time, and to apply the discipline of staying with you, and it does take discipline. With time, and with work, your therapist and you can build, syllable by syllable, image by image, a sense of being known, and sometimes known for the first time.

Once this human bond has been established, or, really, while it is being established, some kind of external supports can help a great deal in restructuring one's life. People with ADD do very well when given support. While you may never get organized on your own, if you feel a part of a team, you will do much better.

We particularly like the idea of a coach. This person may also be a therapist, but need not be. It may be a friend or a colleague, anyone who knows something about ADD and is willing to put in the time—ten or fifteen minutes a day—to coach.

What is an ADD coach? The person is just what the name implies: an individual standing on the sidelines with a whistle around his or her neck barking out encouragement, directions, and reminders to the player in the game. The coach can be a pain in the neck sometimes, dogging the player to stay alert, in the game, and the coach can be a source of solace when the player feels ready to give up. Mainly, the coach keeps the player focused on the task at hand and offers encouragement along the way.

Particularly in the beginning phases of treatment—the first couple of months—the coach can stave off a reversion to old bad habits: habits of procrastination, disorganization, and negative thinking, the most damaging and pernicious of which is the negative thinking. Treatment begins with hope, with a jump-start of the heart. A coach, someone on the outside, can holler at the ADD mind when it starts down the old negative grooves and bring it back to a positive place.

Tips for the Coach

At the beginning of treatment there should be brief (ten-to-fifteen-minute) daily check-ins with the coach, in person or over the phone. The discussion should focus on the practical and concrete—what are your plans? what is due tomorrow? what are you doing to get ready for tomorrow?—as well as on the abstract—how do you feel? what is your mood? These questions can be organized by the initials H.O.P.E. as follows:

H—*Help*: Ask the person you are coaching, what kind of help do you need? Begin by getting an update and seeing what specific assistance is needed.

O—*Obligations*: Ask specifically what obligations are upcoming and what the person is doing to prepare for them. You must ask. If you don't ask, the individual may forget to tell you.

P—*Plans*: Ask about ongoing plans. It is very helpful to remind people with ADD of their goals. They often forget them, quite literally, and so stop working toward them. If they say they don't know what their goals are, try to help them define them. Goals function as a kind of guard against aimlessness, drawing the individual through time toward a desired place.

E—*Encouragement*: The most fun part of the coach's job. The coach should really get into it and not be embarrassed to be rah-rah. The coach is joining a battle against chaos and negativity; the more affirmative he or she can be the better. Don't be daunted by cynicism. It takes a while to undo a lifetime of negativity.

■ ■ ■

Traditional psychotherapy is sometimes indicated for people with ADD because of the problems with self-esteem, anxiety, and depression that build up in the wake of ADD. While the primary problem of ADD is best treated with structure, medication, and coaching, the secondary psychological problems often require ongoing psychotherapy. It is a mistake to treat the primary problems of attention, distractibility, impulsivity, and restlessness and overlook the considerable secondary problems with self-esteem, depression, or marital or family discord.

In doing psychotherapy with adults with ADD, the therapist will help structure sessions; he or she will be quite active. The fundamental rule of psychoanalysis, for the patient to say whatever comes to mind, often leaves the person with ADD at a complete loss. There is so much coming to mind that you don't know where to begin. Or, once you do begin, you don't know where to stop. You may become flooded, not with interesting unconscious material, but with bushels of detritus—useless material that risks turning the psychotherapy into a kind of aimless monologue, going nowhere, frustrating both you and therapist.

If your therapist can provide some structure and direction, you can often get on track. If you have trouble getting started, your therapist might ask a directive question, like "How is that problem with your boss working out?" Or if you start to go off on a tangent that seems to be leading nowhere, your therapist might try to help by bringing you back to the original subject. This is quite counter to what a good therapist usually does in open-ended, insight-oriented psychotherapy. In that kind of therapy the therapist often wishes the patient would get off track, would let go of conscious control to some extent in order to uncover what lies beneath the surface. However, in patients with ADD this approach can backfire, leaving both patient and therapist lost in a meaningless maze made of distractions and incomplete thoughts and images.

If you have ADD, you need the therapist to guide you through your thoughts and associations, helping you prioritize your mental productions and pay attention to what is germane while letting go of what is extraneous. If in the process you let go of a pearl, that is too bad; but it is better than spending the whole therapy shucking pearl-less oysters.

Let me give an example to illustrate this point. At the beginning of a session one of my patients, a forty-two-year-old man in treatment for ADD and depression, said, "Well, I sure won't be needing my wife's money anymore." His reliance on his wife's considerable inherited wealth had become a central issue in therapy because it undermined his sense of independence and self-esteem. In fact, he relied on it only in his imagination, as the couple lived on the incomes each member earned, and they earned about the same amount.

In response to his question I looked interested and said, "Oh, really, why is that?"

"Because I've had a breakthrough. The store has said they will pay me to get special training that will enable me to take over the whole department probably in about a year."

"Really," I said, hoping for more.

"Yes, but I also want to talk to you about the elevator in this building. Why can't they get it fixed? It's a real pain walking up four flights of stairs."

Now at this point I had a decision to make. In psychotherapy with a patient without ADD, I would probably remain silent, or I would ask more about the elevator, thinking in the back of my mind that the patient was inching in on significant transference feelings, feelings about me, his therapist, through his feelings about the elevator, and the pain it caused him to get to me, to our sessions. Why couldn't I make it easier? he might be asking me. Why couldn't I take better care of my building, of my elevator, of my patients, of him? Couldn't I be relied on for that much? Or, looking for past memories or unconscious fantasies, I might ask for my patient's associations to elevators. Sometimes such a question can jar an old memory loose and lead to a whole new and unexpected vein of material. On the other hand, my patient's bringing up the subject of the broken elevator right on the heels of announcing a big promotion certainly could make me wonder if he did not feel conflicted about the promotion. Did the promotion make him think of things that needed repair, like the elevator, like himself? Was he wondering, in the punning way the unconscious often uses, if he were "up" to the job, if he were entitled to "rise" in his field, or if he needed an extra "lift," perhaps from me? With another patient I might have pursued any or all of these ideas.

However, with this patient, I simply said, "I know the broken elevator is annoying. I am told it will be fixed this week. But I'm interested in hearing more about your feelings about the new development at work." It may be argued that in doing this—essentially redirecting the patient back toward what I thought was most important—I lost an opportunity. But I did not want to lose the opportunity the patient had presented at the start of the session in telling about his possible promotion at work. In looking at both opportunities, I decided to take over and choose the promotion as what we should focus on.

Now if the man had responded, "No, I really want to talk about the elevator," I of course would have let him. But he didn't. Instead, he very easily glided back into talking about the promotion, as if that was what he had really wanted to talk about in the first place.

I had to decide whether he brought up the topic of the elevator for hidden reasons we had best look at, or if he brought it up just because it popped into his head, for no significant reason, like a distraction, like the sound of a train whistle outside my window or the telephone ringing in the next office. In making the decision I did, I was taking on the role of distraction censor, a role I often play with my patients who have ADD. The risk inherent in making such a decision for my patient is that I would unintentionally sidestep important material.

Your therapist must make this kind of determination all the time in doing psychotherapy with you, if you have ADD. Even with people who do not have ADD, the therapist must constantly weigh what is heard and consider what to focus on and what to let slide by. However, with patients who have ADD, the therapist has to be more active along these lines than with other people.

In addition, your therapist should take into account your perceptual problems in getting a sense of social situations. Often people with ADD respond inappropriately or awkwardly to other people. Sometimes they appear to be self-centered and remarkably unaware of the needs of others. Consider the following scene as an example.

Dave, a thirty-five-year-old man with ADD paused at the office water cooler for a drink. As he was sipping his spring water, a friend joined him at the cooler. "Hi, Dave," the friend said, filling his conic cup. Dave did not respond. "Be nice to get these estimates out on time, for once, huh? You've done a great job." Dave still didn't say anything. "You must have been here late last night?"

Dave, who had been thinking about how to construct a three-dimensional oval, like an egg, for his daughter's science project, threw his cup in the metal trash basket, saw his friend, grunted, and headed back toward his office. His friend called after him, "Nice talking to you, Dave." Dave didn't stop. His friend registered this encounter as just another example of spacey Dave being spacey Dave.

It is not that Dave was too selfish to acknowledge or hear his friend. It is that he was mentally elsewhere. It would be important for his therapist to know of this tendency and to give practical advice on how to handle social situations. By practical advice I mean concrete pointers such as "When you are at the water cooler, a central stopping place, keep it in mind that other people might walk up to you," or "When you see a friend, don't just grunt, say something, give a real response," or "In conversation, make eye contact and listen before you start to speak." These kinds of counsel—

concrete, obvious, perhaps tedious—can help a person with ADD immensely. People with ADD may not make friends or do well socially simply because *they don't know how*. They don't know the rules. They don't know the steps of the dance. They have never been taught what we all assume everyone learns as second nature. People with ADD may lack this second nature. They may need lessons in how to interact. Social "reading" can be as difficult for these people as the reading of words. As painfully obvious as these social lessons may be to the socially adept, to the person with ADD, who can feel as lost in a conversation as he does in the middle of a written page, these lessons can impart nothing less than the ability to make contact with other people.

Having stressed the importance of "coaching," and the importance of focusing and directing the psychotherapy in working with patients with ADD, let us also make it clear that the work you and your therapist do is not simpleminded. While coaching may sound simple—and, indeed, at its best it is simple, deceptively simple—and while focusing the therapy may sound like a kind of traffic control—stopping this conversation, whistling it over there—the work can also be as subtle, unpredictable, and imaginative as any kind of psychotherapy.

■ ■ ■

While individual therapy marks the starting point for most people with ADD, additional forms of psychotherapy can be extremely helpful, particularly family therapy, couples therapy, and group therapy. The main issues that come up in couples and families were discussed in previous chapters, so we will discuss here only group therapy.

Groups—for any problem, not just ADD—can mobilize positive energy in ways that are truly remarkable. When groups are properly run, they are a safe, cost-effective, and highly successful kind of therapy for ADD. This applies to both children and adults. Indeed, with children individual therapy may not get at the real problems at all, because the problems only come up in groups. The child may sit with his or her individual therapist and happily play games, all the while showing none of the symptoms that cause the big problems in everyday life at school and at home. However, group therapy for children can address the issues as they come up, head on, *in situ*, as it were, in the group. For example, a child who cannot pay attention when other children are around will not show this in individual therapy. Or a child who becomes disruptive when asked to share with other children will not demonstrate this symptom in individual therapy. But in a group these kinds of behavior will appear.

For adults with ADD, group therapy has several advantages. First of all, it gives people a chance to meet and interact with other people like themselves, people who have had to deal with many of the same problems and frustrations in life.

Second, the members of the group can teach each other a great deal. They can talk about their own experiences and share tips and pointers that they have found helpful in their own lives while learning similar information from other members of the group. In a sense, the best therapist for someone with ADD is someone else with ADD, someone who has been there, someone who knows the place from the inside.

Third, a group can validate its members' experiences in ways that an individual therapist cannot do. A group can understand its members and give powerful support. The acceptance one can find in a group can be uplifting.

Fourth, a group can supply a tremendous amount of energy. Groups can be like reservoirs of fuel where members fill up each week.

Fifth, as with groups for children who have ADD, adult groups can re-create the very situations that people with ADD are trying to learn how to cope with. Groups can re-create situations like Dave at the water cooler. Groups create situations where its members must listen to each other, wait their turn, where they must share, where they must keep silent for a period of time, where they must stay put, where they must take responsibility for what they say or do not say, where they can hear feedback as to how they come across to others. As the individual learns to bear with the tension of these feelings in the group, that skill can be carried into the outside world.

Sixth, groups address the problem of disconnectedness. Many people with ADD have trouble finding a place where they feel connected, a part of something larger than self. Although people with ADD tend to be outgoing and gregarious, they can also harbor strong feelings of isolation, loneliness, and disconnectedness. Their stance in life is often one of reaching out but not quite making contact, as if running alongside a speeding train, trying to grasp the hand that is being held out to them to help them on board. Groups can bring people on board. Groups can provide a sense of belonging, a sense of connectedness. Once on board, the individual can feel more a part of things in other areas of his or her life.

To illustrate the power of group therapy in ADD, let me tell a story from one of the groups I conduct. Some time ago I began to organize groups for adults with ADD. I had never done this before, and I had not read of others doing it, but for all the reasons given above, it seemed to me a good idea. To start my first group I announced the idea at a lecture I gave. From the people who signed up, I selected a group of ten men and women, and we started to meet once a week.

I did not know what to expect. Colleagues I mentioned the idea to rolled their eyes and said, "Ten people with ADD in a group?! How can you run herd on that?" Another colleague asked, "Will they ever show up on time?"

Not knowing what would happen, I sat in my office the evening of the first meeting of the group. We were to meet from 7:00 to 8:15. By 7:15 not one of the ten members had appeared. I began to wonder if my own ADD had led me to write down the wrong day. At 7:20 the first member showed up. He burst into the office ready to apologize for being late, but when he discovered he was the first to arrive, he started laughing and said, "Well, what can you expect?" Seven people eventually arrived for that first meeting. Three others left messages saying they had gotten lost on their way to my office.

The ones who did find their way began the most remarkable group I have ever participated in. They came together immediately, united in their desire to find mutual understanding, to tell their various stories, and to "be there" for each other.

I gave the group some basic guidelines: Try to be on time. Don't socialize with each other outside the group. If you are going to miss a session, try to let the group know about it in advance. We contracted to meet for twenty weeks with an option to continue for another ten weeks if people wanted to. I also called the members who had got lost and gave them directions for the following week.

The next session all ten members showed up and on time. They laughed about the trouble they'd had with directions the week before, and started what became a regular practice in the group of giving good-natured kidding as a way of dealing with the problems of ADD. "It's a miracle," they laughed, "that we all got here this week, and on time no less." Their exuberance filled the room even before they knew each other. It was as if, in some intuitive part of their minds, they already knew each other and how important the group would become. From the beginning they were ready for each other.

They began to tell their stories. One by one, not on cue but spontaneously, tales of humor and tales of pain filled the room. They looked around at each other, giving nods of approval and looks of recognition as they would identify with one detail or another that was being related. To be with them was to be with people who had spent their whole lives feeling "different," only now to discover in each other that they were not alone. They laughed back tears, and they faced each others' pain with firsthand understanding, as they told of misunderstandings, frustrations, and lost chances as well as of tips and advice, tricks from the ADD trade.

I didn't have to do a thing. If one member interrupted another member, others would say something like, "Now don't interrupt. Since we all have ADD, we have to be really careful about paying attention to each other." They looked out for each other in this kind of way during every session. I sat back and answered factual questions about ADD now and then, but, by and large, the members of the group did all the work. When I had to miss a few meetings because of prior commitments, the group simply met in my office without me. They asked only if I would bill them for sessions I missed. I said of course not.

Within a few weeks the group had developed a powerful sense of cohesion. One member, who was an aspiring actress, turned down a part in a play because rehearsal time conflicted with group time. Another member, who went on vacation, sent us a postcard. Members gave each other permission to call each other in case of an emotional crisis. I worried this might lead to subgrouping or breakdowns in confidentiality. It never did.

When the option to continue the group for another ten weeks came up, everyone wanted to go on. However, one member stated she could not afford to. Later that week I received a letter without signature or identifying marks. It contained, in cash, the fee for an additional ten weeks of the group. The person who wrote the letter identified him- or herself only as "a member of the adult ADD group."

Now I, who was trained in psychoanalytically oriented Boston, felt racked by a dilemma. What should I do? Do I bring the money into the group? Give it back? To whom? What if the person who had said she could not afford to continue had said that as a way of leaving the group gracefully? Would this put undue pressure on her to continue? What if others felt cheated that they couldn't get a "scholarship" also? What about the group's curiosity as to the identity of the anonymous donor? What about my own curiosity? With these questions swimming through my mind, I called a colleague, experienced in group work, for advice. He felt a bit perplexed as well, but advised me to bring the matter up in the group and see how they handled it.

At the next meeting of the group we decided to go on for ten more weeks and then to stop. At that point I informed the group that I had received an anonymous cash donation to cover the fee of the member who could not afford to continue.

Well, thankfully, the group was not psychoanalytically trained. Their response was to say how generous it was for someone to donate the money, and then they moved on to other topics. I sat there biting my tongue, thinking, Yes, but, don't you want to know *more*? Don't you see the complicated dynamic issues involved here? Shouldn't we analyze the implications of this gift? Etc., etc. However, I didn't let myself make more of the matter than the group did, and so the incident passed into the group's history as this: the group received a generous gift which allowed the group to remain intact for ten more weeks. In retrospect, I do still have all those questions I had originally. But most of all, I see the gift as evidence of just how important it was to the members of the group to be together and, at last, to be understood.

MEDICATION

The various medications that we now use in the treatment of attention deficit disorder can dramatically improve the quality of an individual's life. Just as a pair of glasses help the nearsighted person focus, so can medication help the person with ADD see the world more clearly. When the medication is effective, the results can be truly astonishing and life-changing. However, medication is no panacea. It does not work for everybody who has ADD, and for those it does help, it ameliorates but does not cure the syndrome. Medication should be used only under medical supervision, and only as part of a comprehensive treatment program that includes a careful diagnostic evaluation; education about ADD and associated learning problems; practical suggestions as to how to restructure one's life and manage one's moods; counseling, coaching, or psychotherapy; as well as family or couples therapy as needed.

The following information on medication is intended to supplement conversations with a physician or other counselor. You should never take any medication until you feel you have learned all you need to know about it and you feel comfortable with this course of treatment.

Before beginning a course of medication, you of course want to be sure of the diagnosis. Then you must determine what the target symptoms are so that you will have an objective way of assessing the efficacy of the medication. Typical target symptoms in ADD would include: easy distractibility; an inability to stay focused on a task at work, reading a book, homework, or classroom material; impulsive acts or words; difficulty maintaining attention during a conversation; poor frustration tolerance; angry outbursts; mood swings; difficulty getting organized; chronic procrastination; difficulty prioritizing; a tendency to worry rather than act; a subjective inner feeling of noise or chaos; a tendency to hop from topic to topic or project to project. It is important to try to define the symptoms you want to alleviate as concretely as possible.

Very often at the initial stage of treatment there is great reluctance to try medication. Parents do not want to "drug" their child, or the adult with ADD wants to make it on his own, without the aid of some unknown medication. This hesitancy may be deeply felt and must be dealt with carefully.

Children, particularly boys, often feel that taking medicine is like admitting something scary is wrong with them, admitting they are "retarded" or "crazy" or "stupid," all labels they are struggling to throw off. They also often feel that medication is a crutch they should not need to use. They frequently feel embarrassed or humiliated in taking the medication. It is essential that these feelings be explored and dealt with gently and respectfully. It may take months, even years, before a child—or an adult— feels ready to give medication a try. That is all right. The medication should not be given until the individual is ready to take it. The decision to take medication should never be unilateral and should not be a struggle; it should be bilateral, emerging from a dialogue that lasts as long as it needs to.

Of course, no one is obliged ever to try medication. And no one should try medication without wanting to do so and without a full understanding of the risks and benefits involved. But what too often happens is that one decides against medication on the basis of hearsay, superstition, or gut feeling, not on the basis of fact and science. There is a great deal of misinformation promulgated about the various medications used to treat ADD. For example, it is extraordinary how many false rumors swirl around Ritalin, one of the chief medications used to treat ADD. "It will make you crazy," people whisper to each other. "I saw an article in the paper that said Ritalin turned one man into a homicidal maniac." "Ritalin is just the school's way of lobotomizing children." "Ritalin turns you into a dwarf." These tabloid-headline-type remarks are made frequently. They are utterly untrue.

The fact is that when Ritalin and the other medications used in the treatment of ADD are used properly, they are very safe indeed, and can be as dramatically effective as the right pair of eyeglasses can be for near-sightedness.

Although medication does not always work, when it does work, it works wonders. To decide against it on an informed basis is fine, but to decide against it for irrational reasons is a mistake. The information that follows is offered in the hope of helping to make the decision a thoroughly rational one.

There are two main classes of medication used in the treatment of ADD: the stimulants and the antidepressants. The same medications are used in both children and adults. For both children and adults with correctly diagnosed ADD, some medication will be effective about 80 percent of the time. Finding the right medication and the right dosage can take several months of trial and error, as we do not as yet have a way of predicting what medication in what dosage will help a given individual. It is worth being patient and not giving up too soon, since often an increase in dosage or a change in medication will make a dramatic difference.

When medication is effective, it can help the individual focus better, sustain effort over a longer period of time, reduce anxiety and frustration, reduce irritability and mood swings, increase efficiency by enhancing concentration as well as reducing time lost in distraction, and increase impulse control. These primary effects may lead to secondary effects of increased confidence, a sense of well-being, and greater self-esteem.

The medication does not always work, and even when it does work, sometimes it must be discontinued due to intolerable side effects. In these cases the nonmedication forms of treatment can still produce significant therapeutic gains.

First, let's consider the stimulants. The most common is Ritalin (ge-

neric name, methylphenidate). Others include Dexedrine (dextroampheta-
mine) and Cylert (pemoline). As their name implies, the stimulants act on
neurotransmitters to activate or stimulate the central nervous system. In
ADD this has the effect of helping the individual to focus or attend more
fully than before. They also can have a mood-leveling effect.

A few things the stimulants do *not* do should be mentioned to clear
up common misconceptions. They do not "drug up" or cloud the sensorium
of the individual taking them. They are not addictive in the doses prescribed
for ADD. They do not take away the creativity or "special something" so
many people with ADD possess.

However, there may be side effects. Using Ritalin as an example, the
most common side effects are the suppression of appetite and loss of sleep.
Blood pressure and heart rate may also be elevated. These side effects are
dose-related and may be avoided by lowering the dose. There may be some
nausea and headaches at the outset of therapy; these usually pass within a
few days. In addition, as the medication wears off, the individual may feel
a letdown or change of mood. One can usually accommodate to this by
changing the amount or timing of the dose. One may also feel jittery or
nervous on Ritalin while still getting therapeutic benefits. Sometimes the
addition of a low dose of a medication called a beta-blocker, such as Corgard
(generic name, nadolol), can remove this jitteriness.

Other, far-less-frequent side effects of Ritalin include the development
of an involuntary muscle twitch, or what is called Tourette's syndrome;
growth suppression in children (for which there is a compensatory spurt
in growth when the medication is discontinued); and alteration in blood
count or other blood chemistries, which normalize upon discontinuation
of the medication. These side effects are very rare. In general, Ritalin is an
extremely safe medication when given under proper supervision.

Each dose of Ritalin lasts about four hours (although this may vary
somewhat from person to person). Therefore, Ritalin is given in divided
doses throughout the day. The usual schedule is as follows: first dose with
breakfast, second dose four hours later or with lunch, and third dose about
four or five o'clock in the afternoon. This routine may be varied according
to one's individual schedule. The main point is to have the medication on
board when you need to be focused, and to space each dose by about four
hours.

There is a slow-release form of Ritalin that lasts eight hours, thus allowing one to skip the noon dose. This is particularly helpful in children, who often forget to take their noon dose or don't want to be seen going to the school nurse for medication. However, in many cases the slow-release (or SR) Ritalin does not work as well as the regular Ritalin.

One can take generic methylphenidate or brand-name Ritalin. Brand-name Ritalin is slightly, but only slightly, more expensive; in our experience it works better than the generic methylphenidate.

The therapeutic dose varies from individual to individual. A typical dose of Ritalin would be 10 mg three times a day. One usually starts at 5 mg twice a day to see if the medication is going to be well tolerated. After a few days it can be increased to 10 mg twice a day, then on to three times a day. One can continue to increase the dose until either side effects appear, such as appetite suppression or sleep loss, or until a therapeutic benefit is achieved and target symptoms are relieved.

Sometimes the medication simply does not work no matter what the dose. Other times one gives up too soon, not reaching a high-enough dose to achieve a therapeutic effect. One can increase the dose until side effects occur, but when side effects do occur, the dose should be lowered or the medication stopped. If the medication is stopped, one can try another stimulant or another class of medication, such as the antidepressants, or Catapres (generic name, clonidine), an anti-high-blood-pressure medication that has been found to be useful in treating ADD. It should also be borne in mind that if one stimulant does not work, another stimulant may. The main reason we usually start with Ritalin, as opposed to another stimulant, such as Dexedrine, is that decades ago, when stimulants were first used to treat ADD, many people thought of Dexedrine as a street drug, a drug of abuse. Although when Dexedrine is used properly it is not a drug of abuse, it had a major public image problem. Therefore, most physicians prescribed Ritalin, which had no such image problem. The trend continues to this day.

One should take care not to conclude too quickly that the medication "doesn't work." Often it takes weeks, even months, to find the right dosage and the right dosing schedule. Sometimes a low dose will work, but only if it is given at the right time. Sometimes a small increase in dose will make a great difference. Sometimes the addition of another medication will allow the first medication to work better, such as combining a stimulant with an antidepressant or combining a beta-blocker with a stimulant. This can be a tedious process, like trying on many pairs of shoes until you find the right fit. But it is well worth the effort.

Often the person taking the medication will not be aware if it is working. However, teachers, friends, spouse, or boss may notice dramatic improvement in focusing and productivity. Therefore, the assessment of efficacy should include reports from at least one other person in addition to the person taking the medication. In children, behavioral checklists filled out by the classroom teacher can be particularly helpful. In adults, the assessment is somewhat less formal, but it should be equally objective.

Ritalin, and the other stimulants, should be discontinued for a week or so every four to six months. These periodic "drug holidays" allow one to observe if the medication is still necessary by assessing functioning off medication.

Of the antidepressants used to treat ADD, Norpramin (generic name, desipramine) is the most commonly used because most of the research on the antidepressants in ADD has been done with this medication. It is in the class of drugs called the tricyclic antidepressants. Although it is a completely different substance, chemically, from the stimulants, it has a similar effect upon the target symptoms of ADD. Sometimes, when a stimulant does not work, Norpramin will, and vice versa.

There are several advantages of Norpramin over Ritalin and the other stimulants. First, it can be given in a single daily dosage, thus avoiding the need to remember to take a pill several times a day. (Trying to remember to take medication for ADD brings up a kind of Catch-22: how are you supposed to remember to take the medication that is supposed to help you remember to take your medication?) Second, it does not produce the jagged peaks and valleys some people experience on Ritalin. It is smoother, evener in its action. Third, it is not a controlled substance and so there can be greater flexibility in prescribing; controlled substances cannot be refilled automatically and prescriptions are limited in the amount that can be prescribed at one time. In addition, in some states it is necessary to produce identification to get the prescription for a controlled substance filled.

Common side effects of Norpramin include dry mouth, mild urinary retention, and transient lowering of blood pressure upon standing up, which results in dizziness. People occasionally develop cardiac arrhythmias while taking Norpramin. There have been instances in which these arrhythmias have resulted in sudden death. This is extremely rare and can be watched for by EKGs and by monitoring blood levels. But one should monitor Norpramin carefully, especially at higher doses.

There are two dosing schedules for the use of Norpramin in treating ADD: low-dose and high-dose. With the low-dose approach, first advocated by Hans Huessy and others some years ago, we have found some success. Daily dosage is 10 to 30 mg. At this dosage level, side effects are minimal and the risk of cardiac side effects is minimized. In some patients the therapeutic gain is just as great as with high-dose Norpramin or with Ritalin or other stimulants, and may even be greater. Therefore, before putting patients on the higher-dose schedule, we always give them a trial of the lower dose. Also, the combination of Norpramin at a low dose plus Ritalin can work well and is worth trying before going to the higher dose of Norpramin.

The high-dose schedule is from 75 to 300 mg per day. At these doses, which are built up to gradually, one must carefully monitor blood levels and signs of side effects.

There are several other medications that have been found to be helpful in childhood and adult ADD. These include tricyclics other than Norpramin, such as Pamelor (generic name, nortriptyline) and Tofranil (imipramine) as well as newer medications, such as Wellbutrin (bupropion), Ludiomil (maprotiline), Prozac (fluoxetine)—all three of which are nontricyclic antidepressants—and Catapres (clonidine), which has been mentioned already. Prozac actually has little effect on attention; it is most helpful if there is a component of depression to the ADD. As one can see, if the stimulants or Norpramin do not work, there are other medications one can try.

In addition, there are various medications that can be useful adjunctively, either to treat side effects or to improve the effect of the primary medication. We have already mentioned the usefulness of the beta-blockers, specifically Corgard at a dose of 20 mg per day, to treat the jitteriness or anxiety that is sometimes associated with the stimulants, particularly Ritalin.

There are several others worth mentioning. Many women who have ADD feel that their symptoms get much worse when they are premenstrual. As one of our patients has commented, "I do OK on the medication for most of the month . . . but when I'm juggling twelve balls in the air to get something done, and then PMS arrives, it makes it impossible to continue to function very well."

No scientific evidence linking a proneness to PMS with ADD has been offered. But many of our female patients report unusually severe PMS symptoms. It might be a common accompanying problem. It can restrict a woman's attempts to deal with her ADD and can make any existing anxiety, depression, or mood swings much worse. The addition of serotonin-active drugs like buspirone, fluoxetine, or sertraline (BuSpar, Prozac, or Zoloft) to the treatment regimen can make a great difference to a woman with ADD. These medications can alleviate the typical PMS symptoms and re-regulate the neuroendocrine imbalance wreaking havoc on an already un-balanced system.

If depression coexists with ADD, as it often does, the addition of an antidepressant medication to one of the stimulants can be quite helpful. Ritalin by itself has a mildly antidepressant effect. The addition of Nor-pramin, or one of the serotonin-active medications such as Prozac or Zoloft can help treat the depressive symptoms while the stimulant treats the symp-toms of ADD. One should not usually start the antidepressant at the same time one starts the stimulant. This is because the individual's depression often disappears as the symptoms of ADD go away. However, if the depres-sion persists, an antidepressant medication may help.

Outbursts of rage, tantrums, and even violent behavior sometimes accompany ADD. There are a variety of medications that can treat these symptoms. The mood-stabilizing medications lithium, valproic acid (De-pakote), and carbamazepine (Tegretol) all may help control these outbursts. The beta-blockers nadolol (Corgard) and propranolol (Inderal) can also reduce explosiveness.

If obsessive-compulsive disorder occurs with ADD, the addition of clomipramine (Anafranil) can treat the obsessional symptoms.

The medications used in the treatment of ADD are summarized in the table to the right.

There are emotional issues that underlie the taking of medication, particularly in children, but in adults as well. Many people recoil at the thought of taking medication "for their brains," or their children's brains. It conjures up images of thought control or serious mental illness. It is important to discuss these fears or preconceptions as openly as possible.

The taking of medication for ADD should not be an act of faith but an act of science. Sometimes people ask, "Do you believe in medication as part of the treatment of ADD?" as if medication were a religious principle. We neither believe in it nor disbelieve in it for all people. Rather, we

PRIMARY SYMPTOMS	MEDICATION (Trade Name)	MECHANISM OF ACTION
Inattention Distractibility Impulsivity	Stimulants, including Ritalin, Dexedrine, Cylert	
Minipanic Impulsivity	Antidepressants, particularly Norpramin; also Wellbutrin, Ludiomil, and Prozac, and the alphaagonist, Catapres	Enhance certain neurotransmitters

SECONDARY SYMPTOMS	MEDICATION	MECHANISM OF ACTION
Outbursts of rage Tantrums Violent behavior	Lithium Tegretol Depakote	stabilize mood
	Corgard Inderal	beta-blockers
PMS/Irritability	BuSpar Prozac Zoloft	enhance serotonin
Somatic tension Impulsivity	Corgard Inderal Catapres	beta-blockers alpha-agonist
Obsessive-compulsive symptoms	Anafranil Prozac Zoloft	enhance serotonin
Jittery side effects of Ritalin or other stimulants	Corgard Inderal	beta-blocker

approach it rationally. For most people who have ADD, medication has proven to be extremely useful. For some it has proven to be ineffective. For a very few it has proven to be harmful. If the diagnosis of ADD is carefully made, the best research data we have states that a trial of medication is indicated.

Before starting the medication it is useful to explore all one's feelings about it, in addition to getting as much scientific information about it as possible. As we pointed out earlier, there are many misconceptions and much misinformation about the medications involved in treating ADD.

A few last points about medication must be stressed. Medication is not the whole treatment for ADD. It is a useful and powerful adjunct, but it should never be regarded as the complete treatment. Medication should always be monitored by a physician. One should never take medication without feeling comfortable doing so. Spend time preparing yourself to take the medication—talking about it, getting questions answered—before you start, and your chances of success will be greatly improved.

Practical Tips on the Management and Treatment of ADD

This section offers short, encapsulated bits of advice on how to deal with ADD, practical tips that aim to assist in the day-to-day coping with life with ADD. These tips are culled from our years of experience in working with individuals with ADD, hearing their problems and complaints, and learning from the solutions they devised.

As you read through the following suggestions, you will probably find that you use many of them already; you will find that some of them are obvious or apply to everybody, with or without ADD; you will find that some of them seem irrelevant to your situation; and you will find, we hope, that some of them are new and quite helpful.

A word of caution should be added. Often when people read these tips for the first time, they become excited about incorporating them into their lives right away. After an initial burst of enthusiasm and improvement, however, they find that the old habits associated with their ADD start to creep back into their lives, and they find that the tips, although "correct," are hard to follow consistently. As one patient said, "If I could follow the tips, then I wouldn't need to follow them, because I wouldn't have ADD in the first place." Or as another patient said, "I have my days when I can follow the tips and days when I can't. It's like the old heartbeat, up and down."

It is important, therefore, to keep in mind that the tips are only one part of a treatment program. Very few people with ADD can implement these tips consistently on their own. They need help, either from what we call a "coach," or from a group, or from a therapist, or from some other external source. Do not feel intimidated or disheartened if at first you have trouble putting all these tips to work for you in your life. It will take time, it will require hard work, and it will require encouragement (and forgiveness) from the outside world. But with these considerations in mind, the tips can offer solid, practical help.

FIFTY TIPS
ON THE MANAGEMENT OF
ADULT ATTENTION DEFICIT DISORDER

■

INSIGHT AND EDUCATION

1. Be sure of the diagnosis. Make sure you're working with a professional who really understands ADD and has excluded related or similar conditions, such as anxiety states, agitated depression, hyperthyroidism, manic-depressive illness, or obsessive-compulsive disorder.

2. Educate yourself. Perhaps the single most powerful treatment for ADD is understanding ADD in the first place. Read books. Talk with professionals. Talk with other adults who have ADD. These may be found through ADD support groups or local or national ADD organizations like CHADD. You'll be able to design your own treatment to fit your own version of ADD.

3. Choose a coach. It is useful for you to have a coach, for some person near to you to keep after you, but always with humor. Your coach can help you get organized, stay on task, give you encouragement, or remind you to get back to work. Friend, colleague, or therapist (it is possible, but risky, for your coach to be your spouse), a coach is someone who stays on you to get things done, exhorts you as coaches do, keeps tabs on you, and in general stands in your corner. A coach can be tremendously helpful in treating ADD.

4. Seek encouragement. ADD adults need lots of encouragement. This is in part due to many self-doubts that have accumulated over the years. But it goes beyond that. More than most people, ADD adults wither without encouragement and thrive when given it. They will often work for another person in a way they won't work for themselves. This is not "bad," it just is. It should be recognized and taken advantage of.

5. Realize what ADD is *not*—i.e., conflict with mother, unconscious fear of success, passive-aggressive personality, etc. People with ADD, of course, may have a conflict with their mother or an unconscious fear of success or have a passive-aggressive personality, but it is important to separate the ADD from these other kinds of problems because the treatment for ADD is completely different.

6. Educate and involve others. Just as it is key for you to understand ADD, it is equally if not more important for those around you to understand it—family, job, school, friends. Once they get the concept, they will be able to understand you much better and to help you reach your goals.

7. Give up guilt over high-stimulus-seeking behavior. Understand that you are drawn to intense stimuli. Try to choose them wisely, rather than brooding over the "bad" ones.

8. Listen to feedback from trusted others. Adults (and children, too) with ADD are notoriously poor self-observers. They use a lot of what can appear to be denial.

9. Consider joining or starting a support group. Much of the most useful information about ADD has not yet found its way into books but remains stored in the minds of the people who have ADD. In groups this information can come out. Plus, groups are really helpful in giving the kind of support that is so badly needed.

10. Try to get rid of the negativity that may have infested your system if you have lived for years without knowing that what you had was ADD. A good psychotherapist may help in this regard.

11. Don't feel chained to conventional careers or conventional ways of coping. Give yourself permission to be yourself. Give up trying to be the person you always thought you should be —the model student or the organized executive, for example— and let yourself be who you are.

12. Remember that what you have is a neurological condition. It is genetically transmitted. It is caused by biology, by how your brain is wired. It is *not* a disease of the will, nor a moral failing, nor some kind of neurosis. It is not caused by a weakness in character, nor by a failure to mature. It's cure is not to be found in the power of the will, nor in punishment, nor in sacrifice, nor in pain. Always remember this. Try as they might, many people with ADD have great trouble accepting the syndrome as being rooted in biology rather than weakness of character.

13. Try to help others with ADD. You'll learn a lot about the condition in the process, as well as feel good to boot.

■

PERFORMANCE MANAGEMENT

14. Establish external structure. Structure is the hallmark of the nonpharmacological treatment of the ADD child. It can be equally useful with adults. Once in place, structure works like the walls of the bobsled slide, keeping the speedball sled from careening off the track. Make frequent use of lists, notes to self, color coding, rituals, reminders, files. Also use pattern planning, as described earlier.

15. Use pizzazz. Try to make your environment as peppy as you want it to be without letting it boil over. If your organization system can be stimulating (imagine that!), instead of boring, then you will be more likely to follow it. For example, in setting things up, try color coding. Mentioned above, color coding deserves emphasis. Many people with ADD are visually oriented. Take advantage of this by making things memorable with color: files, memoranda, texts, schedules, etc. Virtually anything in the black-and-white of type can be made more memorable, arresting, and therefore attention-getting with color.

16. When it comes to paperwork, use the principle of O.H.I.O: Only handle it once. When you receive a document or a memo or any kind of written material, try to only handle it once. Either respond to it right away, on the spot, or throw the document away, or file it permanently. *Do not* put it in a TO DO box or pile. For people with ADD, TO DO piles might just as well be called NEVER DONE piles. They serve as little menaces around one's desk or room, silently building guilt, anxiety, and resentment, as well as taking up a lot of space. Get in the habit of acting immediately on your paperwork. Make the wrenching decision to throw something away. Or, overcome inertia and respond to it *on the spot*. Whatever you do with the document, whenever possible, only handle it once.

17. Set up your environment to reward rather than deflate. To understand what a deflating environment is, most adult ADDers only need to think back to school. Now that you have the freedom of adulthood, try to set things up so that you will not constantly be reminded of your limitations.

18. Acknowledge and anticipate the inevitable collapse of X percent of projects undertaken, relationships entered into, obligations incurred. Better that you anticipate these "failures" rather than be surprised by them and brood over them. Think of them as part of the cost of doing business.

19. Embrace challenges. ADD people thrive with many challenges. As long as you know they won't all pan out, as long as you don't get too perfectionistic and fussy, you'll get a lot done and stay out of trouble. Far better that you be too busy than not busy enough. As the old saying goes, if you want to get something done, ask a busy person.

20. Make deadlines.

21. Break down large tasks into small ones. Attach deadlines to the small parts. Then, like magic, the large task will get done. This is one of the simplest and most powerful of all structuring devices. Often a large task will feel overwhelming to the person with ADD. The mere thought of trying to perform the task makes one turn away. On the other hand, if the large task is broken down into small parts, each component may feel quite manageable. (For example, it was only by using this technique that we managed to write this book.)

22. Prioritize rather than procrastinate. If you cannot handle it only once (tip 16), then be sure to prioritize. When things get busy, the adult ADD person loses perspective: paying an unpaid parking ticket can feel as pressing as putting out the fire that just got started in the wastebasket. Sometimes one becomes paralyzed. Prioritize. Take a deep breath. Put first things first. Then go on to the second and the third task. Don't stop. Procrastination is one of the hallmarks of adult ADD. You have to really discipline yourself to watch out for it and avoid it.

23. Accept the fear of things going too well. Accept edginess when things are too easy, when there's no conflict. Don't gum things up just to make them more stimulating.

24. Notice how and where you work best: in a noisy room, on the train, wrapped in three blankets, listening to music, whatever. Children and adults with ADD can do their best under rather odd conditions. Let yourself work under whatever conditions are best for you.

25. Know that it is OK to do two things at once: carry on a conversation and knit, or take a shower and do your best thinking, or jog and plan a business meeting. Often people with ADD need to be doing several things at once in order to get anything done at all.

26. Do what you're good at. Again, if it seems easy, that is OK. There is no rule that says you can only do what you're bad at.

27. Leave time between engagements to gather your thoughts. Transitions are difficult for ADDers, and minibreaks can help ease the transition.

28. Keep a notepad in your car, by your bed, and in your pocketbook or jacket. You never know when a good idea will hit you, or you'll want to remember something else.

29. Read with a pen in hand, not only for marginal notes or underlining, but for the inevitable cascade of "other" thoughts that will occur to you.

■

MOOD MANAGEMENT

30. Have structured "blow-out" time. Set aside some time in every week for just letting go. Whatever you like to do—blasting yourself with loud music, taking a trip to the racetrack, having a feast—pick some kind of activity from time to time where you can let loose in a safe way.

31. Recharge your batteries. Related to number 30, most adults with ADD need, on a daily basis, some time to waste without feeling guilty about it. One guilt-free way to conceptualize it is to call it time to recharge your batteries. Take a nap, watch TV, meditate. Something calm, restful, at ease.

32. Choose "good," helpful addictions, such as exercise. Many adults with ADD have an addictive or compulsive personality such that they are always hooked on something. Try to make this something positive.

33. Understand mood changes and ways to manage these. Know that your moods will change willy-nilly, independent of what's going on in the external world. Don't waste your time looking for someone to blame. Focus rather on learning to tolerate a bad mood, knowing that it will pass, and learning strategies to make it pass sooner. Change sets, i.e., get involved with some new activity (preferably interactive), such as a conversation with a friend, or a tennis game, or reading a book.

34. Related to number 33, recognize the following cycle, which is very common among adults with ADD:

a. Something "startles" your psychological system, a change or transition, a disappointment or even a success. The precipitant may be quite trivial, nothing more than an everyday event.

b. This "startle" is followed by a minipanic with a sudden loss of perspective, the world being set topsy-turvy.

c. You try to deal with this panic by falling into a mode of obsessing and ruminating over one or another aspect of the situation. This can last for hours, days, even months.

    To break the negative obsessing, have a list of friends to call. Have a few videos that always engross you and get your mind off things. Have ready access to exercise. Have a punching bag or pillow handy if there's extra angry energy. Rehearse a few pep talks you can give yourself, like, "You've been here before. These are the ADD blues. They will soon pass. You are OK."

35. Learn how to name your feelings. Many people with ADD, particularly men, get frustrated and angry because they cannot put their feelings into words. With practice and coaching, this is a skill that can be learned.

36. Expect depression after success. People with ADD commonly complain of feeling depressed, paradoxically, after a big success. This is because the high stimulus of the chase or the challenge or the preparation is over. The deed is done. Win or lose, the adult with ADD misses the conflict, the high stimulus, and feels depressed.

37. Learn symbols, slogans, sayings as shorthand ways of labeling and quickly putting into perspective slip-ups, mistakes, or mood swings. When you turn left instead of right and take your family on a twenty-minute detour, it is better to be able to say, "There goes my ADD again," than to have a six-hour fight over your unconscious desire to sabotage the whole trip. These are not excuses. You still have to take responsibility for your actions. It is just good to know where your actions are coming from and where they're not.

38. Use "time-outs," as with children. When you are upset or overstimulated, take a time-out. Go away. Calm down.

39. Learn how to advocate for yourself. Adults with ADD are so used to being criticized, they are often unnecessarily defensive in putting their own case forward. Learn to get off the defensive.

40. Avoid premature closure of a project, a conflict, a deal, or a conversation. Don't "cut to the chase" too soon, even though you're itching to.

41. Try to let a successful moment last and be remembered and become sustaining over time. You'll have to train yourself consciously and deliberately to do this because you'll naturally tend to forget your successes as you brood over your shortcomings or pessimistically anticipate the worst.

42. Remember that ADD usually includes a tendency to overfocus or hyperfocus at times. This hyperfocusing can be used constructively or destructively. Be aware of its destructive use: a tendency to obsess or ruminate over some imagined problem without being able to let it go.

43. Exercise vigorously and regularly. You should schedule exercise into your life and stick with it. It helps you work off excess energy and aggression in a positive way, it allows for noise reduction within the mind, it stimulates the hormonal and neurochemical system in a most therapeutic way, and it soothes and calms the body. When you add all that to the well-known health benefits of exercise, you can see how important exercise is. Make it something fun so you can stick with it over the long haul, i.e., the rest of your life. One particular form of exercise, sexual activity, is very good for ADD.

■

INTERPERSONAL LIFE

44. Make a good choice in a significant other. Obviously, this is good advice for anyone. But it is striking how the adult with ADD can thrive or flounder depending on the choice of mate.

45. Learn to joke with yourself and others about your various symptoms, from forgetfulness to getting lost all the time to being tactless or impulsive. If you can bring a sense of humor to your failings, others will forgive you much more quickly.

46. Schedule activities with friends. Adhere to these schedules faithfully. It is crucial for you to keep connected to other people.

47. Find and join groups where you are liked, appreciated, understood, enjoyed. Even more than most people, people with ADD take great strength from group support.

48. Don't stay too long where you *aren't* understood or appreciated. Just as people with ADD gain a great deal from supportive groups, they are particularly drained and demoralized by negative groups, and they have a tendency to stay with them too long, vainly trying to make things work out, even when all the evidence shows they can't.

49. Pay compliments. Notice other people. In general, get social training if you're having trouble getting along with people.

50. Set social deadlines. Without deadlines and dates your social life can atrophy. Just as you will be helped by structuring your business week, so, too, you will benefit from keeping your social calendar organized. This will help you stay in touch with friends and get the kind of social support you need.

While the tips above refer to treatment in adults, they are also applicable to children and adolescents in many instances. However, there is an important area the tips do not touch upon in the treatment of children, namely the classroom management of ADD. For children with ADD to do well, it is imperative that their teacher understand what ADD is and know how to work with these children in the classroom. The classroom experience can make or break the self-esteem, as well as the intellectual foundation, of children with ADD.

To assist in the classroom, we offer fifty tips written for ADD children in school. Since these tips were written explicitly for the classroom teacher, you may find it useful to share them with your child's school.

Teachers recognize what many professionals do not: that there is no one syndrome of ADD, but many; that ADD rarely occurs in "pure" form by itself, but rather usually shows up entangled with several other problems, such as learning disabilities or mood problems; that the face of ADD changes with the weather, that it's inconstant and unpredictable; and that the treatment for ADD, despite what may be serenely elucidated in various texts, remains a task of hard work and devotion. The effectiveness of any treatment for this disorder at school depends upon the knowledge and the persistence of the school and the individual teacher.

The following suggestions are intended for teachers of children of all ages. Some suggestions will be obviously more appropriate for younger children, others for older, but the unifying themes of structure, education, and encouragement pertain to all.

FIFTY TIPS
ON THE CLASSROOM MANAGEMENT
OF ADD

1. First of all, make sure what you are dealing with really is ADD. It is definitely not up to the teacher to diagnose ADD, but you can and should raise questions. Specifically, make sure someone has tested the child's hearing and vision recently, and make sure other medical problems have been ruled out. Make sure an adequate evaluation has been done. Keep questioning until you are convinced. The responsibility for seeing to all of this is the parents', not the teacher's, but the teacher can support the process.

2. Build your support. Being a teacher in a classroom where there are two or three kids with ADD can be extremely tiring. Seek the support of the school and the parents. Find a knowledgeable person with whom you can consult when you have a problem. (Learning specialist, child psychiatrist, social worker, school psychologist, pediatrician—the person's degree doesn't really matter; what matters is that he or she knows much about ADD, has seen many children with ADD, knows his or her way around a classroom, and can speak plainly). Keep in touch with the parents to ensure you are working toward the same goals. Call on your colleagues for help.

3. Know your limits. Don't be afraid to ask for help. You, as a teacher, cannot be expected to be an expert on ADD. You should feel comfortable in asking for help when you feel you need it.

4. Ask the child what will help. Children with ADD are often very intuitive. They can tell you how they can learn best, if you ask them. They are often too embarrassed to volunteer the information because it can be rather eccentric. But try to sit down with the child individually and ask how he or she learns best. The most insightful "expert" on how the child learns best is often the child himself or herself. It is amazing how often their opinions are ignored or not asked for. In addition, especially with older children, make sure the child understands what ADD is. This will help both of you.

5. Remember the emotional part of learning. These children need special help in finding enjoyment in the classroom, mastery instead of failure and frustration, excitement instead of boredom or fear. It is essential to pay attention to the emotions involved in the learning process.

6. Remember that ADD kids need structure. They need their environment to structure externally what they can't structure internally on their own. Make lists. Children with ADD benefit greatly from having a table or list to refer back to when they get lost in what they're doing.

They need reminders. They need previews. They need repetition. They need direction. They need limits. They need structure.

7. Post rules. Have them written down and in full view. The children will be reassured by knowing what is expected of them.

8. Repeat directions. Write down directions. Speak directions. Repeat directions. People with ADD need to hear things more than once.

9. Make frequent eye contact. You can "bring back" an ADD child with eye contact. Do it often. A glance can retrieve a child from a daydream or give permission to ask a question or just give silent reassurance.

10. Seat the ADD child near your desk or wherever you are most of the time. This helps stave off the drifting away that so bedevils these children.

11. Set limits, boundaries. This is containing and soothing, not punitive. Do it consistently, predictably, promptly, and plainly. *Don't* get into complicated, lawyerlike discussions of fairness. These long discussions are just a diversion. Take charge.

12. Have as predictable a schedule as possible. Post it on the blackboard or the child's desk. Refer to it often. If you are going to vary it, as most interesting teachers do, give lots of warning and preparation. Transitions and unannounced changes are very difficult for these children. They become discombobulated by them. Take special care to prepare for transitions well in advance. Announce what is going to happen, then give repeat reminders as the time approaches.

13. Try to help the children make their own schedules for after school in an effort to avoid one of the hallmarks of ADD: procrastination.

14. Eliminate, or reduce the frequency of, timed tests. There is no great educational value to timed tests, and they definitely do not allow many children with ADD to show what they know.

15. Allow for escape-valve outlets such as leaving class for a moment. If this can be built into the rules of the classroom, it will allow the child to leave the room rather than "lose it," and in so doing begin to learn important tools of self-observation and self-modulation.

16. Go for quality rather than quantity of homework. Children with ADD often need a reduced load. As long as they are learning the concepts, they should be allowed this. They will put in the same amount of study time, just not get buried under more than they can handle.

17. Monitor progress often. Children with ADD benefit greatly from frequent feedback. It helps keep them on track, lets them know what is expected of them and if they are meeting their goals, and can be very encouraging.

18. Break down large tasks into small tasks. This is one of the most crucial of all teaching techniques for children with ADD. Large tasks quickly overwhelm the child, and he recoils with an emotional "I'll-*never*-be-able-to-do-*that*" kind of response. By breaking down the task into manageable parts, each component looking small enough to be doable, the child can sidestep the emotion of being overwhelmed. In general, these kids can do a lot more than they think they can. By breaking tasks down, the teacher can let the child prove this to himself or herself. With small children this can be extremely helpful in avoiding tantrums born of anticipatory frustration. And with older children it can help them avoid the defeatist attitude that so often gets in their way.

19. Let yourself be playful, have fun, be unconventional, be flamboyant. People with ADD love play. They respond to it with enthusiasm. It helps focus attention—the kids' attention and yours as well. So much of their "treatment" involves boring stuff like structure, schedules, lists, and rules, you will want to show them that those things do not have to go hand in hand with being a boring person, a boring teacher, or running a boring classroom. Every once in a while, if you can let yourself be a little bit silly, that will help a lot.

20. Still again, watch out for overstimulation. Like a pot on the fire, ADD can boil over. You need to be able to reduce the heat in a hurry.

21. Seek out and underscore success as much as possible. These kids live with so much failure, they need all the positive handling they can get. This point cannot be overemphasized: these children need and benefit from praise. They love encouragement. They drink it up and grow from it. And without it they shrink and wither. Often the most devastating aspect of ADD is not the ADD itself, but the secondary damage done to self-esteem. So water these children well with encouragement and praise.

22. Memory is often a problem with these kids. Teach them little tricks like mnemonics, flash cards, etc. They often have problems with what Dr. Mel Levine, a developmental pediatrician and one of the great figures in the field of learning problems, calls "active working memory," the space available on your mind's table, so to speak. Any little tricks you can devise—cues, rhymes, codes, and the like—can help a great deal to enhance memory.

23. Use outlines. Teach outlining. Teach underlining. These techniques do not come easily to children with ADD, but once they learn them, the techniques can help a great deal in that they structure and shape what is being learned as it is being learned. This helps give the child a sense of mastery *during the learning process*, when he or she needs it most, rather than the dim sense of futility that is so often the defining emotion of these kids' learning process.

24. Announce what you are going to say before you say it. Say it. Then say what you have said. Since many ADD children learn better visually than by voice, if you can write what you're going to say as well as say it, that can be most helpful. This kind of structuring glues the ideas in place.

25. Simplify instructions. Simplify choices. Simplify scheduling. The simpler the verbiage the more likely it will be comprehended. And use colorful language. Like color-coding, colorful language keeps attention.

26. Use feedback that helps the child become self-observant. Children with ADD tend to be poor self-observers. They often have no idea how they come across or how they have been behaving. Try to give them this information in a constructive way. Ask questions like, "Do you know what you just did?" or "How do you think you might have said that differently?" or "Why do you think that other girl looked sad when you said what you said?" Ask questions that promote self-observation.

27. Make expectations explicit.

28. A point system is a possibility as part of behavioral modification or a reward system for younger children. Children with ADD respond well to rewards and incentives. Many are little entrepreneurs.

29. If the child has trouble reading social cues—body language, tone of voice, timing, and the like—try discreetly to offer specific and explicit advice as a sort of social coaching. For example, say, "Before you tell your story, ask to hear the other person's first," or, "Look at the other person when he's talking." Many children with ADD are viewed as indifferent or selfish, when in fact they just haven't learned how to interact. This skill does not come naturally to all children, but it can be taught or coached.

30. Teach test-taking skills.

31. Make a game out of things. Motivation improves ADD.

32. Separate pairs and trios, whole clusters even, that don't do well together. You might have to try many arrangements.

33. Pay attention to connectedness. These kids need to feel engaged, connected. As long as they are engaged, they will feel motivated and be less likely to tune out.

34. Give responsibility back to the child when possible. Let him devise his own method for remembering what to put into his bookbag, or let him ask you for help rather than your telling him he needs it.

35. Try a home-to-school-to-home notebook. This can really help with the day-to-day parent-teacher communication and avoid the crisis meetings. It also helps with the frequent feedback these kids need.

36. Try to use daily progress reports. These may be given to the child to hand on to his parents, or if the child is older, read directly to the child. These are not intended as disciplinary, but rather as informative, and encouraging.

37. Physical devices such as timers and buzzers can help with self-monitoring. For example, if a child cannot remember when to take his or her medication, a wrist alarm can help, rather than transferring responsibility to the teacher. Or during study time, a timer placed on his desk can help the child know exactly where the time is going.

38. Prepare for unstructured time. These kids need to know in advance what is going to happen so they can prepare for it internally. If they suddenly are given unstructured time, it can be overstimulating.

39. Praise, stroke, approve, encourage, nourish.

40. With older children, suggest that they write little notes to themselves to remind them of their questions about what is being taught. In essence, they can take notes not only on what is being said to them, but what they are thinking as well. This will help them listen more effectively.

41. Handwriting is difficult for many of these children. Consider developing alternatives. Suggest learning how to type. Consider giving some tests orally.

42. Be like the conductor of a symphony. Get the orchestra's attention before beginning (You may use silence, or the tapping of your baton, to do this.) Keep the class "in time," pointing to different parts of the room as you need their help.

43. When possible, arrange for students to have a "study buddy" in each subject, with phone number (adapted from Gary Smith, who has written an excellent series of suggestions on classroom management).

44. To avoid stigma, explain to the rest of the class and normalize the treatment the child receives.

45. Meet with parents often. Avoid the pattern of meeting only when there are problems or crises.

46. Encourage reading aloud at home. Read aloud in class as much as possible. Use storytelling. Help the child build the skill of staying on one topic.

47. Repeat, repeat, repeat.

48. Encourage physical exercise. One of the best treatments for ADD, in both children and adults, is exercise, preferably vigorous exercise. Exercise helps work off excess energy, it helps focus attention, and it stimulates certain hormones and neurochemicals that are beneficial. Suggest exercise that is fun: either team sports, such as volleyball and soccer, or individual exercise the child can do alone, such as swimming, jumping rope, or jogging.

49. With older children, stress preparation prior to coming into class. The better idea the child has of what will be discussed on any given day, the more likely the material will be mastered in class.

50. Always be on the lookout for sparkling moments. These kids are far more talented and gifted than they often seem. They are full of creativity, play, spontaneity, and good cheer. They tend to be resilient, always bouncing back. They tend to be generous of spirit, and glad to help out. They usually have a "special something" that enhances whatever setting they're in. Remember, there is a melody inside that cacophony, a symphony yet to be written.

Common Problems in the Treatment of ADD

The treatment of ADD varies considerably from person to person. Depending on the severity and complexity of the situation, the treatment may last from a few sessions to several years. Sometimes the treatment consists just in making the diagnosis and providing some education. Sometimes the treatment becomes very involved, requiring years of individual and family therapy, various medications, and much persistence and patience. Sometimes there is spectacular improvement; sometimes the change is so slow that it is difficult to recognize. There is no one recipe for the treatment of ADD. Each case presents its own problems and requires its own solutions. But there are general principles one can follow, and they have been outlined in this chapter.

In addition, there are particular obstacles one encounters frequently in the treatment of ADD. What follows is an analysis of ten of the most common.

1. Certain key individuals in the person's life—teacher, parent, spouse, employer, friend—do not accept the diagnosis of ADD.

They do not "believe in" ADD, and they do not want to talk about it. It almost seems to go against their religion or core ethics. They make the person with ADD feel like a fraud or a faker. Such a disbelieving response can undermine both the hope that begins with the diagnosis and the treatment. One often hears variations on the theme of "There's no such thing as ADD. It's just an excuse for being lazy. Put your energy into buckling down and working harder instead of pursuing bogus diagnoses."

Dealing with this response can be tricky. It is best that the individual with ADD not take the chief responsibility for handling it, because that usually leads to a struggle. It is wiser for the professional making the diagnosis to address whatever skepticism or disbelief may arise among those involved with his patient—be they extended family, spouse, teacher, employer, or friend.

The name of the game is education. Give the people the facts. Stay with the facts, confronting superstition, rumor, hearsay, prejudice, and misinformation with fact. Try to avoid inflammatory debate. Often those objecting to the diagnosis will be using their objections to conceal an emotional agenda. They may be angry with the person being diagnosed. They may resent him for all his past sins, and they don't want to see him get off with just a diagnosis. They want punishment. So they will grow angry at the notion of ADD, and try to discredit it. At these moments it is best to stay with the science, to stay with the facts we have about ADD. At some point one may need to address the angry feelings for what they are: angry feelings. They usually derive from past annoying behavior on the part of the person with ADD. These angry feelings are totally understandable and valid; however, they should not be used to invalidate a correct diagnosis of ADD.

2. After an initial burst of improvement, progress slows.

Often when the diagnosis of ADD is made—particularly in adults—there is an initial period of euphoria: at last there's a name for all the suffering the person has endured through the years. And usually there is an initial spurt of emotional growth as the treatment begins. However, after some months, the growth curve begins to level off, and the individual may become despondent. This is normal and understandable. The beginning of treatment is exciting, and it is disappointing to confront the fact that the treatment does not make all of life's problems go away. It is at this point of dismay that support is crucial—from a therapist, from a support group, from friends, from family, from books. The individual needs help to stay on course and not revert to old habits of negative thinking and self-sabotage.

3. The person with newly diagnosed ADD does not want to try medication.

His reasons are not quite clear, but he has a strong, negative reaction to the idea of medication. This is very common, both in adults, children, and parents of children. Understandably, no one wants to take medication unless it is necessary. Any medication, but particularly medication that affects the brain, deserves special care. No one should take medication against their wishes (unless they are mentally incompetent), and no one should be bullied into taking medication.

If the individual strongly objects to taking medication, he should not take it. However, before making this decision, it is best to get all the facts and make a scientific, rather than a superstitious, decision. Sometimes it takes months or even years before a person decides to try medication. Everyone has their own timetable. But the medication stands a much better chance of working if it is taken with a full understanding of its measured benefits and risks.

4. No medication seems to work.

The key here is to keep trying. Since the field of treatment for ADD, particularly in adults, is young, and since new medications are being developed all the time, and old medications are being tried in new ways, we are still operating largely on a trial-and-error basis. There is as yet no way to predict with certainty who will respond to what medication for the treatment of ADD. If one medication does not work, another one may. If the second does not work, a third may yet. And changes in dose and timing of dose can also make a big difference. It can take many months to find just the right medication, dosage, and dosing schedule.

Some people are exquisitely sensitive to medication. This is not a problem as long as it is recognized. Some people cannot tolerate anything but the tiniest dose of any medication. When they get a headache, they take a quarter of an aspirin. Just a sip of coffee keeps them up all night. So it can be with the medications used for ADD. Ten milligrams of Norpramin, a very small dose, may be too much and may make some people feel too activated. They may need to take 10 mg every other day, or, as one of my patients does, cut the pill in quarters and take 2.5 mg a day. It is important to keep this dosing sensitivity in mind, because some who could benefit from microdoses of medication give up too soon, thinking they cannot tolerate the medication at all.

It can be very frustrating for the patient—and the doctor—as they try to find just the right medication, or combination of medications, and the right dosage, but it is important to keep trying.

5. In filling some prescriptions, some pharmacists, in their attempt to comply with federal drug regulations, make consumers feel as though they are obtaining illicit drugs.

Looking up from behind the counter, the pharmacist's eyes seem to say, "You want Ritalin? What are you, some kind of drug dealer?" This is because of the association between Ritalin and "speed" in some people's minds. Until it is widely known that Ritalin is a safe, effective, and non-habit-forming treatment for ADD in adults, this unfortunate situation will probably continue to exist.

6. You can't find other people who understand what it feels like to have ADD.

One of the hardest parts about having ADD can be the feeling of being alone, of being "different," of feeling misunderstood. An excellent way to deal with this problem is to join a support group. These groups bring people together, supply information, build confidence and camaraderie, and over time reduce one's sense of loneliness or isolation. Most parts of the country now have active ADD groups. You can consult your local pediatrician, psychiatrist, neurologist, or hospital to locate these groups, or you can call the organizations listed above or at the end of this book.

7. It is difficult to decide whom to tell about ADD, and difficult to decide how to tell about it.

It should be possible to talk about having ADD without encountering suspicions or disbelief. However, this is rarely the case. People who know nothing about what ADD is—and that includes most people—can easily misunderstand a description of ADD. They may think it is an excuse for being lazy, or that it means the person is mentally ill, or that it is just a fancy word for stupid. In telling other people about ADD, one should anticipate these misunderstandings and not be thrown off by them. Have information ready with which to correct the misconceptions. Try not to get defensive, but rather be sympathetic with the other person's point of view. They have never heard of ADD and at first it sounds pretty fishy. "You mean, there's a neurological condition to explain why you're late, forgetful, impulsive, and disorganized? Give me a break," they may say. Be patient. Over time you will be able to explain it to them, and you may find they start thinking of other people who have it, maybe even themselves.

Bringing it up in the workplace can be particularly tricky. There is a law now to protect against discrimination on the basis of disabilities, and this includes ADD. The Americans with Disabilities Act of 1990 (ADA) makes it unlawful to discriminate in employment against a qualified individual with a disability. ADD is considered a disability that is guaranteed protection under this law. (For further information about this very significant law, write to the Equal Employment Opportunity Commission, 1801 L Street, NW, Washington, DC 20507, or telephone 202-663-4900.)

However, one may still fear the kind of discrimination that is hard to pin down, the kind of discrimination that invisibly can undermine one's career without being explicit enough to file a grievance over.

The best way of dealing with this situation is to find your way slowly. Make inroads, form alliances, and when you feel you have some basis of trust, bring up the subject of ADD in the abstract. Do some advance educating before you volunteer the fact that you have it yourself. It is well worth doing this, because if your boss can understand what ADD is, it can make your work life much more satisfying and productive. It is simple to devise an ADD program for the workplace as long as the workplace is receptive to it—and remember, an employer is bound, under law, to be receptive to what are called "reasonable accommodations" in the workplace. The same kinds of strategies that work in the classroom—structure, lists, reminders, breaking large tasks down into small, elimination of time limits, reduction of distracting stimuli, encouragement, and support—help a great deal in the workplace as long as the environment is receptive. And not only does the law mandate that the employer be receptive, it is also in the employer's best interest: people with ADD are hard, energetic workers. Tapping into their true potential is like harnessing rushing rapids to a hydroelectric turbine.

8. It is impossible to find a knowledgeable clinician in your area to diagnose and/or treat ADD or you can't find information on ADD.

There are several good places to go for information on where to get treatment. First, there is your state medical society, as well as your state neurological, pediatric, and psychiatric societies. Second, any medical school in your area can help you find a specialist in ADD. Just ask for the department of neurology or the department of pediatrics or the department of psychiatry or child psychiatry. Third, there are several organizations and newsletters devoted to ADD. These are excellent sources of information as well as support groups. We offer a partial listing here and a fuller listing at the end of this book.

Children with Attention-Deficit Disorders (CH.A.D.D.), a national organization, is a robust and active group offering information and support to all people involved with ADD. CH.A.D.D. and its indefatigable staff have been at the forefront of advocating both politically and socially for all those with ADD. Although originally founded to help children with ADD, CH.A.D.D. has now expanded to include adult ADD as well. The address of its headquarters is 499 NW 70th Avenue, Suite 308, Plantation, FL, 33317. Telephone: (305) 587-3700.

The Attention Deficit Information Network (AD-IN) is another excellent national organization devoted to helping people with ADD. Its address is 475 Hillside Avenue, Needham, MA 02194. Telephone: (617) 455-9895.

ADDendum is a newsletter for adults with ADD. For more information, write to its editor, Paul Jaffe, Box 296, Scarborough, NY 10510.

The ADDult Support Network is an innovative organization that publishes a newsletter for adults called the *ADDult News*. Address: 2620 Ivy Place, Toledo, OH 43613.

Challenge, Inc., publishes an excellent newsletter on ADD. Address: Box 488, West Newbury, MA 01985. Telephone: (508) 462-0495.

The Orton Dyslexia Society is a national organization devoted to the treatment of dyslexia in children and adults. The society and its highly distinguished directors and advisors are active in promoting the understanding of ADD, particularly as it interfaces with dyslexia. Address: Chester Building, Suite 382, 8600 LaSalle Road, Baltimore, MD 21204-6020. Telephone: (301) 296-6232.

The Appendix to this book contains more listings.

9. Attempts at structuring keep falling apart.

Once the individual understands the importance of structure and goes to the trouble of setting up a solid system of organization for himself, he often finds that the system keeps collapsing, or that his attempts to abide by the system repeatedly fail. This is where a coach can be invaluable. Rather than letting the system collapse, the coach can help the individual revise the system, or can offer encouragement to stay with the system. It is not surprising, after all, for it to take a while for the new system to start to work; it is replacing a lifetime of no system. However, the person with ADD can get discouraged very quickly, not wanting to experience another failure, and so back away. At these moments the coach can intervene, offering reassurance, support, and hope.

_____

10. There are lingering feelings of shame and embarrassment about having ADD.

This is a very common reaction, particularly if the syndrome is not explained properly. We tend to stigmatize any condition that effects the brain. However, with support and education the individual should come to realize that ADD has as many advantages as disadvantages, that there are many highly successful people in the world who have ADD, that the company of Mozart, Edison, Einstein, and Dustin Hoffman isn't bad, and that the most dangerous stigma comes from within. People with ADD should stand up and be proud. While their lives may be full of struggle, their contributions to the joy and humor, as well as the productivity, of this world are great.

▪ 9 ▪

A Local Habitation and a Name

THE BIOLOGY OF ADD

Attention deficit disorder lives in the biology of the brain and the central nervous system. Although environmental factors do influence the course of ADD over a lifetime, most practitioners in the field now agree that the characteristic problems of people with ADD stem from neurobiological malfunctioning. It is our understanding of the biological component of the syndrome that has revolutionized our thinking about ADD in the past decade and shaped our ability to treat it as effectively as we can today.

We still have much to learn. The exact mechanism underlying ADD remains unknown. There is no single lesion of the brain, no single neurotransmitter system, no single gene we have identified that triggers ADD. The precise workings of the brain that underlie ADD have so far escaped us, in part due to the extraordinary complexity of the attentional system.

The attentional system involves nearly all structures of the brain in one way or another. It governs our consciousness, our waking experience, our actions and reactions. It is the means through which we interact with our environment, whether that environment is composed of math problems, other people, or the mountains on which we ski.

Still, we have been able to take some steps toward defining, in terms of the anatomy and chemistry of the brain, the underpinnings of ADD.

269

With every step forward we become more sure what the disorder is not: it is not willful misbehaving, it is not a moral failing, it is not a lack of trying nor an inability to take an interest in the world. Neurobiological data now show that the syndrome is rooted in the central nervous system.

How psychologists and medical researchers, building on one another's insights over the past century, have come this far in defining the nature and causes of ADD is a fascinating story of deduction and persistence.

Where the story began is impossible to say. Certainly, the symptoms of ADD have been with us as long as history has been recorded. However, the modern story of ADD, the story of bringing those symptoms out of the realm of morality and punishment and into the realm of science and treatment, began somewhere around the turn of the century.

In 1904 one of the world's most prestigious medical journals, the British journal *Lancet*, published a little doggerel verse that might be the first published account of ADD in the medical literature.

The Story of Fidgety Philip

"Let me see if Philip can
Be a little gentleman;
Let me see if he is able
To sit still for once at the table."
Thus Papa bade Phil behave;
And Mama looked very grave.
But Fidgety Phil,
He won't sit still;
He wriggles,
And giggles,
And then, I declare,
Swings backwards and forwards,
And tilts up his chair,
Just like any rocking horse—
"Philip! I am getting cross!"
See the naughty, restless child
Growing still more rude and wild,
Till his chair falls over quite.
Philip screams with all his might,

Catches at the cloth, but then
That makes matters worse again.
Down upon the ground they fall,
Glasses, plates, knives, forks and all.
How Mama did fret and frown,
When she saw them tumbling down!
And Papa made such a face!
Philip is in sad disgrace . . .

Fidgety Phil has had many incarnations in popular culture, including Dennis the Menace and Calvin from "Calvin and Hobbes." Most everybody knows a little boy who bangs into things, climbs to the top of trees, scales the furniture, beats up on his siblings, talks back, and displays all the characteristics of being out of control, maybe a little bit of a bad seed, despite the generosity and best efforts of the parents. How can this be explained? And how is it that this person has existed throughout the centuries?

The story might start with the earlier-mentioned George Frederic Still, M.D., who in 1902 described a group of twenty children who were defiant, excessively emotional, passionate, lawless, spiteful, and had little inhibitory volition. This group consisted of three boys for every girl, and their troubling behaviors all had appeared before the age of eight. What was most striking to Still was that this group of kids had been raised in benign environments, with "good-enough" parenting. Indeed, those children who had been subject to poor child-rearing were excluded from his analysis. He speculated, in light of the adequate rearing these children received, there might be a biological basis to the unbounded behavior, a genetically inherited proneness toward moral corruption. He gained confidence in his theory when he discovered that some members of these children's families had psychiatric difficulties such as depression, alcoholism, and conduct problems.

While it was certainly possible that the pathology was psychological only, and was passed down from generation to generation as a kind of family neurosis, Still proposed that genetics and biology should be considered at least as much as free will in assessing the cause of these children's problems. This was a new way of thinking.

Although it would be decades before there was conclusive evidence bearing Still out, his new way of thinking was pivotal. In the nineteenth century—and before—"bad" or uncontrollable behavior in children was seen as a moral failing. Either the parents or the children or both should be held responsible. The usual "treatment" for these children was physical punishment. Pediatric textbooks from that era are full of descriptions of how to beat a child and exhortations on the necessity of doing so. As clinicians began to speculate that neurology, rather than the devil, was governing behavior, a kinder, more effective approach to child-rearing emerged.

The puzzling contradiction between upbringing and behavior in this population of children captured the imagination of turn-of-the-century psychologists. Still's observations supported the theory of William James, the father of American psychology. James saw the deficits in what he called inhibitory volition, moral control, and sustained attention as being causally related to each other through an underlying neurological defect. Cautiously, he speculated on the possibility of either a decreased threshold in the brain for inhibition of response to various stimuli, or a syndrome of disconnection within the cortex of the brain in which intellect was dissociated from "will," or social conduct.

The trail of Still and James was picked up in 1934, when Eugene Kahn and Louis H. Cohen published a piece called "Organic Driveness" in the *New England Journal of Medicine*. Kahn and Cohen asserted that there was a biological cause for the hyperactive, impulse-ridden, morally immature behavior of the people they were seeing who had been hit by the encephalitis epidemic of 1917–18. This epidemic left some victims chronically immobile (as those described by Oliver Sacks in his book *Awakenings*) and others chronically insomniac, with impaired attention, impaired regulation of activity, and poor impulse control. In other words, the characteristics plaguing this latter group were what we now take to be the diagnostic triad of ADD symptoms: distractibility, impulsivity, and restlessness. Kahn and Cohen were the first to provide an elegant description of the relationship between an organic disease and the symptoms of ADD.

At about the same time, Charles Bradley was developing another line of evidence linking ADD-like symptoms to biological roots. In 1937, Bradley reported success in using benzedrine, a stimulant, to treat behaviorally disordered children. This was a serendipitous discovery that was quite counterintuitive; why should a stimulant help hyperactive children become less stimulated? Like many important discoverers in medicine, Bradley couldn't explain his discovery; he could only report its veracity.

Soon this population of children would be labeled MBD—minimal brain dysfunction—and treated with Ritalin and Cylert, two other stimulants that were found to have a dramatic effect on the behavioral and social symptoms of the syndrome. By 1957 there was an attempt to match the symptoms of what was by then called the "hyperkinetic syndrome" with a specific anatomical structure in the brain. Maurice Laufer, in *Psychosomatic Medicine*, placed the location of dysfunction at the thalamus, a midbrain structure. Laufer saw hyperkinesis as proof that the work of the thalamus, which was to filter stimuli, had gone awry. Although his hypothesis was never proved, it did promote the conception of the disorder as one defined by an overactivity of a part of the brain.

Throughout the sixties, clinical skill with the hyperkinetic population improved, and the clinician's powers of observation grew more attuned to the nuances of the children's behavior. It became more apparent to the clinician's eye that the syndrome somehow was due to genetically based malfunctioning of biological systems rather than to bad parenting or bad behavior. The definition of the syndrome has evolved through family studies and statistical analysis of epidemiological data that absolve parents and children of blame (although the pernicious and unfair tendency to blame parents and children persists to this day among the ill informed).

By the early seventies the definition of the syndrome included not just the behaviorally evident hyperactivity, but also the more subtle symptoms of distractibility and impulsivity. By then, we knew that ADD clustered in families and was not caused by bad parenting. We knew that the symptoms were often improved by the use of stimulant medication. We thought we knew, but couldn't prove, that ADD had a biological basis, and that it was genetically transmitted. However, this more accurate and encompassing view was not accompanied by any major new discoveries related to the biological causes of the syndrome.

Due to the lack of further biological evidence, some people argued that ADD was a mythical disorder, an excuse contrived to exonerate reprobate children and their parents. As is usually the case in psychiatry, the intensity of the debate was inversely proportional to the availability of factual information.

As in a good mystery, the journey from suspicion to proof, from speculation to empirical evidence, from Kahn and Cohen to Paul Wender and Alan Zametkin and Rachel Gittleman-Klein and the other current researchers, has been riddled with false leads, multiple possibilities, contradictory findings, and many gut reactions of all kinds.

One of the first attempts to unite the effects of the stimulants with what we know about the brain was made by C. Kornetsky, who in 1970 proposed the Catecholamine Hypothesis of Hyperactivity. Catecholamines are a class of compounds that includes the neurotransmitters norepinephrine and dopamine. Since the stimulants affect the norepinephrine and dopamine neurotransmitter systems by increasing the amount of these neurotransmitters, Kornetsky concluded that ADD possibly was caused by an underproduction or underutilization of these neurotransmitters. Although this hypothesis is still tenable, biochemical studies and clinical tests of neurotransmitter metabolites in urine over the past two decades have not been able to document the specific role of the catecholamines in ADD.

No single neurotransmitter system may be the sole regulator of ADD. Neurons can convert dopamine into norepinephrine. Many of the drugs that act on the catecholamines act on serotonin. Some of the drugs that act on serotonin can act on norepinephrine and dopamine. And we can't rule out the role of other neurotransmitters like GABA (gamma amino butyric acid), which have showed up in some biochemical studies. The most likely possibility is that the effect of dopamine and norepinephrine and serotonin is key and drugs that alter these neurotransmitters will have the most telling effect on the symptomatology of ADD.

So can we say that ADD is a chemical imbalance? Like most questions in psychiatry, the answer is yes and then again no. No, we have not found a good way to measure the specific imbalances in the neurotransmitter systems that may be responsible for the ADD. But yes, there is enough evidence that neurochemical systems are altered in people with ADD to state that the problem derives from the chemistry of the brain. Most likely, it is a dysregulation along the catecholamine-serotonin axis, a dance where one misstep by one partner creates a misstep by the other, which creates another misstep by the first. Before they know it, these dance partners are out of step not just with each other but with the music—and who is to say how it happened?

Alan Zametkin and his colleagues at the National Institutes of Mental Health may not have defined how it happened, but they did demonstrate for sure that it was happening, that the biochemical dance was different in the brains of people with ADD as compared to the brains of people without ADD. Zametkin created a bridge where before there had been only a leap of faith. His work is so important that it is worth a close look.

Zametkin's study in 1990 examined activity in the brain in adults with and without ADD. The study did this by watching how the brain uses glucose, its energy source, during a continuous performance task. The use of glucose is a good marker of metabolic activity. Continuous performance tasks are tests that have been designed specifically to measure attention and vigilance to stimuli. In Zametkin's study, subjects had to indicate if and when they heard particular tones, using a push-button apparatus hooked up to a computer. This test was administered to twenty-five adults who had a childhood history of hyperactivity and were diagnosed with ADD according to Wender's Utah Criteria. All of these adults, eighteen of whom were men and seven of whom were women, were the biological parents of children with ADD. They were matched to a group of fifty controls who did not have ADD but who shared the same demographic characteristics as themselves.

To measure glucose metabolism Zametkin's group used PET scans. The PET, or positron emission tomograph, can be described as an expensive camera that records the radioactivity given off by the brain after it has used radio-labeled glucose during a specific task. Through computer manipulation, a composite of numerous data points are assembled into an image that we can look at and use for comparisons. What Zametkin found using this technique was a deficit in glucose uptake, and hence energy use in the brains of subjects with ADD as compared to controls. Overall, the ADD group metabolized glucose at rates 8 percent lower than the control group.

The reduction in glucose uptake was widespread throughout different regions of the brain. Most informative is that the decrease in metabolic activity was largest in the prefrontal and premotor regions of the brain. The frontal region is the major regulator of behavior. It keeps impulses in check, allows us to plan and anticipate, and serves as the place where we initiate behavior. It gets input from the lower brain, which regulates arousal, screens out irrelevant stimuli, and serves as the seat of fight-or-flight reactions. It receives input from the limbic system, the seat of emotion, hunger, thirst, sexuality, and other physiological impulses. And it probably is the site of working memory, the combination of moment-to-moment experience and long-term memory. Thus the frontal lobes synthesize sensory and cognitive information, they orchestrate attention, and they function as the gateway to action.

As Zametkin pointed out, the results of the PET scans indicating depressed frontal lobe activity are consistent with what other researchers have claimed to be the functional neuroanatomy of ADD. Both J. A. Mattes and C. T. Gualtieri have speculated that the frontal lobes were involved in ADD because of the similarity between ADD symptoms and frontal-lobe syndromes resulting from injuries or lesions to the frontal areas. This observation was codified by the work of G. J. Chelune in 1986 as the frontal-lobe hypothesis, which posited that hyperactivity and impulsivity are basically a form of disinhibition. According to this hypothesis, many of the symptoms of ADD arise because the brain loses its ability to put on the brakes sufficiently. This is due to disturbed inhibition in the cortex, or outer layer, of the brain. Without cortical inhibition, the brain fails to block inappropriate responses and fails to send out appropriate inhibitory messages. According to Chelune's frontal-lobe hypothesis, the cortex of the frontal lobe is where the action is—or isn't—in ADD. Inhibition breaks down; impulsivity and hyperactivity rise concurrently.

In addition to giving support to Chelune's hypothesis, Zametkin's findings also support the 1984 work of H. C. Lou and his colleagues, who found decreased blood flow in the frontal regions of the brain in people with ADD. Lou's study also indicated a deficit in blood flow in the right hemisphere of the brain as compared to the left. This is intriguing, as some researchers think that ADD is related to right-hemisphere dysfunction. The right hemisphere generally controls our so-called executive or decision-making capacities, our visual-spatial abilities, and our ability to process many sources of stimuli simultaneously. Some specific deficits associated with right-hemisphere dysfunction include topographagnosia (getting lost a lot!) and social-emotional learning disabilities. Martha Denckla, a specialist in the neuropsychiatry of learning disabilities, points out that right-hemisphere problems could prevent one from grasping configurations of many details, "getting the big picture," so to speak. Certainly, the picture that is painted of right-hemisphere disabilities sounds just like the complaints we hear from patients about always losing their keys, always getting lost, never paying attention to the big picture, and never quite understanding other people.

Is there accordance between what may be the functional neuroanatomy of ADD and the role of specific neurotransmitter systems? Yes, indeed. The prefrontal areas of the brain are rich in catecholamines, and some research has shown that aged monkeys whose prefrontal cortices are deficient in dopamine and norepinephrine perform poorly in delayed-response tests. Delayed-response tests, like continuous-performance tests, measure attention and vigilance; they also measure the functioning of working memory. In addition, dopamine forms a pathway between the motor center and the frontal regions of the brain, and another pathway from the limbic center to the frontal regions of the brain. Dopamine neurons from these lower areas pass through the central frontal lobe to reach the prefrontal cortex. This doesn't prove anything, but it does suggest a role for dopamine in connecting motor activity, emotion, attention, and impulse control, since dopamine neurons run through the regions of the brain that regulate these functions.

Recently, it has been speculated that dopamine may even regulate the overall output of the cortex. A problem with the use of the catecholamines by the frontal areas would account for the lack of impulse control, the attention problems, and learning problems. And although it is more than probable that other neurotransmitters and other brain structures influence the expression of ADD, the catecholamine-frontal area relationship is too clearly illustrative of ADD characteristics to dismiss.

Interestingly enough, the role of working memory may be significant in the ADD syndrome. As investigated and defined by Patricia Goldman-Rakic, working memory could be the cause of many of the clinical manifestations of the syndrome, since working memory controls our ability to review our past experience, evaluate our current experience, and plan for the future. Rakic vividly describes what would happen if working memory were to fail: the world would be viewed by the brain as a series of disconnected events, like a series of unrelated slides, rather than as a continuous sequence, like a movie. We have heard the world as poignantly described by our patients with ADD, sometimes in the same words. Life seems discontinuous. There is no sense of history. Each new experience is met cold.

As is known by clinicians who work with the ADD population, and by parents of ADD children, and by adults who have ADD, one of the most frustrating aspects of ADD is the inability to profit from one's experience, the inability to focus on consequences, the inability to navigate through tasks or social situations or the world at large by using what has been learned previously. If working memory is expressed in the frontal areas of the brain, and if the frontal areas of people with ADD are underactive, could we conclude that people with ADD have impaired working memory? Probably not conclusively. Yet future research might prove this, as our methods of investigation and measurement become more sophisticated.

■ ■ ■

What none of this explains is why ADD seems to run in families and seems to be passed down through the generations. Most of the studies that have examined the familial risk of ADD have been epidemiological, either looking at the incidence of ADD in parents, offspring, and siblings, or looking at its preponderance among fraternal and identical twins. The work of Joseph Biederman and colleagues has shown that up to about 30 percent of parents of ADD children have ADD themselves. Other researchers have found a similar rate of ADD among parents. Research also indicates that relatives of ADD children have a greater risk for ADD than the relatives of controls. No research to date has been able to investigate the statistical likelihood that ADD adults will have ADD children, though existing research, and scientific intuition, leads us to believe that if you have ADD, there is certainly an increased probability that one of your children will have ADD. What we cannot do as yet is put a number on that increased probability.

Twin studies repeatedly find higher rates of ADD in identical twins as compared to fraternal twins. What does this really mean? Fraternal twins are genetically related in the same way as siblings are—the only difference being that fraternal twins share the same environment for the first nine months of development. Identical twins, on the other hand, share not only the same prenatal and postnatal environment, but also the same genetic material. A higher incidence of ADD in people who share the same genetic blueprint, versus those who share everything but, means that the genetic makeup of the individual must be influencing the expression of the disorder. One large study (127 sets of identical twins and 111 sets of fraternal twins) recently found that in 51 percent of the identical sets both twins had ADD, while only 33 percent of those in the fraternal group shared the ADD diagnosis.

We might wonder why we don't see 100 percent concordance in identical twins. Nobody seems to know the answer. Identical-twin studies of most genetically based disorders, including schizophrenia, show about a 50 percent concordance rate. The ADD twin studies reflect this same pattern and are considered to be valid evidence that there is a genetic predisposition to the disorder.

The strongest evidence for the genetic underpinnings of ADD may be yet to come. As we saw when looking at the progression of research into the neurobiology of ADD, solid scientific inquiry usually begins with speculation, advances through testable hypotheses and replicable findings, and culminates in empirical evidence. The work of Biederman and others confirms that something genetic is happening in this disorder. But what is it? One of the first clues might be contained in a controversial 1991 study published in the *Journal of the American Medical Association* by a nationwide team of investigators headed by David Comings and Brenda Comings. This study considered the role played by a particular dopamine receptor in neuropsychiatric disorders. The receptor, called the D2 receptor, is made by a particular gene. The gene has been implicated in early-onset hereditary alcoholism. Scientists have postulated that it may be associated with a number of other psychiatric disorders.

The team used a sample of more than three hundred people. They discovered that the gene was found more frequently in patients with Tourette's syndrome, ADD, autism, and alcoholism than in those without. The investigators do not claim in their report that the gene is the primary cause of the preceding disorders. But they do claim it is a modifying gene—a gene which makes some neuropsychiatric disorders worse if these disorders already are present, due to some unknown, primary gene. The Comings team concludes that their study supports a genetic basis for ADD. Although some researchers do not agree with the findings for various technical reasons, the study may signal the next wave of sophistication determining the genetic basis of ADD by linking it with other kinds of disorders. For example, if one base gene governs a certain brain formation, it may be that other modifying genes can produce a variety of syndromes by playing variations, so to speak, on the formation governed by the basic gene.

At the least, current evidence supports the contention that ADD is a syndrome of genetic origin where one's biological system has experienced some kind of change—be it chemical, neuroanatomical, or maturational—and has been rendered out of balance. It is the lack of balance, the dysregulation of the body's neurobiological system, that impairs one's ability to pay selective attention to one's surroundings. The world becomes a land without street signs, the individual a car in bad need of a tune-up. The vastness of the attentional system partially accounts for the variation of ADD "types." Where one individual needs an oil change, the next needs spark plugs replaced. Where one individual is withdrawn and overwhelmed by stimuli, the next is hyperactive and can't get enough stimuli. Where one is frequently anxious, the other is depressed. To compensate, each develops his or her own coping strategies that developmentally add to, or subtract from, the brain's various subsystems. So Mr. A becomes a stand-up comedian, and manic. Ms. B becomes an architectural wizard with obsessive-compulsive traits. Their offspring become a sculptor and a stunt pilot. None of them can balance their checkbook. And all of them wish they had more time in the day.

With such diversity in the disorder, can we encompass and describe ADD in a way that is in line with research and clinical experience, and also allows us to illustrate and sort out the many symptoms and test results that we find in ADD? There are several schools of thought on the best way to understand the actual deficit in attention that plagues individuals with ADD. Each has its merit and each can serve as a metaphor for the syndrome. For instance, Paul Wender, in the early seventies, proposed that ADD was due to a decreased activation of the brain's reward center and its connections. He believes the ADD person's insensitivity to consequences arises from an inability to be "conditioned" with praise and punishment because of lowered activity in the neural systems that modulate reward-and-punishment responses. Wender's argument is compelling, since it explains so many of the behavioral problems we see in ADD, and is consistent with neuroanatomical and neurochemical studies.

Russell Barkley similarly describes the primary problem in ADD as a deficit in the motivation system, which makes it impossible to stay on task for any length of time unless there is constant feedback, constant reward. Barkley's work is often misunderstood and taken to mean that the child or adult is unmotivated and, therefore, lazy. But there is a difference between labeling someone as unmotivated and labeling someone as lacking the biological predisposition to stay on task without frequent reminders: one is a value judgement, the other a description of a neurological disorder. "There is no ADD while playing Nintendo," Dr. Barkley is fond of saying, not meaning, of course, that the child will be motivated only in desirable situations, but that the rapid, ever-compelling, visually complex nature of the video game, and its constant rewards, sufficiently engage the child to rivet attention.

Low activity in the frontal areas of the brain could explain the breakdown in goal-directed behavior and self-regulation as described by Barkley. If there is a problem in maturation or a problem in regulation of the frontal lobes and the systems that feed into them, the internal cues that keep us on task and focused on an outcome would not be loud enough or strong enough or good enough. There is another group of researchers that views the deficits in attention as a problem with arousal in the brain system. This group similarly believes that the messages ADD folks are getting are not loud enough or good enough, but they believe it's due to the receipt of external cues, or to the lack of receipt of external cues, rather than due to a lack of internal ones.

Larry Silver, a renowned figure for many years in the field of ADD, describes the syndrome as a faulty filter system in the lower parts of the brain known as the reticular activating system. In Silver's model this injured filter system, which is regulated by the catecholamines, doesn't screen out irrelevant information and sensory stimuli as efficiently as it should, thereby letting everything that registers at the desk of the reticular activating system arrive in the rooms of the frontal regions of the brain. The individual is bombarded, taking care of ten thousand guests in a hotel built for one thousand, on overload all the time, receiving messages about every minute aspect of his or her experience. It is no wonder, then, that the individual would be distractible or, as Silver would argue, inclined to withdraw from it all and shut the damned hotel down.

Another way to understand ADD is to think in terms of underarousal of the brain system. According to this view, the person with ADD does not receive enough input from the lower area of the brain to the frontal areas. Thus the distractible, hyperactive, and risk-taking behavior of ADD attempts to heighten the level of arousal in the frontal cortex. The optimal-arousal theory, as this is sometimes called, underlies some very effective and innovative learning strategies. Sydney Zentall believes that heightening the power of relevant stimuli allows the child to learn much more effectively. Because children with ADD notice and usually attend to novel stimuli, a key to educating these kids is to "dress up" educational lessons and tools with colors, animation, and diversity, while limiting all extraneous stimuli and opportunities for distraction. We have seen this strategy work in adults with ADD, as well. For example, color-coded notes, files, keys, etc., often help the adult get organized. Dr. Zentall, describing the management of her own ADD, talks of carrying small toys around in her pocketbook with which to amuse herself during boring meetings or times of low stimulation. One of the most engaging and lively of all researchers in the field of ADD, Zentall has concocted many practical ways to enhance novelty and stimulation in everyday life, such as taking notes on her own thoughts while listening to other people talk, doing at least two things at once while listening to a lecture, or adding as much color and other visual pizzazz to one's surroundings as possible.

The model for ADD that seems to fit best from our point of view, however, comes from the school of thought that thinks more in terms of inhibition and disinhibition than motivation or arousal. Chelune, Gualtieri, Lou, and a number of other researchers and clinicians have framed ADD as an inability to stop receiving messages rather than as an inability to receive the right messages. These people always feel a press for the next thing and the next thing and the next thing. The ADD individual is captive to the events of the external world. Although the difference may seem semantic, it is significant in the way we describe ADD. It stresses that the positive components of the syndrome will assist the problematic ones. Instead of framing the syndrome as an inability to pay attention to cues, this definition focuses on the ability of someone with ADD to pay attention to many more cues than the average person. Instead of describing ADD as an inability to concentrate, this model presents it as the ability to concentrate on everything. The world always is alive and ripe with sources of interest. This analysis is supported by the scientific findings and also has the benefit of removing the stigma of laziness and the burden of guilt with which ADD people have struggled most of their lives. It allows them to start considering their strengths, rather than dwelling on weaknesses.

The disinhibition model fits with what we know about the functional neuroanatomy and the neurochemistry of the brain. As noted earlier, the frontal cortex and its associated systems and neurotransmitters are crucial for the process of inhibiting behaviors, thoughts, actions, emotions—the impulses with which we all live but which some of us regulate more easily than others. If there is a problem in maturation in the frontal systems in ADD, or a problem in regulation of the dopamine system that feeds into the frontal areas, ADD very well could be described as a problem with inhibitory capacity.

·If ADD is a problem with inhibiting, we can understand the phenomenon of time collapsing in on itself for people with ADD: instead of being able to carve out discrete activities that would create a sensation of separate moments, the person cannot stop the relentless flow of events. Everything runs together, unbraked, uninhibited. We hear the ADD adult so painfully describing the verbal rush, the inability to stop the words, and the verbal paralysis, or stuttering, derived from the inability to stop the thoughts long enough to find the words. The social intrusiveness that is so characteristic of those who have ADD is the inability to stop at the other's boundaries. The failure to form intimate relationships is the inability to pause long enough even to listen to the other person, let alone to understand and respect the other's needs. The impulsivity, the lack of planning, and the outbursts are the inability to restrain the flow of action and feeling.

We also see people with ADD hyperfocusing on an activity, like rock-climbing or driving or work, probably because it allows them to forget about the expectations associated with "time." Our patients frequently report that they are their most calm when completely caught up in the thrill of it all, whatever the "all" may be. It could be fun, a catastrophe, or a life-or-death crisis. These situations allow the ADD person not only to get into forward motion, but also to forget, to disregard that they need brakes in the first place. In an emergency, it's full speed ahead. What a relief.

The clinician's challenge is to find a way to allow the ADD person to put on the brakes. From a biological perspective, one of the most successful strategies has been the use of medications. The medications employed to treat ADD interact with the catecholamine system in such a way as to correct the dysregulated attentional processes and stop the rush of experience. As detailed in chapter 8, the medications commonly used include the stimulants and the tricyclic antidepressants. The stimulants—Ritalin, Cylert, Dexedrine—act on the catecholamine system. The tricyclics—desipramine and imipramine—act on the catecholamine system and on the serotonin system, with the greatest effect being on norepinephrine. Both types of drugs increase the levels of the neurotransmitters they affect, allowing more of the particular neurotransmitter to be available for use by the brain.

Because we do not know precisely what is causing the ADD, we cannot know exactly where the drugs are working. They could work at the beginning or at the end of the line, in the lower brain or in the cortex. If they work in the lower part of the brain, and effect the modulation of arousal, they might be up-regulating the entire system and letting only relevant stimuli make its way to the frontal lobes. If they work directly in the front regions of the brain, they might awaken an otherwise sleepy cortex. Wender speculates that the drugs work in the middle of this loop, in the limbic system. He proposes that the action of norepinephrine in the limbic system is impaired, and since incoming stimuli from the lower brain must pass through the limbic system before reaching the frontal lobes, it is possible that a problem in regulation of this area would cause the disinhibition in the frontal regulatory processes.

Either way, we feel the effects of the drugs in the cortex, the treetops of our brains. The drugs enhance the functioning and use of neurotrans-mitters in the frontal regions and smooth out regulatory and attentional functioning. Their effectiveness has been documented in numerous studies, through numerous means. The use of stimulants generally improves scores in continuous-performance tests, school performance, behavioral rating scales, and self-reports.

And the effect is immediate, unlike the drug action in almost any other neurobiologic disorder. The immediacy of action indicates that the drugs have a direct effect at the synaptic level, the cellular juncture where one neuron passes a message to the next. Right away they improve the way one brain cell communicates with another, as if they have come along and swept out the blockage in the synapse. Other medications that effect the brain, such as those used to treat depression, schizophrenia, panic, and anxiety, work to reset the neuronal network. They gradually change receptor sensitivity to neurotransmitters, or otherwise change the structure of the neuronal communication system. They work as traffic coordinators instead of street sweepers, rerouting information along different channels.

It may be that the stimulants create an equilibrium in the chemistry of the frontal regions of the brain without requiring the whole system to change. This allows tonic control of the frontal systems; that is, the job of the frontal lobes becomes easier and less prone to interruptions. Inhibiting thoughts and feelings and actions becomes easier. The beginnings and endings of moments in time become clear, and deliberation, planning, and pausing finally become possible. Life becomes continuous rather than disjointed.

■ ■ ■

In many ways, our understanding of the biology of ADD is still in its first chapter. The next few decades will be more exciting as our ability to test, measure, and evaluate the biological processes implicated in neurobiologic disorders expands. Although it is doubtful we will find the magic bullet that can rid an individual of ADD, one day our methods of treatment might be sophisticated enough so that the frustrations and uncertainties of living with the syndrome will be eased, and those with ADD can draw confidently on their thoughts.

■ ■ ■

ACKNOWLEDGMENTS

One of the great pleasures of writing this book was the help and encouragement we received from many sources.

Our patients helped us first of all. They created this book. By teaching us about ADD and by giving us their stories to share with others, they gave of themselves in a most personal way. We hope this book lives up to their generosity.

Many other individuals helped us. We thank Sandra Freed Thomas, past president of CH.A.D.D., a national ADD organization, for her encouragement from the start; Jill Kneerim, our agent, for her disciplined guidance; Susan Grace Galassi for her early reading of the manuscript and Jonathan Galassi for his support all along; Priscilla Vail for all her help, particularly with the dyslexias and other language problems; the late Carol Rinzler, for so many kinds of help; the team at Pantheon, including our editor, Linda Healey, for her suggestions which were always helpful and for her exacting and imaginative reading of the manuscript which improved it greatly, her assistant, Jennifer Trone, for skillfully keeping us focused while seeming to remain unobtrusive, and Fred Wiemer for his superb copy editing.

We are thankful to Lyn, Tom, and Tim Bliss for many helpful suggestions; James Hallowell for his persistent skepticism which helped us keep a balanced view; Ellen D'Ambrosia for her warm support; Peter Metz for his invaluable consultations, freely given no matter how busy he was himself; Kevin Murphy, Russell Barkley, and the rest of the staff of the University of Massachusetts Medical Center ADD Clinic for their help and advice on ADD in adults; Betsy Busch for her always useful advice; Edward Khantzian for his most helpful ideas regarding ADD and addictions; Paul Wender for his encouragement and counsel; Catherine Leveroni, Andrea Miller, and the rest of John Ratey's staff at Medfield State Hospital for their tireless attention to many details.

We are indebted to Lisa Poast for the list of support groups that appears in the Appendix; Elizabeth Leimkuhler for many observations on ADD in adults; Leopold Bellak, for an early conversation that helped start us thinking; John and Ben Hallowell, for encouraging their little brother to write; and our wives, Sue George Hallowell and Nancy Blackmore, for their ideas and their support, patience, and enthusiasm for this project from beginning to end.

—E. M. H.
—J. J. R.

■ ■ ■

Where to Find Help

If you believe that you, or someone you know, may have ADD and you would like additional information, a good place to start is your own physician. If your doctor is not expert on the syndrome, he or she can probably point you in the right direction. The local medical society or psychological society is another good resource, as is any medical school in your area. The departments of psychiatry, psychology, child psychiatry, neurology, pediatrics, and family medicine would be the most likely departments to have experts.

If you still have trouble finding help, we offer this appendix as an additional resource. However, we cannot emphasize too strongly the following point: *Do not diagnose and treat yourself. Get professional consultation.*

Organizations to Contact for Information About ADD

National Attention Deficit Disorder Association (ADDA)
1788 Second Street, Suite 200
Highland Park, IL 60035
(847) 432-ADDA (2332)

ADDA provides educational resources on Attention Disorders to individuals and support organizations.

Adult ADHD Clinic
University of Massachusetts Medical Center
Department of Psychiatry
55 Lake Avenue North
Worcester, MA 01655
(508) 856-2552

This clinic, under the direction of Kevin Murphy, Ph.D., serves adults. U. Mass. also has an internationally famous clinic for treatment and research in childhood ADD under the guidance of Russell Barkley, Ph.D.

Adult Attention Deficit Foundation
132 North Woodward Avenue
Birmingham, MI 48009
(313) 540-6335

CH.A.D.D.
(Children and Adults with Attention Deficit Disorder)
499 NW 70th Avenue, Suite 308
Plantation, FL 33317
(305) 587-3700
Fax: (305) 587-4599

CH.A.D.D. is the national and international nonprofit parent-support organization for children and adults with ADD.

SOME STATE ADVOCACY GROUPS

ADD Advocacy Group
8091 South Ireland Way
Aurora, CO 80016
(303) 690-7548

CH.A.D.D. National State Networking Committee
499 NW 70th Avenue, Suite 308
Plantation, FL 33317
(305) 587-3700

This committee offers guidance and expertise in the formation of CH.A.D.D. state councils throughout the country, which can serve as advocacy groups.

Organizations to Contact for Information About Learning Disabilities and Dyslexia

Orton Dyslexia Society
8600 LaSalle Road
Baltimore, MD 21204-6020
(301) 296-0232

A great and proud organization full of dedicated individuals, the Orton Dyslexia Society has stood strong for many decades advocating for research, education, and equality.

A packet of information on Dyslexia is available for $4.00.

ERIC Clearinghouse on Adult Career and Continuing Education
(800) 848-4815

This "hotline" can provide important information about employment possibilities, career changes, educational resources, etc.

National Network of Learning Disabled Adults
(602) 941-5112

National Center for Learning Disabilities
381 Park Avenue South, Suite 1420
New York, New York 10016
(212) 545-7510

National Information Center for Children and Youth with Disabilities
(NICHY)
P.O. Box 1492
Washington, DC 20013-1492

Northeast Conference on Learning Disabilities and Mental Health
P.O. Box 271336
West Hartford, CT 06127-1336
(203) 232-6112

Annual conference with workshops, research presentations, and topics related to LD/ADD and MH. Sponsored by Learning Disabilities Association of Connecticut, 139 North Main Street, West Hartford, CT 06107.

Self-Help Clearing House
St. Claire's Riverside Medical Center
Pocono Road
Denville, NJ 07834
(201) 625-9565

Provides local and national referral services and carries support-group listings.

Learning Disabilities Association of America
4156 Library Road
Pittsburgh, PA 15234
(412) 341-1515

Newsletters

ADDendum [for adults with ADD]
c/o C.P.S.
5041-A Backlick Road
Annandale, VA 22003
Paul Jaffe, Editor

This quarterly publication for adults with ADD includes reviews of recent research, interviews and articles by leading researchers and clinicians specializing in adult ADD, question-and-answer columns, and articles and poetry written by adults with ADD. In addition, *ADDendum* has available a nationwide listing of Adult ADD support groups.

This publication is available at a cost of $25.00 per year for four issues.

ADDult News
c/o Mary Jane Johnson
ADDult Support Network
2620 Ivy Place
Toledo, OH 43613

This newsletter includes substantive articles about issues relevant to adults with ADD, as well as a listing of resources and support-group announcements. *ADDult News* welcomes letters, comments, personal stories, poems, and artwork.

This publication is available at a cost of $12.00 per year for 4 issues.

CH.A.D.D.ER and CH.A.D.D.ER BOX
CH.A.D.D. National Headquarters
499 NW 70th Avenue,, Suite 308
Plantation, FL 33317
(305) 587-3700
Fax: (305) 587-4599

CH.A.D.D.ER: A biannual, twenty-five-page-plus newsletter that frequently contains articles written by leading researchers and clinicians for adults with ADD.

CH.A.D.D.ER BOX: A monthly newsletter with several issues per year devoted solely to adult ADD concerns.

Challenge
P.O. Box 448
West Newbury, MA 01985

A bimonthly published by ADDA, this newsletter occasionally has articles about ADD in adults.

The Rebus Institute Report
198 Taylor Boulevard, Suite 201
Millbrae, CA 94030

A quarterly newsletter published by the Rebus Institute, a nonprofit research institute devoted to the study and dissemination of information related to adults with learning difficulties and ADD. The newsletter includes employment-related issues, ADA (see below) information, book reviews, news reports, and announcements.

Offices to Contact for Information About the Americans with Disabilities Act, Equal Employment Opportunity Issues, and Educational Rights According to PL94-142 (also called Individuals with Disabilities Education Act—IDEA) and Section 504)

Equal Employment Opportunity Commission
1801 L Street, NW
Washington, DC 20507
(202) 663-4900
(800) 800-3302

Contact the EEOC about employment issues related to the Americans with Disabilities Act. Title I of ADA prevents an employer from discriminating against a qualified individual with a mental or physical disability with regards to job-application procedures, hiring, discharge, compensation, advancement, job training, and other conditions and privileges of employment.

Department of Justice
Office of Americans with Disabilities Act
Civil Rights Division
P.O. Box 66118
Washington, DC 20035
(202) 514-0301

Contact the Department of Justice about "public accommodation" issues, as defined by the Americans with Disabilities Act. Title III of the act prohibits any private entity that owns, leases, or operates a place of public accommodation (e.g., restaurants, retail stores, colleges and graduate schools) from discriminating against an individual on the basis of disability.

Office of Civil Rights
U.S. Department of Education
400 Maryland Avenue, SW
Washington, DC 20202-4135
(202) 401-3020

Contact OCR with issues pertaining to Section 504 of the Rehabilitation Act (1973), and the Individuals with Disabilities Education Act (IDEA), both of which provide guidelines for the rights of individuals with ADD in public school settings.

The Rebus Institute
198 Taylor Boulevard
Suite 201
Millbrae, CA 94030

The Rebus Institute has printed information about the relevance of ADA to LD and ADD adults, especially as to how the new act relates to employment situations.

Readings and References About ADD in Adults

The following list contains books and other resources that we think will be helpful in learning more about ADD and LD in adults and children. It is only a sample, however, of the many excellent and informative publications that are available about attention deficit disorder. Perhaps it can serve as your starting point. The books are presented alphabetically by author.

Inside Attention Deficit Disorder. Susan Alfultis. 1991. Subtitled "A Collection of Thoughts and Feelings on ADD by an Adult Who Lives It," this personal account of ADD is thought-provoking and helpful. Available through ADDA.

Attention Deficit Hyperactivity Disorder: A Handbook for Diagnosis and Treatment. Russell Barkley, Ph.D. Guilford Publications, New York, New York, 1990. This comprehensive text details the history of ADD, the developmental course of the disorder, its relation to cognitive and emotional maturation, its impact on the family, and its implications for adulthood. It discusses evaluative, diagnostic, and treatment methodologies, and provides a solid understanding of the research that has been done in the field.

ADHD: What Do We Know? and *ADHD: What Can We Do?* Two videos by Russell Barkley, Ph.D., available through Guilford Press Videos, Guilford Publications, Inc., 72 Spring Street, New York, NY 10012.

Psychiatric Aspects of Minimal Brain Dysfunction in Adults. Leopold Bellak, editor. Grune and Stratton, New York, NY, 1979. This book was written before MBD and ADD were taken to be much the same thing. A classic in the field, the book is now out of print.

CH.A.D.D.ER, Special Edition: The Adult with ADD, written specifically about adult issues, available through CH.A.D.D.

Medications for Attention Disorders (ADHD/ADD) and Related Medical Problems. Edna Copeland. Reviews the neurophysiological basis of ADD and the mechanism of action of the drugs commonly prescribed for ADD. Written for the parent, educator, and others who may not have a comprehensive background in psychopharmacology.

Maybe You Know My Kid: A Parent's Guide to Identifying, Understanding and Helping Your Child with Attention Deficit Disorder. Mary Cahill Fowler. Birch Lane Press, 1990. Takes the reader on one family's journey toward discovering their child was not willfully misbehaving, but had attention deficit hyperactivity disorder. May help the adult in identifying childhood patterns consistent with ADD.

Ritalin: Theory and Patient Management. Lawrence L. Greenhill, M.D., and Betty B. Osman, Ph.D., editors. 1991. Mary Ann Liebert Press, 1651 3rd Avenue, New York, NY 10128. A reference book on the many issues related to the use of Ritalin: the action of Ritalin on the central nervous system, the use of Ritalin to decrease impulsive behavior and increase cognitive performance, the pharmacological treatment of ADD in adults, and many more chapters by leaders in the field.

Attention Deficit Disorder: A Different Perception. Thom Hartmann, Underwood-Miller, Novato, CA, 1993. An interesting theory.

Hyperactive Children Grown Up, Lily Hechtman, Ph.D., and Gabrielle Weiss, Ph.D. The Guilford Press, New York, NY, 1986. Hechtman and Weiss have followed children with ADD for the past three decades. The book summarizes the findings of their landmark longitudinal studies and integrates their findings with that of other research in the field.

Learning Disabilities: Proceedings of the National Conference. James F. Kavanaugh, and Tom J. Truss, editors. York Press, Parkton, MD, 21120, 1988. Excellent collection.

You Mean I'm Not Lazy, Stupid, or Crazy?! A self-help book for adults with ADD. Kate Kelly and Peggy Ramundo. Tyrell and Jerem Press, Box 20089, Cincinnati, OH 45220, 1993. Written by and for ADD adults, this book includes tips on coping with, organizing, and living the life of an ADD adult.

Attention Deficit Disorder and the Law: A Guide for Advocates. Peter S. Latham, J.D., and Patricia H. Latham, J.D. 1992. A clear and comprehensive overview of the rights of ADD individuals according to PL 94-142, IDEA, the Social Security Act, ADA, federal, state, and case law. Available through JKL Communications, 1016 16th Street, NW, Suite 700, Washington, DC 20036.

Keeping A Head in School. Mel Levine, M.D. 1991. This book offers practical advice, studying strategies, and hope for the grammar-school and high-school student with ADD. Includes an overview of learning disabilities and problems, an explanation of different learning styles, and creative methods that can be employed to accomplish goals.

Diagnosing Learning Disorders: A Neuropsychological Framework. Bruce B. Pennington. Guilford Press, New York, NY, 1991. A superb overview. Written more for the professional than the lay reader.

The Boy Who Couldn't Stop Washing. Judith Rapoport. E.P. Dutton, New York, NY, 1989. This book articulates the etiology, and the trauma, of obsessive-compulsive disorder. It has struck may chords for adults with ADD.

Smart Kids with School Problems: Things to Know and Ways to Help. Priscilla Vail. New American Library, New York, 1987; *Learning Styles: Food for Thought and 130 Practical Tips.* Priscilla Vail. Modern Learning Press, Rosemont, NJ, 1993; and *Emotion: The On/Off Switch for Learning,* Priscilla Vail, Modern Learning Press, Rosemont, NJ, 1994. Priscilla Vail brings a special combination of warmth, hard-nosed practicality, and strong prose to all her writing. These three titles are but a suggested sample.

Attention Deficit Disorders in Adults: Practical Help for Sufferers and Their Spouses. Lynn Weiss, Ph.D. Taylor Publishing Company, 1992. Emphasizes the ways in which ADD symptoms appear in adults. Reviews treatment and coping strategies and includes a list of clinicians across the country who specialize in treating adults with ADD.

The Hyperactive Child, Adolescent, and Adult. Paul Wender, M.D. Oxford University Press, 1987. Dr. Wender, one of the true innovators in all of contemporary psychiatry and pioneer in the field of ADD, presents here an overview of ADD in childhood, adolescence, and adulthood. He discusses evaluation procedures and treatment approaches developed from his lifetime of work in the field. Written for the parent, health-care professional, or adult with ADD.

Educational Vendors

A.D.D. WareHouse
300 NW 70th Avenue, Suite 102
Plantation, FL 33317
(305) 792-8944

The Attention Deficit Resource Center
1344 Johnson Ferry Road, Suite 14
Marietta, GA 30068

Support Groups

We are grateful to Lisa Poast of Bellingham, Washington, for putting together the following list of support groups for adult ADD around the country. The list cannot be complete, because new groups are being formed all the time.

Alabama
BIRMINGHAM
John Larson
(205) 823-5910

Arizona
PRESCOTT
Marcia Brehmer
(602) 636-5160
SCOTTSDALE
Attention Deficit Disorder Clinic
(602) 423-7770
TUCSON
Della Mays
(602) 293-0533

California
ALAMEDA COUNTY
CH.A.D.D. of Alameda County
(510) 581-9941
ARCADIA (PASADENA AREA)
Melissa Thomasson, Ph.D.
(818) 301-7977
CONTRA COSTA COUNTY
Pat and Monte Churchill
(510) 825-4938

Rita Wilson
(510) 524-3953

LONG BEACH
Patreen Bower, M.S., M.F.C.C.
Sue Griffith, M.A., Psy. Asst.
(310) 493-1496
NEWPORT BEACH
Joan Andrews, L.E.P.
(714) 476-0991
PALO ALTO
Kitty Petty
(415) 329-9443
ROSEVILLE (SACRAMENTO AREA)
CH.A.D.D. of Roseville
and Greater Sacramento
(916) 782-5661
SAN JOSE
Karen Neale, M.A.
(408) 395-1348

California Spouse Support Group
CONTRA COSTA COUNTY
Monte Churchill
(510) 825-4938

Colorado
DENVER
Don Lambert
(303) 424-5272

FORT COLLINS
Lou Hartmeister
(303) 221-1835

Maxine Jarvi
(303) 223-1338

For additional listings of Colorado
Support Groups, contact:

Ralph Myers, editor
Add Vantage
(303) 287-6944

**Colorado Spouse Support
Group**
PERL-MACK
Pamela Stone
(303) 277-1059

Connecticut
EAST HAMPTON
Cathy Ziegler
(203) 267-6807
NEW HAVEN
CH.A.D.D. of New Haven
County
(203) 888-1434
WEST HARTFORD
Michael Kissane
(203) 277-8669

Florida
GAINESVILLE
Elias Sarkis, M.D.
(904) 331-5100

Bob Newman
(904) 374-9207
PLANTATION
Diana Kennedy
(305) 726-4590

Georgia
ATLANTA
Larry Melear, Ph.D.
(404) 971-4763

Illinois
BLOOMINGTON
Ron Ropp, Rel.D.
(309) 829-0751
CHICAGO (NORTHWEST
SUBURBAN)
Becky Booth
(708) 303-1189

Indiana
PORTAGE (NORTHWEST
INDIANA)
Teresa Gross
(219) 465-0447

David Shultz
(219) 232-6690

Iowa
IOWA CITY
Don Walker
(319) 337-5201

Kansas
OVERLAND PARK
Avner Stern, Ph.D.
(913) 469-6510

Maine
SCARBOROUGH
Lindy Botto
(207) 883-2528

Maryland
MONTGOMERY COUNTY
Kathleen G. Nadeau, Ph.D.
(301) 718-8114

Massachusetts
BARNSTABLE
John Welles
(508) 428-2102
BOSTON
John Patrick Moir
(603) 881-5540
GREENFIELD
Lori Roy
(413) 773-5545
LYNN
Linda Harrison
(508) 535-3131
PLYMOUTH
Linda Greenwood
(508) 747-2179
WESTON
John Patrick Moir
(603) 881-5540

Michigan
ANN ARBOR
Jim Reisinger
(313) 426-1659
GROSSE POINTE
Gerhard W. Heinen
(313) 886-8907

LANSING
Eric Shotwell
(517) 543-9683
NOVI
Fred Michaelson
(313) 348-2656
SOUTHFIELD
Chuck Pearson
(313) 540-6335
TROY
Kathleen A. Van Howe
(313) 939-1112

Minnesota
MINNETONKA
William Ronan, LICSW
(612) 933-3460

Missouri
KANSAS CITY AREA
Avner Stern, Ph.D.
(913) 469-6510
ST. LOUIS AREA
De Paul Health Center
Adults with ADD Support Group
(314) 344-7224

Montana
GREAT FALLS
David Walker
(406) 727-2137

Dennis Patton
(406) 454-1964

New Hampshire
CONCORD
Sarah Brophy, Ph.D.
(603) 226-6121

NASHUA
John Patrick Moir
(603) 881-5540

New Jersey
LONG BRANCH
Robert LoPresti, Ph.D.
(908) 842-4553

Phyllis Wolff, M.S.W.
(908) 870-5215

New Jersey Spouse Support
Group
LONG BRANCH
Robert LoPresti, Ph.D.
(908) 842-4553

Phyllis Wolff, M.S.W.
(908) 870-5215

New Mexico
ALBUQUERQUE
Attention Deficit Disorder Clinic
(505) 243-9600

New York
LONG ISLAND
Joan B. Ellis
(516) 244-3665
MANHATTAN
Barbara Andersen
(914) 378-3295
NEWBURGH
Jim Nowack
(914) 562-1283
ROCHESTER

Greater Rochester Attention
Deficit Disorder Association
(GRADDA)
(716) 251-2322
WHITE PLAINS
Susan G. Salit, M.S.W.
Charlotte Tomaino, Ph.D.
(914) 472-2935

New York Spouse Support
Group
NEWBURGH
Jim Nowack
(914) 562-1283

Ohio
CINCINNATI
Kate Kelly, R.N., M.S.N.
(513) 861-8519
TOLEDO
Jan Menzie
(419) 841-6603
XENIA (DAYTON AREA)
Bettylou Huber
(513) 862-4573

Madge Jones
(513) 897-4380

Oklahoma
OKLAHOMA CITY
CH.A.D.D. of Central Oklahoma
(405) 722-1233
TULSA
Shelley Curtiss
(918) 622-1370

Juan Wilson
(918) 486-5035

Pennsylvania

BRYN MAWR
Jerry McCrone
(215) 647-8807
LANCASTER
Judy Mansfield
(717) 656-9515
NORRISTOWN (MONTGOMERY COUNTY)
Joan Kempton
(215) 565-8676
PHILADELPHIA
Rose St. Julien
(215) 732-4639

Harvey Kravetz
(215) 732-9541
TELFORD (BETWEEN ALLENTOWN AND PHILADELPHIA)
Ginger Varley
(215) 723-8587

Texas

AUSTIN
L.D.A. of Austin
(512) 477-5516
DALLAS
ADD Treatment and Research Center
(214) 980-7488

Larry Steele
(817) 498-6842
HUMBLE (HOUSTON AREA)
Karen Kasper
(713) 288-6758

Virginia

FAIRFAX COUNTY
Kathleen G. Nadeau, Ph.D.
Susan Biggs, Ed.D.
(703) 642-6697
NEWPORT NEWS
Jody Lochmiller-Jones
(804) 930-1931

Mark Jacob
(804) 874-7992
ROANOKE
Debra Maxey
(703) 772-8672

Washington

BELLINGHAM
Lisa F. Poast
(206) 647-6681

Thomas Melo, B.A.
(206) 647-5523
OLYMPIA
Ron Jones, P.A.
Cheryl Adams, M.A.
(206) 754-4801
SEATTLE
W. J. McNabb, Ph.D.
(206) 609-3470

Carol Lee Crabill
(206) 246-9752
TACOMA
Cynthia Hammer
(206) 752-0801

Brian Howell
(206) 759-2914

Wisconsin
WAUKESHA (MILWAUKEE AREA)
Paul Rembas
(414) 542-6694

Canada
CAMPBELL RIVER, BRITISH COLUMBIA
Loring Kuhn
(604) 923-7405

NEW WESTMINSTER, BRITISH COLUMBIA
Attention Deficit Disorder Support Association (ADDSA)
(614) 524-9183

OTTAWA, ONTARIO
Mark Turcotte
(613) 231-7646

■ ■ ■

The Adult ADD Association wishes to thank Paul Jaffe, editor of *ADDendum,* and Mary Jane Johnson, editor of *ADDult News,* for their contribution to this listing, and more importantly, for their documentation in their newsletters of the development of support groups for adults throughout the country over the last three years.

■ ■ ■

Changes and/or additions may be sent to:
Lisa F. Poast
Adult ADD Association
1225 East Sunset Drive, Suite 640
Bellingham, WA 98226

■ ■ ■

INDEX

318   *Index*

  masking of, 9, 36, 51
  primary vs. secondary, 16, 52, 106
  severity and duration of, 6, 43
  variability of, 9, 10–11, 82
  see also specific symptoms

tactlessness, 114–15
teachers, xi
  evaluation and treatment recommended by, 31, 35–36, 56, 131
  exasperation of, 16–17, 24, 61, 65
  guidelines for, 219–20, 224–25, 254–62
  parents and, 16–17, 24, 48, 50–51, 130, 145
  progressive yearly comments of, 61–64, 198
  scolding and punishment by, 7, 11–12, 17, 23, 24, 168
Tegretol (carbamazepine), 172, 242, 243
temperament, x, 7, 9, 49, 52
tenacity, 11, 16, 18–19, 215
Test of Variability of Attention (TOVA), 206
tests:
  for ADD, 25, 29, 33, 39, 41–42, 50, 51, 84–85, 115, 169, 195, 205–7
  blood, 199–202
  diagnostic, 202
  doing poorly on, 17, 50
  doing well on, 24, 42, 78
  inkblot, 205
  intelligence, 41–42, 46, 50, 78, 171, 205
  memory, 169
  neuropsychological, 39, 41–42, 50, 84–85, 115, 159, 169, 205–7
  reading-comprehension, 169
  thyroid function, 202

thyroid dysfunction, 42, 72
time management, 30, 222
Tofranil (imipramine), 241, 283
topographagnosia, 276
Tourette's syndrome, 203, 238
transference, 30
traumatic events, 154, 168, 183–84
treatment, xi, 215–68
  active process of, 217, 245–62
  common problems in, 262–68
  components of, 19–21, 30, 98–99
  comprehensiveness of, 19, 30, 94, 235
  development of insight in, 31, 115–16
  diagnosis and, 15, 20, 39–40, 206–7, 216
  duration of, 19, 116
  educational process in, 19, 20, 30, 121, 141–42, 216–20, 235, 245–47
  emotional and supportive aspects of, 19, 20, 30–31, 144, 146, 224, 225–27
  guidelines for, 219–20, 224–25, 244–68
  initial phase of, 15, 26, 106, 227, 236
  maintaining hope in, 147, 158, 216
  mood management in, 21, 99, 105–6, 124, 236, 238, 250–52
  patience and perseverance in, 6, 14–15, 25, 106, 146–47
  performance management in, 247–50
  progress of, xii, 15, 21, 67, 85, 106
  resistance to, 30, 67, 236–37
  self-, 25–26
  staying on track in, 30–31, 100, 106

structure in, 19, 20, 30–31, 43,
91–92, 94, 99, 102, 221–25,
227–28
success of, 21, 25–26, 29–31, 40,
57–59, 94, 100–101, 102,
105–6, 154
synopsis of, 20–21
testing as, 206–7
see also drugs, treatment of ADD
with; psychotherapy
tricyclic antidepressants, 240–42,
283
anticholinergic properties of, 40
tutoring, 55, 129, 131, 141, 161,
164, 218, 224
Type A personalities, 11, 181, 182–
83

underachievement, 9
scholastic, x, 5, 23, 27–28, 31–32,
35–36, 38, 44, 47–48, 55, 61–
65, 78, 126, 130–31, 166, 174
sense of, 73
work-related, 4–6, 26–27, 147
underactivity, 9
Ury, William, 139–41
Utah Criteria, 76–77, 198–99, 202,
275

Vail, Priscilla, 36, 160–62
valproic acid (Depakote), 242, 243

Wechsler Intelligence Scale for Children (WISC), 41–42, 205
Weiss, Gabrielle, 70n
Weiss, Lynn, 71
Wellbutrin (bupropion), 241, 243
Wender, Paul, ix, 70n, 71, 76–77,
199, 220, 274, 275, 280, 284
willfulness, 13, 16
withdrawal, 88–91, 93–94, 104,
111–12, 153

work:
difficulties with superiors at, 4–5,
10, 21, 86, 89
dismissal from, 4, 5, 10, 171
emphasis on abilities vs. limitations
in, 31
formulating manageable tasks in,
30, 92
formulating new organizing principles for, 31
frequent job changes and, 3, 7, 10,
108, 147, 171
frustration in, xi, 4–5, 15–16,
97
high-pressure, 8
intensity in, 8, 85–86, 108, 110,
179–80
lack of follow-through in, 4, 6, 8,
11, 26–27, 28, 29, 36, 95–96,
130–31, 154
overcommitment to, 102
problems connected with, xi, 3, 4–
5, 18, 21
short periods of, 30
simultaneous projects of, 11, 26–
27, 73
underachievement in, 4–6, 26–27,
147
World of the Gifted Child, The (Vail),
162
worry, 75, 84–85, 105
organizing around, 155–56,
159
sharing of, 146
writing, problems with, 97, 159–61,
163, 168

Y chromosome, 152

Zametkin, Alan, 71–72, 274–76
Zentall, Sydney, 281–82
Zoloft (sertraline), 242, 243